STAN BOWLES

STAN BOWLES

FourFourTwo | *great footballers*

Steve Bidmead

Published in Great Britain in 2002 by
Virgin Books Ltd
Thames Wharf Studios
Rainville Road
London W6 9HA

A catalogue record for the book is available
from the British Library.

ISBN 0 7535 0672 6

Typeset by TW Typesetting, Plymouth, Devon

Printed and bound in Great Britain by
Mackays of Chatham PLC

Contents

Acknowledgements

Former footballers, managers and chairmen (and one legendary TV presenter) who helped to tell the tale: Garry Birtles, Tony Book, Stan Bowles, Tony Currie, Mervyn Day, Gerry Francis, Don Givens, Paul Hince, Emlyn Hughes, Terry Hurlock, Chris Kamara, Martin Lange, Brian Little, John McGovern, John Robertson, Dave Sexton, Ernie Tagg, Peter Taylor, Dave Thomas 1, David Vine, Frank Worthington.

Work colleagues, and those who have provided useful information or assistance: Matt Allen, Ralph Allen, Becky Allin, Dr Roy Bailey, Cormac Bourne, Ewan Buck, Paul Carpenter, Prof. Steve Cooper, Jon Crampin, Paul Finney, Michael Hann, Ian Jameson, Martyn Jones, Louis Massarella, Richard Pendleton, Sam Pilger, Steve Russell, Richard Scott, Dr George Sik, Mike Skyte, Hugh Sleight, David Steel, Mat Snow, Dave Thomas 2.

To all the inspirational, talented and gullible servants of the mighty *FourFourTwo* magazine, past and present. Seriously, thanks for everything – you are great people to work with as well as to learn from. A special mention to Jon Crampin and Kris 'Drink-while-you-think!' Adams for the darts therapy – playing against you two always does me the world of good! Also, to Jonathan at Virgin Books, a QPR and Stan Bowles fan – hope you enjoy the read.

And a very special thank you to Laura, without whose staggering show of support and vitally important help this book would not exist. (Of course, you may soon be cursing her!) This is dedicated to Laura, and to my mother and brother who, despite being many miles away, ensure I never forget my Swansea roots ('You're turning all *English*, you are!').

Steve Bidmead
February 2002

Introduction

Six months of research into Stan Bowles' life has affected me. Just recently, I walked past the bookie's down the street from my flat and for the first time in my entire life my thoughts wandered to the ten-pound note in my back pocket. Thankfully, my momentum carried me past the grubby but oddly alluring doorway and on to the pub, where I resolutely refused to buy myself anything stronger than half a shandy. Which I sipped slowly.

Furthermore, during the writing of this biography I have become something of a rebel – or so I'd like to think – even breaking one of the cardinal rules of story-telling: I have started, more or less, in the middle. But before you throw this book in the bin, let me explain, at the same time giving a taste of what's to come.

Stan Bowles was once beaten up in a Belgian police cell. He had two fist-fights with Malcolm Allison in nightclubs. He occasionally drove around in an ambulance. He walked out on England. He failed to turn up for Nottingham Forest's European Cup final in 1980. He isn't welcome at Gamblers Anonymous after laughing at other people's stories, then arranging a game of cards. Just about all his ex-team-mates call him 'the best player I ever played with'. He faked his own retirement to make some cash from a national newspaper. He posed with topless models. His mates beat up journalists. He claims he once kicked the FA Cup off its stand. He made a fool of himself on a national TV programme. He was sacked by two different clubs within the space of two months. After one of many court appearances, he had a fling with the court secretary. He broke European goalscoring records. He only ever won one trophy, gambled away almost a million pounds and ended up in a psychiatric hospital.

Stan Bowles was not your run-of-the-mill footballer, therefore he does not deserve a run-of-the-mill biography. This book takes a comprehensive look at his footballing life, focusing on the best and worst bits – and there are lots of both – with the aim of putting Stan the Man into context and reliving a notorious, riotous career.

I was determined this should not simply be autobiography number two, but I thought Bowles should at least know I was writing a book about him, so I spoke to him, essentially to find out what he'd been up to in the years after football. I found him eager to help, kind and extremely entertaining. And looking remarkably fit and youthful. Over a pint or three before lunch in a Celtic-mad pub a couple of streets behind Brentford's Griffin Park ground, we chatted about the brilliant highs and alcoholic lows of his career and I quickly discovered why so many people were prepared to forgive his numerous indiscretions. His piercing sky-blue eyes and cheeky grin are charming, his conversation confident, welcoming and, despite the occasional, disarming pause for thought, mesmerising. I think it's called charisma.

On a number of occasions, though, my research virtually ground to a halt because, surprisingly, not much has been written about Bowles, and many alternative sources of information proved erratic (Internet), elusive (team-mates) or pricey (£250 for a twenty-minute chat with an ex-professional is over the top). However, the lurid stories I knew I'd soon be writing about provided many hours of entertainment, though I was initially plagued by a few nagging doubts – particularly over the fact that despite his ability and the myriad colourful anecdotes, he grossly underachieved in the game.

This biography kicks off at Queens Park Rangers, the club where Bowles made his name and enjoyed most success. It investigates numerous spectacular stories at the west London club and his greatest moments there, as well as attempting to answer the thirty-year-old question: was Bowles better than his predecessor in the famous QPR number 10 shirt, Rodney Marsh? It's a question not just the QPR faithful but many football fans have asked countless times.

It also treads carefully through the treacherous path of the rest of his career, before QPR and after. Why did things go so horribly wrong at Manchester City and Bury? How did he end up playing for Crewe, at the time probably the worst team in the Football League? Who gave him his chance to return to the big time with a move to Carlisle? Why did the legendary disciplinarian Brian Clough at Nottingham Forest decide to take a chance on this notorious maverick who hated authority? Why did Bowles refuse to go to the European Cup final? When Forest tired of him, he went to Leyton Orient but despised every minute of it. In the end, he found rest and relaxation at Brentford, but a few years later he had quit football and was lying in a psychiatric ward. What went wrong? His controversial international career under various England managers is covered too. Should he have won more than his five England caps? Why did he storm off the pitch when playing for his country and head straight to his favourite dog track? Did gambling ruin Bowles' chances at the highest level?

The text goes on to profile the men who shaped his career, for better or for worse – those who gave him his opportunities and lived to regret it, and those who learnt how to harness his talents and get the best from him. Another chapter looks into the problems of addiction in the game, in Bowles' era and today, examining the make-up of compulsive behaviour and the changing faces of football. Finally, we catch up with Bowles as he is today, 'playing life' with abandon, as ever.

One of the first true tabloid stars of football, Bowles' countless colourful anecdotes and heaven-sent left foot mean he will never be forgotten. He represents both the best and worst sides of football – a monumental talent wasted and unfulfilled. Some of his behaviour cannot be condoned, but it's still funny. Though, perhaps like all footballers, Bowles never wanted to be a role model, he has become a symbol of sorts: a player with the world at his feet who seemed not to know that he was throwing it all away, and who to this day insists he would do exactly the same again; a hero to each new generation of supporters who probably never saw him play but sympathise with his attitude to life and, through him, live out a fantasy of rule-breaking and rowdiness. Though the reality may be different, many people would claim they would rather earn a fraction of what Michael Owen gets today just to enjoy the rollercoaster lifestyle Bowles exemplified and, for the most part, enjoyed. And to those who saw him play, including those who played alongside him, he is simply one of the very best.

The fact that he never fulfilled his enormous potential makes him the perfect legend. His all-too-human flaws make him larger than life. This biography refuses to reel off season after season, goal after goal, which would not do his extraordinary talents justice anyway. Rather, it deals with the most important and entertaining aspects of a varied career on and off the field. QPR, Forest, the other clubs, England, addiction – the events that have made Stan Bowles a legend.

The truth, of course, is that everybody loves a rogue, and probably always will. Though 'Rogue of the Century' George Best has something of a monopoly on adoration in this field, having won the most hearts with his good looks and tragic addiction, Stan Bowles isn't too far behind him. Never particularly a woman's man (though he's lost a few), he treated football simply as a means of earning money to put on the races. There are, probably as a result, a few clichés that have followed Bowles around for more than three decades, and many football fans have heard them: 'If Stan could pass a bookie's like he could pass a ball, he'd be a rich man' (Crewe boss Ernie Tagg invented that one); 'Stan Bowles has gone for more walkabouts than the average aborigine'; 'Stan could sell a dummy better than Mothercare'. And two classic quotes: 'I lost half a million quid on gambling, booze and women – the rest I wasted'; and 'I was penniless again. I'd blown the lot on vodka and tonic, gambling and fags. Looking back, I think I overdid it on the tonic.'

Football fans across the country have long debated the exact rankings in the pantheon of football's 'bad boys'. If talent is the main criterion, then Bowles is, at worst, in the top five; if it's making headlines, Bowles is in the top three. There's been little serious competition in recent years. Eric Cantona performed that kung-fu kick, Gazza had his problems with wife Sheryl, Stan Collymore had Ulrika Jonsson, Duncan Ferguson served a little spell in prison for inappropriate use of the head – all unpleasant events, though, that have marred the image of football more than Stan Bowles and his sense of humour ever did. Paul Merson was so apologetic and tearful about his multiple addictions that he came out smelling of roses. But bad boys don't cry.

Chastised and worshipped in equal measure, Bowles has been mysteriously ignored by biographers until now. Still, that is the whole point of this effort: to fill that gap on every football fan's bookshelf.

1 Officially the Worst Superstar Ever!

You couldn't have picked a worse person to represent football on television!

PAUL HINCE, FRIEND AND FORMER TEAM-MATE

In 1976, Stan Bowles was at the height of his powers. Queens Park Rangers had just enjoyed the best season in their history, finishing just one point behind champions Liverpool in Division One, and Bowles was the star of the show.

Having refused to travel with the team for a lucrative April tour of Israel (one of many no-shows that bedevilled the course of his controversial career), Bowles was invited by the BBC to appear on *Superstars*, a popular television show where top sporting celebrities of the era battled it out against one another in a series of challenges. Things did not go well. The *Superstars* story, passed on by word of mouth over the years, doesn't exactly do Bowles any favours. It is the one story, perhaps more than any other, which people associate with the player. It overshadows some of his greatest and most famous moments on the pitch.

Just about every publicity event Bowles has ever staged – from drugs confessions and false retirements to photo shoots with topless models – has been undertaken with the sole aim of getting cash to use and abuse at the White City dog track in London, and this occasion was no different. Though the outlook was bright, everything fell apart at the seams at just the wrong moment.

The BBC, buoyed by the star's apparent enthusiasm, forwarded Bowles £500. He claims that he also managed to get another £500 from QPR, telling his club that the

Beeb would not advance him any cash. That £1,000 quickly disappeared, as usual, so he lost interest in the project. However, QPR team-mate and fellow trouble-maker Don Shanks, who was acting as Bowles' manager for the day, got a further £500 – the second half of the original fee – in exchange for a guarantee that his unreliable charge would definitely turn up. (At that point in his career, Bowles rarely went anywhere without Shanks, getting into trouble at every turn.) That money was quickly parted with at White City too, and once again Bowles couldn't see the point of going through with *Superstars*.

Still, Shanks borrowed a friend's car (Bowles has never learnt to drive), plus a bit of cash for petrol, and they made it to the hotel where the competitors were meeting – a little late, but at least they made it. Desperate for some more money, Shanks spun an unfeasible yarn about writing off his Jaguar on the way and having to hire a Morris Marina, and received more money from the BBC to cover the expense, though whether this is really how the affair proceeded is anybody's guess. As one of Bowles' friends once confided, 'He can't remember much about the seventies!' Bowles, with Shanks at his side, duly met up with all the other competitors, including prolific striker Malcolm 'Supermac' Macdonald, who had moved from Newcastle to Arsenal that summer for £333,333. Hellos and formalities over, he started on the lager at the hotel. Then came the wine, and the brandy and the cigars. It was the small hours of the morning before the pair managed to haul themselves to bed.

Recording for the programme – and in retrospect Bowles must be eternally thankful that it wasn't going out live – started early the next morning, but Bowles was in no fit state to get up, let alone take part in two days of sporting challenges in front of the cameras. The hilarious shambles that followed has gone down in television legend. It is impossible to imagine today's top sportsmen – Alan Shearer or Michael Schumacher, say – agreeing to risk injury (as well as humiliation) on a TV programme, but in this case it made for spectacular viewing. As the programme's main presenter David Vine confirmed, the show was watched avidly by people around the world. 'We worked out,' he explained, 'that it was the most-watched television series in the world. It was watched by an average of over fourteen million in 1976 in Great Britain, and the total audience, with the European and world competitions, was over 300 million. It was unbelievable.' *Superstars* was essential viewing for all sports fans, and it made stars of contestants such as the impressive judoist Brian Jacks. If any of the contestants slipped up, though, they did so in front of millions of viewers. There was no turning back.

'From the world of international sport come . . . the Superstars!' Vine cried out beneath his badly ironed hair, introducing the competition for the Wilkinson Sword Trophy. Cue satisfyingly over-the-top blaring seventies theme tune. 'From England and Queens Park Rangers, Stan Bowles!' Bowles, all wispy hair and pale skin, looked by far the least 'Superstarish' of the ten eager contestants, among whom stood the Formula One hero and dedicated playboy James Hunt, who happily admitted, 'I'm only here for the beer!' As events transpired, Hunt and the others were in fact taking it very seriously. They were there to win. Bowles, it seemed, was there just to keep them all amused.

Introductions completed, the competition began in earnest.

EVENT 1: 100-METRE SPRINT
Some of the competitors had been in training for the show for weeks, even months, determined not to show themselves up on national television, but not Bowles. When asked by the late TV presenter Ron Pickering before the first event how he thought he'd fare, he replied, somewhat uneasily, 'I'm not too good.' He could have been talking about his hangover. 'I'm all right over fifty metres, though,' he added with a half-hearted smile.

The ten sporting guests could choose which eight of the ten events they would take part in, and nearly half of them pulled out of the sprint because of hamstring concerns. The remaining selection of stars, heroes and fine athletes settled into their blocks and looked down the track with steely, determined eyes. Bowles looked at the ground with bleary eyes, accidentally 'getting set' before the 'get set' order came.

When the starting pistol fired, they burst from the blocks like bullets. Bowles chalked up his first points of the competition by coming in fourth (out of six), at least twenty metres behind Macdonald, the programme's record holder at the event from a previous appearance. Nevertheless, two points were better than none, as Bowles was about to find out.

EVENT 2: 125-METRE CANOE SPRINT

Champion boxer John Conteh had been doing a lot of solo training for this one, almost drowning himself in his attempts to perfect the technique. While out practising on a local river he had capsized and got trapped in his canoe. Crying out for help and frantically flapping his arms, an elderly lady had spotted him, recognised him and cheerfully waved back before carrying on along the path. Bowles, on the other hand, was scared of water. 'There's Stan Bowles,' muttered Vine, 'who hates the water almost as much as he hates flying. He's not looking forward to this at all.' Indeed, Bowles looked as though he wished to be rescued from the nightmare he had (almost) woken up to.

As the race began, Bowles quickly dropped to the back, seemingly unsure what the oars were actually for. Wobbling, he disappeared from shot as the cameras followed the canoes at the front. There was another flash of him when the camera angle briefly changed; he appeared to be cutting wildly across into another lane. 'Bowles is all over the place!' a stunned Vine reported. 'He's in an awful lot of trouble, he's already cut across one lane.'

The race finished quickly, with various judo, squash and rugby stars streaking across the finishing line. Then the camera cut to where Bowles should have been, only to find the white hull of an overturned canoe and a mop of drenched hair paddling, with some effort, away from it. As he stumbled on to the riverbank, he could at least draw some cold comfort from the fact that his football rival Macdonald, whom he thought of as a glory hunter, had also capsized – when Bowles crashed into him.

In his autobiography Bowles' recollection of many of these events is, understandably, slightly distorted. He claims he was drawn in the end lane and that his canoe was somehow swamped by the wake from the safety boat. Through a disastrous display of steering he did in fact end up in the end lane, but was in fact originally drawn in the middle. At least the next event was on dry land.

EVENT 3: WEIGHTLIFTING
'Now for the hard stuff,' Pickering warned with a smile, indicating a stage laden with dumb-bells and multi-coloured weights. Bowles pulled his back on his first attempt – which, unsurprisingly, was not shown in the final cut of the programme – and was forced to withdraw from the event. Macdonald returned to form, finishing third behind Gareth Edwards and reigning 'European Superstar' and Olympic hurdling champion David Hemery. As David Vine recalled, Bowles may well have popped down to the pub at this stage for a quick 'hair of the dog' before resuming his challenge.

EVENT 4: CYCLING
Maybe his back was still sore, but Bowles did not feature in the televised stages of this event either. Indeed, he seemed to be in grave danger of disappearing from the programme altogether. That said, he was still (somehow) eighth on the overall scoreboard, those early two points keeping his head above water.

EVENT 5: TENNIS
Although Bowles later claimed to have been drawn against former Wimbledon junior champion J.P.R. Williams, he actually faced squash player Jonah Barrington, who – and this is good evidence of how seriously *Superstars* was taken – had staged an 'angry walk-out' when recording a

show for the previous year's series. In a surprisingly tight first-round contest, which Barrington won, Bowles' performance was enough to earn another point. Unluckily, despite that point, he slipped to last place on the leaderboard. Worse was yet to come.

EVENT 6: PISTOL SHOOTING

Bowles was fast becoming a sideshow all of his own. For this round the contestants were required to fire live ammunition at human-size targets at a distance of fifteen metres. Some of them managed to get virtually maximum points, shooting with Lee Harvey Oswald-like precision in or around the central ten-point circle, but not Bowles. As the game progressed, David Vine, resplendent in stripy shirt and horrific tie, digressed to alert viewers to a 'remarkable incident'. The footage showed Stan Bowles lifting the pistol, shooting at the target, missing completely, then lowering the gun and accidentally shooting a hole in the table it was resting on. They showed the replay a few times, closing in on Bowles' expression – a mixture of stunned silence and slightly embarrassed grin.

'Yes, it's gone right through the table,' Vine remarked with a chuckle as a grinning Bowles stuck his finger into the hole, 'but the target's not on there!' He added, 'Everybody got away safely.' The rest of the competitors, after a split second of shock, fell about laughing at Bowles' clownish ineptitude. The QPR forward seemed to be running out of events in which to score some points and avoid a humiliating last-place finish.

EVENT 7: SWIMMING

Despite a distinct aversion to water, Bowles' greater aversion to losing triumphed, and he won four points in the pool. A practice swim before the event had clearly calmed his nerves. Despite his painful-looking tight black trunks, he finished third out of four contestants after a monumental battle with Welsh rugby star J.P.R. Williams, and miraculously moved into ninth place overall with seven points.

EVENT 8: FOOTBALL SKILLS

Both Bowles and Malcolm Macdonald were understandably barred from this round, where the celebrity guests had to dribble through poles and attempt to score against a goalkeeper, which was a shame. It would have been another opportunity for the Queens Park Rangers star to put Macdonald in his place, and it would also have provided the programme's producers with the kind of display of excellence they wanted.

EVENT 9: THE GYM

This was not just any gym, it was an army training gym, and the contestants were expected to go through hell in the pursuit of points. Bowles didn't even take part, and judging by the agonised expressions over the subsequent ten minutes he made the right decision. With Pickering drifting around in his glaring yellow jacket and flowery shirt, the contestants had to do as many parallel bar dips (imagine lowering yourself into the bath fifty times, but with your feet in mid-air) and as many squat thrusts as they could – all watched, just for extra effect, by army officers. At the end of the torture, most of the contestants collapsed in exhaustion. Bowles was absolutely nowhere to be seen.

EVENT 10: STEEPLECHASE

He showed up for the final event, though, his last chance. On the starting line he looked the picture of elegance and professionalism, with his bright yellow T-shirt hanging out and an impish 'what the hell is going on?' expression on his face. 'Bowles has only got seven points but he really has been quite a character,' Pickering said, almost by way of an obituary, 'full of gags and cracks.'

Bowles leapt out of the blocks and sprinted off into third place. His slight frame, however, was clearly not meant to undertake such endurance events, especially with a hangover, and he eventually trotted home in sixth, miles behind the winner but miles ahead of thirteen-stone Macdonald. Sixth place was not good enough for any points so a historic new record low, just seven points out of a possible eighty, was set.

At the official award ceremony, a representative from sponsors Wilkinson presented the winner – Hemery again – with a large silver sword. They should have given Bowles a smaller one for his own personal achievement, but then again, so dismal was his performance, he might have fallen on it. The inspiring, trumpety music returned and Bowles' first and, not so astoundingly, last appearance on *Superstars* was over. The programme, aired on 10 November 1976, can be viewed at the British Film Institute in London, where they keep a library of television's greatest moments. The seven points Bowles accumulated remained a *Superstars* record, the lowest tally ever. He is still quite proud of that fact.

'The *Superstars* appearance was absolutely hilarious,' recalled Bowles' former team-mate at Crewe and Manchester City, Paul Hince. 'He can't swim. He never did any weights. He used to hate training. He couldn't run. They used to say that the quickest thing on a football pitch is a brain, and that's what Bowlesy had, but he was even slower than he looked. He never had any pace, certainly not in a race on TV against world record sprinters or whoever it was! I think he was hospitalised at the end of the first day! You couldn't have picked a worse person to represent football on television!'

Presenter David Vine looks back on that episode fondly. 'First of all, when I saw Stan coming in I thought, "Er, this is going to be interesting." I wouldn't have put any money on him! And thank God I didn't, because there was a lot of betting on *Superstars*. A few beers the night before would have accounted for his appearance, and I think he had a fair few during the day as well. He disappeared at one point and we couldn't find him. I think he'd gone for refreshments at the local pub!' Other competitors took things more seriously, however. 'There was socialising,' Vine continued, 'and they all used to say they were only there for a laugh. But by the end of the first day they weren't talking to each other. They were all working on their plans for the next event and training in hiding.' Though Bowles' version of secret training – in the pub – was slightly different to his opponents'.

'They took it desperately seriously,' Vine added. 'It was a matter of life and death to them, quite honestly. Bernhard Russi, the Swiss Olympic skier, won the 100 metres one time and he was jumping up and down and going bananas, saying, "This is the greatest moment of my life!" I said to him, "Come on, Bernhard. You won the downhill skiing at the Olympics!" And he said, "Yes, but I know I can do that. Look who I've just beaten in the 100 metres! I've beaten my heroes!" So they took it very seriously. That's why it worked so well, and why they were stars.

'Now Stanley, I don't know if he took it very seriously, but if he did it didn't work! All the other competitors thought that Stan was great to have around and he tried – there's no question of that. He was never invited back but we had a lot of laughs with him. He might not have come first, but he tried his best. It just shows that some people can do it and some people can't. He certainly made his mark. One of the most amazing performances we'd seen, and yes, he was last by quite a long way. His two greatest performances were probably the canoeing, when he collided with Malcolm Macdonald and they both sank, and of course the pistol shooting, when he nearly shot his foot off! Footballers generally weren't too bad, but not as good as we expected, quite honestly. Macdonald got the all-time 100-metre record – he was incredible, incredible. He was on the show a lot. Mick Channon, Colin Bell, Peter Shilton, Kevin Keegan, of course. Bobby Moore was at Crystal Palace for the very first one in 1973. Finished sixth overall – he wasn't very good, Bobby.'

Keegan was another football star who, like Bowles, might have wished he'd stayed in bed. In the same 1976 series, in Bracknell, Keegan fell from his bike at pace, knocking himself unconscious. 'Horrendous crash. Horrible,' Vine remembered. 'I've still got pictures of it at home. You've never seen anything like it – his back was torn to shreds and he was unconscious. Half an hour later he got up and carried on, but he's still got the scars to this day. Terrible state he was in. He said that he thought he'd killed himself, and I tell you what – the organisers thought he had too.' In a recent interview Keegan was asked what the worst moment of his career was. Failing as England manager? No, he replied, falling off his bike on *Superstars* was worse – perhaps because of the humiliation as much as the pain, and the fact that the incident will never be forgotten.

'It was a great series,' said Vine. 'Working with the late, great Ron Pickering, we used to commute to the Bahamas or Hong Kong, but the money ran out and Chipping Sodbury wasn't quite the same! The line-ups were incredible, and money meant nothing to them.' To all but one, perhaps? 'Yeah, he [Bowles] was probably there not for the beer but for the cash, but there wasn't much about on *Superstars* in those days. That's why it'll never come back – they could never get the insurance. Can you imagine the young captain of England bike-racing on a mud-track in Rotterdam or something?'

Today's footballers are wrapped in cotton wool and, under constant scrutiny, rarely veer from the well-rehearsed media path taught at their clubs. The 1976 Superstars, however, were ready and willing to take substantial risks – not usually a problem for Bowles as a heavy gambler – in order to prove their sporting value. As Grand Prix driver James Hunt boasted on the show, 'We [Formula One drivers] live on a higher plane. If a footballer makes a mistake, he misses a penalty. If a cricketer makes a mistake, his bails come off. If I make a mistake, I'm a mark on a wall somewhere.' So Hunt was not the partner in crime Bowles might have thought he was. He might have claimed to be there for the beer but was actually just as hungry to prove himself as the others. Bowles, on the other hand, seemed to start the show on the lowest plane he could find and, as the events progressed, embarrassingly, stunningly, hilariously, he fell off.

Incredibly, according to David Vine's extensive memory archive, Stan Bowles, despite registering the programme's

lowest ever final score, was not in fact the worst competi-
tor the programme ever witnessed. 'The worst was a
Dutch basketball player,' Vine insisted. 'His greatest
moment was on the parallel bars. People like [judo legend]
Brian Jacks would do 120 or so; this basketball player
went down for the first one and never came back up!'
Scant consolation for Bowles, then. 'I was impressed,
though,' Vine emphasised, clearly unwilling to be too
critical of the QPR striker's performance, 'by the way he
carried on. He did his best. He was a hell of a laugh. He
was always telling us stories about dog racing. I remember
a comment about his greyhound – he said he'd sold it
when he found out he could run faster than it!' And this
is Bowles' success, even in failure. He could shrug his
shoulders, crack a few jokes and move on. 'I was proud of
the fact that the *Daily Mail* said we were putting the fun
back into sport,' Vine added. If there is any fitting epitaph
to Bowles' career, it would be 'At least he had a good
laugh'.

It is fair to say that while this story, and countless
similar tales of woe, often portray Bowles as the 'loveable
rogue', his footballing prowess has been unfairly neglect-
ed. It's important to recall the moments of sublime skill
that turned him into a celebrity in the first place. He
would later go on to break another record: scoring more
goals in a single UEFA Cup campaign than any player
before him. It was one of many highlights in an eventful
career that oppose the self-imposed low points that
blighted his life publicly and privately.

The *Superstars* story sums up Bowles' career rather
succinctly. Coming as it did bang in the middle of his
playing days, in 1976, it found him in the public eye as
one of the country's best, most famous and popular
footballers. He was on one of the world's most popular
shows. And he got so drunk that he completely messed
things up, leaving the nation with a legacy that will stay
in the annals of TV sporting history for ever. The story
features that endearing hint of tragicomedy essential to
the making of a 'maverick' and shows Bowles, as ever, not
having the sense or discretion to stay off the lager for one

night. He might not have won the competition if he'd been completely sober, but it's typical of the man that he lost in such a spectacular fashion. There's no point doing anything by halves, as they say.

2 Start of the Affair: QPR, 1972–75

*Stan could sometimes be seen going to the betting shop
before the game in his kit, then walking down South Africa
Road trying to get back in the ground on time.*

STEVE RUSSELL, QPR FAN

As the star of the Queens Park Rangers team throughout
much of the 1970s, Stan Bowles would turn up in the
dressing room on Saturdays at a quarter to three, get
changed and go straight out on to the pitch to entertain
his audience. No warm-up, no 'psyching-up' or mental
preparation was required. Until a quarter to three he
would have been watching the horse racing upstairs in the
lounge or at the bookie's. 'I could get away with it,' he said
with a grin, 'simply because if I had been left out of the
team at that time, when I was flying and probably the best
player around, there would have been murders from the
crowd. So although the managers didn't like it, they
accepted it.'

'That was just Stan,' confirmed Don Givens, Bowles'
partner in the QPR attack. 'In those days we never went
for a warm-up, and at about twelve minutes to three Stan
would turn up, then at three minutes to three we'd be out
on the pitch. He'd been watching the 2.45 race somewhere or at the bookie's just by the ground. Betting was a
big part of his life, but as his team-mates, that didn't
interest us. I played a lot of golf, but to the other boys that
didn't mean a thing. As long as you can do your best when
you're playing then everybody's individual interests are
their own.'

'Stan could sometimes be seen going to the betting shop
before the game in his kit, then walking down South

Africa Road trying to get back in the ground on time,' recalled lifelong fan Steve Russell. 'He was an instant star. He took the number 10 shirt, which nobody wanted [after Rodney Marsh had vacated it], and he made it his own. He was just fantastic, the fans took to him straight away. He was a magical character and he scored wonderful goals. You thought the ball was glued to his foot he had such close control. You don't see so much of that these days. He also brought a bit of humour. When he used to take corners he'd sit on the wall around the pitch at Loftus Road and he'd be taking his time, chatting to the fans.'

Bowles' status as the fans' favourite and his eventual return to the big time in Division One came after a few painful years in the doldrums, and he was determined to enjoy his well-deserved moments of glory. QPR had shelled out to bring him to London, and now he was about to start repaying them numerous times over.

Following a few turbulent years at Manchester City, Bowles' career had hit rock bottom until he dragged himself back into the game and joined Carlisle. There were plenty of clubs watching his progress. 'All of a sudden there were scouts in Carlisle to watch me,' he remembered. 'I should have originally gone to Crystal Palace but they dropped out at the last minute and QPR came in. We'd played them down at Shepherd's Bush and apparently the chairman, who turned out to be a good friend of mine, Jim Gregory, said, "They've lost 4–0 but that kid from Carlisle was the best player on the pitch. We'll go and buy him." So he made the money available to come and buy me.'

Back in the summer of 1971, however, Gregory had been looking for buyers for the club, and it was only because no offers were received that he remained in charge. The signing of Bowles from Carlisle in September 1972 helped to instil a newfound enthusiasm in Gregory and the new striker looked just as good as Rodney Marsh, Gregory's previous adopted son at QPR – if not even better. 'It was a lot of money to Carlisle at the time, £112,000,' said Bowles, thinking back to the moment when Queens Park Rangers made their bid to take him to

London. 'So the deal was done the same day. I even left the same day, moved into digs in Acton, and I was a Rangers player.'

By this stage in his career he was taking football more seriously than ever before, even believing, as many people were telling him, that with some dedication he could soon become an England player. Rangers was his fifth club and he was still just 23 years old when he signed. It was a huge opportunity to prove himself after wasting the first years of his senior career at Manchester City. After City had sacked him (for reasons discussed later) he went to Bury, Crewe and Carlisle, rebuilding a shattered career with impressive self-motivation and per-severance, aided by firm-but-fair managers Ernie Tagg and Ian MacFarlane. With QPR set to gain promotion to Division One along with an impressive Burnley side, it was Bowles' second bite at the big cherry.

Queens Park Rangers were not a big club in 1972, but they had big plans. When Bowles arrived, at the same time as Don Givens and winger Dave Thomas, QPR were spending a fortune to try to get into the First Division. These three players, bought at the start of the 1972/73 season, played a big part in turning the club into many people's favourite second team, and although the crowds at Loftus Road would never match those at Old Trafford or Anfield, Rangers became a very trendy club to be at. As Bowles insisted throughout his long career, London was the place to be. 'It was all pretty easy,' he recalled nonchalantly. 'Being around people like the Quality Street Gang [villains he knew from Manchester] I wasn't bother-ed about going to different places. I could mix quickly and I knew a lot of people in London by then anyway. Within a couple of days at QPR me and Gerry Francis hit it right off and that was it, I was settled in.'

Over the years Bowles developed a number of close relationships, not only with the adoring fans but with QPR players and staff, but none was so productive on the pitch as his understanding with midfield maestro and soon-to-be England captain Gerry Francis. 'It was a special relation-ship on the pitch,' Bowles agreed, 'and we became friends as well. We're still friends now. He said after my first week, "I'd heard a lot of stories about you but I didn't realise you was this good!' "

When he arrived in London few people realised just how consistently brilliant Bowles could be. QPR fans had been missing the talented Rodney Marsh – another player with flair, cockiness and imagination to spare – whose career had taken him in the opposite direction with a big-money transfer to high-flying Manchester City. Bowles arrived at Loftus Road, claimed Marsh's hallowed number 10 shirt, and never looked back. 'I scored over a hundred goals for Queens Park Rangers,' Bowles said, 'but my game was more about entertaining the crowds. Obviously I wanted to win, but entertaining was drilled into you as a youngster at Manchester City. It was simply, "We want to win but we've got to entertain this crowd otherwise they'll go mad." And they're still like that at City now, the fans like to see it. QPR was similar. They've always had good attacking players right through their records.'

If fans and team-mates didn't know that Bowles was such a massive talent, they would certainly soon be aware that he was a big gambler. Just before he signed, pictures appeared in the newspapers of Bowles with his empty pockets turned inside out, promising never to gamble again. 'Nobody knew I was a gambler in the early days,' he said, a hint of irritation in his voice. 'Those pictures in the paper with me saying I'm giving up gambling were just to get me out of a bit of trouble.' Over the years, Bowles would feature in more newspaper columns for non-football reasons than he did for his exploits on the pitch, many of the stories publicity stunts he had set up for himself or was offered. As with the *Superstars* fiasco, though, all too many of them backfired spectacularly.

The first serious trouble he got into after joining Rangers, however, was certainly not planned. Bowles was actually quite fortunate to avoid a jail sentence because of it, a feat his acquaintance Carlisle Peter failed to achieve. At the end of 1972, a few months into Bowles' first season in London, he and Don Shanks, who was then playing for Luton Town and whom Bowles had got to know through a shared love of the Hackney dog track, found themselves in trouble just for stopping to buy a burger from a Wimpy in Holborn, central London. After a successful afternoon at the track, they had parked their borrowed van on the pavement. Bowles laughed as he picked up the story. 'We was outside this Wimpy bar facing Snow Hill police station, believe it or not. Don Shanks parked on the pavement and of course the police have spotted it. I went off to get a paper and I was coming out of the newsagent's when I noticed the fairly unusual sight of Don lying on the floor surrounded by a group of men pointing guns at his head. My immediate thought was, "Shit, did we pay that Wimpy bill?" The cop asked us a thousand questions. They laughed when we said we were professional footballers. When they searched our pockets they found I had on my person a packet of mints, one of those small blue bookies' pens and £1,800 in cash. Don had 25p and a packet of beef-flavoured Monster Munch. I used to be banker for our gambling forays as Don and me always pooled our money. He begged the copper to write down £900 each.

'It turned out that the Transit van – which I'd borrowed off a mate called Carlisle Peter – had stolen plates on it. We went to the Old Bailey over it because it had been used in an armed robbery. Pete had nothing to do with that but he eventually got three years for changing the plates. He got us out of it, or we'd have been in trouble. He told them it was nothing to do with us. I'm still in touch with Carlisle Peter. He goes to Manchester so I see him there quite a lot. He's been in the nick about four times since then. I think every now and again he likes to go in and have a lie down!' Bowles claimed that Carlisle Peter had been involved in a number of 'small-time robberies' and at the time of the arrest was going to Jersey, on the run from the police.

The papers went to town on Bowles. The Queens Park Rangers manager at the time, Gordon Jago, was upset and embarrassed by the incident, although a public apology was later issued by the police. The judge dismissed the case against them on the grounds that the court had been misled, but the pair were not fully exonerated until March

1973, by which time QPR were progressing very well in the League.

Since his debut in the 1972/73 campaign, a 3–0 win over Nottingham Forest on 16 September 1972, Bowles netting the second goal, hopes of promotion were increasingly high. The team certainly had the personnel to go up, and by the New Year they were one point behind eventual champions Burnley. They ensured a promotion place with five games of the season left to play.

It didn't take Bowles long to get himself into trouble yet again, on this occasion, as Bowles recalled with another laugh, even making the *News at Ten* for a prank that went very, very wrong. With promotion already tied up, Bowles apparently decided to have some end-of-term fun during the last game of the season. The opponents were Sunderland, who had just won the FA Cup 1–0 against the previous year's winners, Leeds United, at Wembley. The Sunderland fans were delighted to see the trophy on display at the side of the pitch as their players ran out at a Roker Park packed with 43,265 happy faces. Their League season, however, had not gone all that well – they eventually finished in sixth position in Division Two, four places behind QPR – and with the promise of top-flight football in a few months' time Bowles' side was rampant, even taunting Sunderland players to get the ball off them. What really annoyed the supporters, however, was when Bowles – who, as he recalled, had had a little bet with a team-mate – kicked the ball at the treasured cup, knocking it clean off its stand at the side of the pitch.

'Even if I had missed I think it would still have caused trouble,' he said. 'All the Sunderland fans ran on to the pitch and we were taken off for forty minutes.' In fact, it was about ten minutes. 'Then the police got involved because I was "inciting a riot" and Jim Gregory didn't want us to go back on. We beat them 3–0 and we were taking the piss because they'd won the Cup. They were still celebrating so they weren't quite with it, if you know what I mean.

'It caused a lot of trouble. I got a lot of f***ing hate mail after that. They were going to kill me and do this or that.

There were letters stacked up at the stadium and the club secretary said, "I can't handle this." I just told him to sling them in the bin. They were not too happy with me at all. It was on the *News at Ten*! It was the lead story! The cup came right off the stand and got a bit of a dent in it! Luckily enough we were all about on the halfway line when they all come on the pitch. It was like the f***ing Taliban running at you! There was thousands of them and all the players dived down the tunnel while they sat down on the pitch. We had to stay in Sunderland overnight and we weren't allowed to leave our hotel. There were police walking round everywhere and they weren't happy either. I've not been back since. We [QPR] played them when we was in the Premiership, when Les Ferdinand was playing at Shepherd's Bush, and I still got a bit of stick then! It was a laugh, but it didn't go down too well at all.'

It is worth mentioning that the incident is recorded briefly in no less a publication than *The Official History of Queens Park Rangers Football Club*, a studious and reliable tome if ever there was one, though its version is slightly different to Bowles'. It reads: 'The Rokerites' tempers were not helped by Rangers winning 3–0 and [burly QPR defender] Tony Hazell knocking the cup off its stand with a clearance.' Separating fact from pub anecdote is occasionally a challenging matter, but Bowles has always been eager to please his public, and the fans want funny stories. It is, after all, sensible to maintain the level of interest appropriate to a legend, or a maverick, or whatever label you want to stick on him. This kind of story bumbles around in the air, flying from pub to pub, office to office and sofa to sofa, morphing and changing ownership over the years. How does that saying go? Flies around shit, bees around honey. Though Hazell's implied end of the bargain here is massively unfair – he really wasn't 'shit' in any context – the best stories do get attached to the best players, and they often keep hold of them.

Regardless of who actually knocked the FA Cup off its table, 1972/73 was a very successful season for the Second Division club. Two of the new signings finished as top scorers: Don Givens with 26 (23 League, 3 Cup) and

Bowles with 18 (17 League, 1 Cup). Bowles' goals came from 39 appearances and included the side's only hat-trick of the season, against Swindon Town in February. The attendance for QPR's first home match of the season, against Sheffield Wednesday (a 4–2 victory), was just 12,977; compare that to the final home attendance of the season of 22,187 for the visit of Fulham (a 2–0 victory). Queens Park Rangers' achievement in winning promotion was partly due to fielding the same players for practically each game – the same eleven started in the last fourteen League matches, with the exception of John Delve replacing Bowles on two occasions. Gerry Francis played in every match that season, bagging nine goals, while Mick Leach, a forward until Bowles' arrival, scored twelve times from central midfield.

TOP HALF OF DIVISION TWO, 1972/73

	P	W	D	L	F	A	Pts
Burnley	42	24	14	4	72	35	62
Queens Park Rangers	**42**	**24**	**13**	**5**	**81**	**37**	**61**
Aston Villa	42	18	14	10	51	47	50
Middlesbrough	42	17	13	12	46	43	47
Bristol City	42	17	12	13	63	51	46
Sunderland	42	17	12	13	59	49	46
Blackpool	42	18	10	14	56	51	46
Oxford United	42	19	7	16	52	43	45
Fulham	42	16	12	14	58	49	44
Sheffield Wednesday	42	17	10	15	59	55	44
Millwall	42	16	10	16	55	47	42

In the FA Cup they had also acquitted themselves well, reaching the fifth round where they met an ebullient Derby County and a prolific Kevin Hector. Derby had won the First Division in 1971/72 and put QPR in their place. The League Cup was less enjoyable for Bowles' side: they went out at the first hurdle to West Bromwich Albion and an unlucky Dave Clement own goal. It had been an eventful season.

For much of his time at Loftus Road so far Bowles had been using Valium, an addictive drug, to keep himself relaxed. However, his lifestyle and tendency to pick up bad habits meant that what started as an innocent experiment turned into many years of physical and mental self-abuse. 'I used to take Valium a lot. I was on it for about six or seven years,' he said soberly. 'Just to calm me down because I used to get a bit agitated. I used to buy fifty off my mate Johnny Hanlon for a tenner. I was banging at it at one time, doing about four or five a day. Plus with the drink, it makes you disorientated, or whatever they call it. The doctor at QPR got me off them because he just wouldn't give me any. It wasn't my nerves with the football. I was having a few panic attacks at the time. The doctor round here [Brentford] won't give me any. I mean, I could get some if I wanted, but I'm still trying to get off them.'

It turned out later in his career that the panic attacks were caused by his alcohol intake, a compulsion which eventually landed him in a psychiatric ward. While Bowles is happy to talk and laugh about his gambling and the lurid tales of scraps with managers and going into hiding, even to open up about his broken marriages, he is withdrawn when mention of drink and drugs comes up. Even if he tries to shrug his shoulders and proffer a typical 'but it doesn't bother me', the painful experiences will not be forgotten. It is in harsh contradiction to the fun-loving, hard-living legend many assume Bowles to be that he cannot fully ignore his mistakes. None of the mavericks, despite their big box of magic tricks, can claim to be able to turn back the clock.

The 1973/74 season, though, was definitely not a season to try to forget. The last time Rangers had ventured into the top flight, in 1968/69 with Rodney Marsh the star and manager Alec Stock at the helm, they had been utterly humiliated, winning four games and accumulating just 18 points from 42 matches. This time around, however, the side was more settled and experienced. Jago went into the transfer market cleverly once more to sign Arsenal centre-back Frank McLintock, who had captained the Gunners to their 1971 League and FA Cup Double.

This season also saw the introduction of the rule whereby three, rather than two, teams were relegated, so Bowles and his team-mates needed to hit the ground running. With First Division football back on the agenda, the fans flooded back to Loftus Road, but in their first five games they witnessed four draws and one defeat, to Manchester United at Old Trafford. Not spectacularly promising, but then again not spectacularly bad either. Then came the breakthrough: a 3–2 win at home to West Ham United. This victory sparked a run of goals from Stan Bowles – nine in eleven League games between 22 September and 1 December – to help Rangers on their way. The fifteenth match of the season, a 3–0 home win over Coventry City with Bowles, Francis and Terry Venables scoring, gave QPR eighteen points, equalling the total amassed in the First Division by the club during the entire 1968/69 season.

Although the goals continued to flow throughout the second half of the campaign, too many goalless draws and home defeats meant that QPR could not clamber much further up the table. By the end of the season and a 1–1 draw with Arsenal on 30 April 1974, Bowles getting the important goal, Rangers had played enough good football to earn eighth place in Division One.

TOP HALF OF DIVISION ONE, 1973/74

	P	W	D	L	F	A	Pts
Leeds United	42	24	14	4	66	31	62
Liverpool	42	22	13	7	52	31	57
Derby County	42	17	14	11	52	42	48
Ipswich Town	42	18	11	13	67	58	47
Stoke City	42	15	16	11	54	42	46
Burnley	42	16	14	12	56	53	46
Everton	42	16	12	14	50	48	44
Queens Park Rangers	**42**	**13**	**17**	**12**	**56**	**52**	**43**
Leicester City	42	13	16	13	51	41	42
Arsenal	42	14	14	14	49	51	42
Tottenham Hotspur	42	14	14	14	45	50	42

By finishing joint third highest scoring side in the division – Givens (fifteen), Francis (nine) and Leach (nine) weighing in with their share of the goals – Queens Park Rangers had more than exorcised the ghosts of 1968/69. Bowles, who finished with 22 in 51 appearances and numerous assists, was the catalyst for much of their good work, and his 19 goals in the League meant he was the third highest Division One scorer, behind Southampton's Mick Channon and Leicester's Frank Worthington. Bowles didn't miss a single match during a season which included an FA Cup run to the sixth round, where they went out to Leicester City having beaten Chelsea, Birmingham and Coventry along the way, and a League Cup run to the fourth round which saw them hammered 3–0 by Third Division Plymouth Argyle at Loftus Road.

Bowles was the focal point. In fact, during all his years at QPR he never once made an appearance from the subs bench. If he was fit and he turned up for the match, then he would play from the start. Occasionally he'd pull a temporary disappearing act over some financial argument with chairman Jim Gregory, maybe put in a transfer request, and therefore not play at all, but whichever side of Bowles was being displayed, there was no place for him on the bench. Everything was either black or white with Stan Bowles. His career, though, was reaching ever higher peaks. At the end of the 1973/74 season he had been called up to the England team. Unless his controversial, fiery personality got in the way, there seemed to be no stopping the young striker.

The summer signing of another central defender, Dave Webb from Chelsea, was offset by the exchange of Ian Evans and the ambitious and tactically astute midfielder Terry Venables for Crystal Palace's Don Rogers. Despite the fact that the 1974/75 season eventually further consolidated QPR's reputation as a dangerous side in Division One, a terrible goal-shy start to the new season saw manager Gordon Jago quit in early October for American side Tampa Bay Rowdies and Dave Sexton arrive from Chelsea. Sexton dragged Rangers from the foot of the table with four wins in his first six games in charge. He sold Tony Hazell to Millwall and bought Don Masson from Notts County and Don Shanks from Luton Town. QPR clearly had a penchant for Dons!

As January 1975 got underway, Sexton's side had forced itself into mid-table. Bowles was fast establishing himself as an international star, but the goals started to dry up and he finished the season with a disappointing twelve in total, ten in the League and one each in the FA Cup and League Cup. Don Givens fared better, scoring 21 in all; Leach got just two, while Francis, reliable as ever, managed ten. Queens Park Rangers finished in eleventh place.

TOP HALF OF DIVISION ONE, 1974/75

	P	W	D	L	F	A	Pts
Derby County	42	21	11	10	67	49	53
Liverpool	42	20	11	11	60	39	51
Ipswich Town	42	23	5	14	66	44	51
Everton	42	16	18	8	56	42	50
Stoke City	42	17	15	10	64	48	49
Sheffield United	42	18	13	11	58	51	49
Middlesbrough	42	18	12	12	54	40	48
Manchester City	42	18	10	14	54	54	46
Leeds United	42	16	13	13	57	49	45
Burnley	42	17	11	14	68	67	45
Queens Park Rangers	**42**	**16**	**10**	**16**	**54**	**54**	**42**

There are a number of unsubstantiated stories from this stage in his career that Bowles keeps up his sleeve for special occasions, worth mentioning here purely for their comedy value. Like the time he went to a meeting of the local Gamblers Anonymous, laughed at everyone else's tragic stories, then arranged a game of blackjack. He thought that as they were all big losers he'd have a good chance – but of course, as even Bowles admits, at the end of the night they had taken his money.

Then there was the occasion when he was in the bookie's and two armed men burst in and stole the money he had just handed across the counter. 'It was like chucking a vindaloo straight down the khazi instead of consuming it first,' he once complained.

On another day, Bowles and Shanks found themselves at Epsom race track on yet another quick money-making venture. The idea was to do a picture special for the papers of Bowles' dream: to ride a Derby winner. The horse turned out to be in an extremely bad mood, and took off with a panic-stricken Bowles, who'd never ridden before, on its back. The horse eventually stopped, as did Bowles' screams of terror, and strolled past the finishing line, allowing the photographs to be taken. As he has confirmed, and as numerous team-mates testify, there was not much Bowles wouldn't do for a pocketful of cash.

Before the drink and drugs became a serious problem, however, Bowles was busy wrapping the press around his little finger. While he was often criticised, occasionally vilified, by some journalists, he always knew how to make a few quid out of them. 'I once did a drugs confession in the *Daily Star*,' Bowles reminded me with a chuckle, 'but that was just to get money. Brian Woolnough gave me £500 and I told him I took drugs. It was all bollocks, but I still managed to get in trouble with the FA over it!'

Not one to be put off, Bowles was soon going to the papers again. 'I knew Brian Madley of the *Sunday People* quite well, and one day I said to him, "Look, Brian, give me £500 and I'll give you an exclusive." He asked me what it was, and I said, "I'm retiring. I want the money in readies today and then you can put it in your paper." So he told me to come down to the office, we done the story, he gave me the money and two days later [on 22 April 1975] I came out of retirement! It was f***ing mad. He never spoke to me for about twenty years. The last time I bumped into him was at QPR, and he came up to me with his bad leg and walking stick and said, "You bastard! I nearly lost my job over you!" So I said, "Yeah, and what about all the aggravation you gave me?" It was just my way of getting back at the press. You could do things like that.' Not many players did do things like that, though.

Generally speaking, Bowles' unique brand of naivety and cheekiness endeared him to the reading public and the journalists who wrote the stories, but there was another side to Bowles' relationship with the press, as the chapter about his notorious England career demonstrates in gruesome detail. There are plenty of examples of the prickly relationship between top sports stars and the people who make a living writing about them. In Bowles' heyday, when rock 'n' roll footballers were sticking two fingers up at anyone who'd watch, press attention was beginning to turn into the clumsy, oafish monster it is today. There was back-stabbing and invention, invasive reporting and bad feeling aplenty. 'Mike Langley,' growled Bowles, still visibly annoyed with the former *News of the World* reporter. 'A mate of mine once grabbed him round the throat in front of Herbert Chapman's bust at Highbury! He dug me out [criticised me] in one of his articles saying we don't ever want this man back playing for England – he walked out on our country and all this bollocks. For some reason he was writing about Herbert Chapman's bust and my mate Mad Mick just grabbed him. He shit himself!'

Langley, like many journalists, had criticised Bowles for walking out of the England hotel after being subbed in a Home Nations match against Northern Ireland in May 1974. Much like the England managers of the day did to Bowles, he has pretty much forgiven Langley, and even approached him when writing his autobiography in the mid-1990s. 'He still wasn't all that complimentary, but I let it go ahead, do you know what I mean? He still stuck to his story – more or less what he was saying all them years ago.' Bowles shrugged. 'And I still see Mad Mick now, by the way, and he's got plenty of money. He's got a lot of property and jewellery shops now, so he's not as mad as he makes out.'

Even though Bowles was aware that his position meant he was accorded certain privileges, the assault on Langley was a particularly shocking incident, and one that suggests he was a man not afraid to risk getting himself into serious trouble. Or, as was the case on a number of incidents, letting his mates (some people call them 'minders') risk getting into trouble on his behalf.

There was a hint of Liam Gallagher in his attitude to press intrusion. 'You had half a chance then because there wasn't as many cameras about as there are today. People like Beckham can't even go to the shops. They know they're being photographed. We didn't have that so much in them days. I didn't have a problem with the press because I got round them by saying, "Well, you can follow me anywhere you want. I don't give a f**k." So they were like, "Oh, he doesn't give a f**k if we follow him. Where's the fun in that?" That worked out pretty well.' And there was more than a hint of the rock star in his private life. Like George Best, but maybe with a little less success, Bowles transcended football and had a personality outside it. He was a publicity magnet who surfed the waves of media attention in order not to be drowned by them, all the while trying to enjoy the trappings of A-list celebrity. The first generation of rock 'n' roll footballers outgrew football, and so did Bowles' cravings.

Even back in the 1970s there was rarely the amount of socialising within football clubs as many people assume; most players usually had families to go home to and other interests to occupy themselves. As Gerry Francis underlined, 'We were great friends, me and Stan, but we didn't always socialise. Stan would go off gambling and I was more into the women, so we used to go our own ways. There were times when we'd go out together, but he had his mates and I had mine.'

'I wasn't socialising with footballers – I never did, really,' Bowles confirmed. 'Don Shanks was my mate, but he wasn't really a footballer anyway! Charlie George was another, and I still see him to this day. But apart from that there was no footballers. There was a few people in the rock game who I got on with, like Phil Lynott from Thin Lizzy. I spent a lot of time with Phil – he used to live just up the road from me. Some of the Sex Pistols used to go to QPR matches because they were all from White City. Phil Collins, too. I've met loads of them sort of people.

'The day [in November 1976] Don Revie resigned on the plane coming home from Rome – we'd got beat 2–0 by Italy – I got a bit drunk on the plane because he'd resigned and we all had champagne and that. Elton John, who was on our plane, invited me to a party back at his house in Hertfordshire. I was happy at first because no one really knew he was a f***ing poof. I was up for it. So my mate picked me up from the airport and he said to me, "You can't go to Hertfordshire!" I said, "What's the matter? What do you mean?" And he said, "He's a bandit! He's a f***ing shirt-lifter!" Anyway, I swerved that invite. I've got a picture of me at the airport with Elton John and it looks like he's got his hand up my arse! My daughter's got it now, and I've told her to keep hold of it and not to show it to anyone, ever!' Never one to hold back with a good story, Bowles chuckled as he recalled his embarrassment. His opinions are certainly 'old school' – some would venture a more damning analysis of his reaction to Elton John's sexuality – and there's no doubting his standing as a 'man's man': never afraid to speak out, to throw in a few 'f***ing's for emphasis, to challenge authority or to crack a few gags about it afterwards.

Glen Matlock, the original bass player with rebellious punk band the Sex Pistols, has always been an ardent QPR and Stan Bowles supporter. 'Bowles was the greatest,' he once told *FourFourTwo* magazine. 'He was such an entertaining player and so talented. The fans loved him because he always liked to put on a show when he played and you always knew he was one of us. He was a bit of a villain, and I suppose he was a real rock 'n' roll character, but that's why I admired him, because he had that streak in him that always wanted to cause trouble.

'I actually got to play football with Bowles a few years back when we played in a five-a-side tournament at Wembley. Elton John had organised this competition and there was us lot [the Sex Pistols], the Stranglers and Rod Stewart, and every side was allowed to have a former professional player. We managed to get Stan Bowles to play for us. There were eight thousand people watching. Stan Bowles has got the ball, so I thought, "Right, I'll make a run here." So I'm shouting across to Stan to pass, and Brian Moore's commentary [on the PA system] is, "Bowles beats one player, he beats another player, he beats a third player . . ." Meanwhile I'm trying to cut across him to make some space, and Stan shouts, "Get out of the f***ing way!" But I couldn't, and his shot goes wide. I felt so embarrassed.'

Such a great footballer that he makes even rock stars feel humble in his presence, Bowles' extravagant skills on the pitch have always been mirrored off it. He summed up his lifestyle in just a few simple sentences: 'A typical day would start with training, and then I'd go off to the races. If not, the betting shop. I'd have a few drinks later on, go to the dogs, and then start it all over again the next morning. It was like that for quite a few years.' At this he laughed for a second, which showed that he does now realise his lifestyle was privileged in some ways and foolish in others, certainly never normal. 'I didn't have a problem with it, though,' he added simply, 'because at the end of the day they could never say that I didn't produce on a Saturday.'

Simplicity is appropriate to Bowles because he was never interested in the complexities of fame, or even of life. While all those around him might have been tearing their hair out, the most laid-back figure in any room – with the help of a few pills now and again – would be Stan Bowles. But, as with any way of life, it was impossible to ignore indefinitely the monotonies and necessities. Like paying bills. 'They [QPR] used to give the wife a few quid for bills, but that didn't last long. That was their idea, not mine. I was six months ahead of my wages so I was borrowing all the time. Because I was gambling so much I needed money every day, and I could demand it every day, otherwise I wouldn't play. Well, I would have played, but I'd just rear up.'

Queens Park Rangers, and especially chairman Jim Gregory, seemed to know what was best for Bowles, even if the player didn't know himself. While Gregory couldn't do much about his unprecedented 'fake retirement' announcement in a Sunday newspaper – an incident which Bowles claimed Gregory found 'hilarious' – he knew how to deal with Bowles' constant transfer requests. 'He used to sling my transfer requests in the drawer and say, "Yeah, all right." The *Daily Express* had him saying I'd put in 32 transfer requests, and I said, "No, it was 33 actually." That amused him. None of them were really serious. It was every time I used to run out of money. If he didn't lend me any money I used to play up a bit, but it all worked out in the end. He'd give me an extra few quid on a Monday, £200 in cash. Some of the players – well, Don Masson – found out. I don't know how because I certainly didn't tell him, but he went to Jim saying, "If he's getting £200 I want £200." But Jim said, "Well, you're not as good as him." F**k off, basically.'

Gregory also had a very individual way of handling enquiries from other clubs, as Hamburg discovered when they travelled to London to offer Bowles a contract. 'Hamburg tried to sign me before Kevin Keegan. We had a meeting at the Royal Lancaster Hotel in Bayswater. We were supposed to meet them about ten in the morning and I was there, but there's no Jim. So I go out the back and ring him up because it's now about eleven o'clock, and he says, "What's up?" I tell him, "Well, we're supposed to be meeting the Germans this morning." He said, "I don't like the f***ing Germans. Do you want to go to Hamburg?" I said, "Well, no, not really." He said, "Right, I'll give you two grand Monday morning, and come over for f***ing Sunday lunch. Now, just f**k off out the back!" And that's what I done. That was the end of that transfer. I didn't want to go anyway.'

It was just as well for QPR that Bowles' 1975 retirement was a wind-up, that none of his transfer requests was wholehearted and that he didn't want to move to Germany, because things were about to get very exciting at the club. After a few years of mid-table mediocrity, QPR were about to challenge the likes of Liverpool and Manchester United for the League title, with Bowles at the heart of their wonderful attacking style of play. Though off the pitch his life was as turbulent as ever, his football was reaching a level rarely seen in the English game. His wife Ann filed for divorce in 1975, just as Bowles' greatest ever season was about to commence, but he convinced her to change her mind and went on to play some of his best football, thriving in these inhospitable conditions.

Manager Dave Sexton saw that his continental ideals were starting to pay dividends on the pitch. Sexton, who now works alongside Sven Goran Eriksson as chief scout in the England set-up, recalled that it was not difficult to work with Bowles or any of the other players at QPR. 'I'd been at Chelsea as manager since 1967 but I ended up getting the sack. Immediately Jim Gregory got in touch with me and asked if I'd like to go there because they had just lost Gordon Jago, and this meant I could still commute from Brighton as I'd been doing over the years. So it all worked out very well.'

The team Sexton inherited practically picked itself and was clearly capable of challenging at the top end of the table. They were old heads playing enthusiastic football, with Bowles the magician at the front. 'It was a real pleasure because there were about four or five captains,' Sexton said. 'People who had been captains before – which is unusual, because it's hard enough to find one to take that bit of responsibility. Stan had been there a couple of years before I arrived and they were a very good and experienced team. There were people like Frank McLintock and Dave Webb and a number of very experienced players coming to the end of their careers. Of course, the captain then was Gerry Francis, who was captain of England as well, so they had a hell of a playing staff. It was mature with some good youngsters like Dave Thomas. They all had international reputations, except Dave Webb.

'From my point of view it was a very good succession to go from Chelsea to QPR. At Chelsea the expectations were very high and there was pressure to do well. But QPR were a much humbler club and were grateful for any sort of success. So I enjoyed not having the strain and also working with such good players. It was a mostly joyous three years at QPR. It was great for me because, having finished disastrously at Chelsea after so many years, it was a wonderful pick-up. Quite a few of the players were in the England and Scotland sides, so they were brilliant to work with, that's for sure.'

Sexton knew not to get involved in Bowles' financial queries, and chairman Jim Gregory always dealt with them quickly anyway. 'Only once was I made aware of a money thing,' Sexton recalled, 'but that died down so it must have been sorted out. Stan and Don Shanks were always there when you walked past the offices at the club, waiting to get in for something or other. Shanks was a good lad. I think they enjoyed themselves. Had a bit of fun.'

'Dave Sexton was probably my favourite manager to work with,' Bowles revealed. 'At first we didn't get on at all, but the more I got to know him the more I got to like him. Sometimes his training sessions were really boring, just complicated and boring. He was just working to make us into a better side, but I was a bit impatient.'

Sexton's experience of Bowles remained purely based on football, and he was keen to paint a utopian picture of the player widely regarded as a legendary bad boy. It is almost refreshing to hear that Bowles, despite all his 'misdemeanours', was committed to improving his game, or at least to staying fit enough to maintain his towering levels of performance, even if he did sometimes find Sexton's sessions 'boring'. 'He was a fit lad and I had no problems with Stan whatsoever,' Sexton insisted. 'No problems with training – he'd do it standing on his head. I think he enjoyed it. His problems came off the field, and they were taken out of my hands because of Jim Gregory, who was looking after him. I didn't have any clashes with him, especially not on the training field because he was always very good, no problem. He was supposed to have had a fight with Frank McLintock once, when Stan tried to bite his ear off, but I missed that. In fact, Gerry Francis was the one who used to turn up late for training, and he was the captain. Stan wasn't one of those. I never had any trouble with him apart from one period when he fell out with his missus. I remember picking up the paper one day [in January 1976] and seeing a photo of Stan with a topless girl. His wife got really incensed and walked out on him. Went back up north. That's the only bit of bother I remember. Otherwise he was a pleasure to work with because he loves football. Most good footballers you don't have trouble with because they want to be part of a good team, and he was one of those. The main thing about Stan is not his gambling or whatever, it's the fact that he loves football. First and foremost.'

Bowles' strike partner at QPR, Republic of Ireland international Don Givens, also recalled that Bowles' football life, away from the public glare and in between the arguments, financial demands and front-page appearances, was quite normal. 'He did have the odd "24-hour flu", as we used to call it,' Givens said with a laugh, referring to Bowles' tendency to disappear without reason, 'but that was on the very odd occasion. And because of his well-known liking for a bet, his lifestyle was very different to mine. When he was at the training ground or out on the pitch there was never a problem. He was very easy to get along with. All the boys knew he'd have a bet, but he was just a good laugh.'

After so many years, Sexton was keen to take the focus away from any kind of glorification of Bowles' off-field activities and, rightly, to give credit for what he was capable of with the ball at his feet. 'Obviously I'd seen Stan play so I knew he was very clever. I'd sum Stan up simply by saying that he was a bloody good footballer. He had a good football brain. I know he was a goalscorer, but probably his passing was his strongest asset – a very clever passer of the ball. He was clever on the ball, but his distribution was even cleverer. He'd bring more people into the game and then come up with the goals as well.'

Since Bowles had joined the club, QPR had been promoted to Division One and had finished eighth and eleventh in the top flight in consecutive seasons. Now, they were about to take their fans' breath away with one of the most closely fought and finely balanced seasons in the history of English football. And Stan Bowles, of course, was in the thick of it.

3 European Record-breaker: QPR, 1975–79

We must have been doing something right to be giving Liverpool a run for their money.

DAVE SEXTON, QPR MANAGER

'Dave Sexton used to say to me, "Stan, you've got to start thinking about other parts of your game now." Tracking back, or whatever they call it,' Bowles admitted, thinking back to that amazing 1975/76 season. 'And I used to listen to him and then just go out and do my own thing. That's how I worked it out: I'd listen to him and then think, "F**k it." Once I was out there on the pitch my own mind took over. And I would always produce.'

'He enjoyed working with me,' Sexton said, 'because it was a very attacking side, which suited Stan. It would have been a pleasure to play in that team for anybody. They enjoyed the success because we made a bit of a name for ourselves.'

Even before the first League game of 1975/76, Bowles' and QPR's best ever season, the side was in devastating form, beating West German champions Borussia Moenchengladbach 4–1 and Portuguese champions Benfica 4–2 in friendlies. John Hollins had arrived from Chelsea to add another dimension and some renewed competition to Rangers' midfield.

Sexton had a keen interest in Dutch and German tactics and training methods, and he took the squad to a small town near Hamburg called Hennef for those pre-season friendlies. 'We used to go to Germany every pre-season to all the top sides,' Bowles recalled, 'because Dave Sexton was fascinated by the way their coaching was done. That's probably why we did so well in Europe later on. We played a bit of a continental style. Everything was on the floor with them. Holland still try to do it today. But then it was quite unusual for an English team to do it. We played that style in the League.' Sexton is enthusiastic to this day about that style of play. 'I was very much into the Dutch system,' he said with a smile, 'so we modelled ourselves on that. Keeping it on the ground. We were one of the first British teams to do that. Because it suited us, we had the players to do it. Don Masson was a revelation, his passing was fantastic, and he deservedly got himself into the Scottish international side – he was a real clever player and he demanded the ball. You can't have eleven people like that or it would be chaos! But he had enough personality, even among that crowd, and with all the senior players, to get us started off in attack – to get the ball off the defence and get us going forward again.'

Sexton's appreciation of the continental style proved well-founded during that 1975/76 season: Bayern Munich had just won their third consecutive European Cup, beating St Etienne in Glasgow. While not quite able to emulate Bayern's all-conquering performances or the 1974 Holland side's 'Total Football' approach to the game, Sexton ensured that his team played attacking and flowing football – a style of play that would take them to the top of the table. With so many gifted ball players, they could afford to leave themselves a little short in defence and to focus on scoring more goals than their opponents.

The opening game of the season, on 16 August 1975, couldn't have been more testing – against Liverpool, runners-up the previous season – but QPR's self-confidence proved to be justified, swashbuckling midfielder Gerry Francis scoring what turned out to be the BBC's Goal of the Season in a 2–0 victory in front of more than 27,000 fans. Their third game of the new season, after drawing with Villa, was a 5–1 thrashing of reigning champions Derby County, a match which featured a Stan Bowles hat-trick.

Suddenly, QPR found themselves at the top of the table, with Sexton's assertions that they were capable of winning the League, which had originally seemed unrealistic, ringing in the players' ears. Furthermore, the consensus among press and public was that Stan Bowles should definitely be in the England side.

QPR's optimistic and almost universally popular League challenge continued at full steam. Throughout the course of this long, thrilling season they were impossible to beat at home, notching up memorable scorelines against the likes of Everton (5–0) and Wolverhampton Wanderers (4–2) as well as more than a few notable away results, including victories over Spurs, Newcastle and Aston Villa.

When the return fixture against Liverpool eventually came round, on 20 December, Bowles, four days short of his twenty-seventh birthday, was returned to the side after briefly being dropped following a row over his gambling, which would occasionally interfere with his and the team's preparations for games. Liverpool got their revenge, beating QPR 2–0, a painful result that was followed by two games in two days: against Norwich City on Boxing Day (a 2–0 win) and Arsenal on the 27th. During this latter game, Bowles, sick of being man-marked wherever the team travelled, wound himself up and was eventually booked for an offensive gesture to one of the linesmen. Arsenal won the game 2–0, knocking an exhausted QPR's confidence off-track. There was not much to celebrate that week.

A renewed assault on the Division One summit was still not out of the question, however, and Bowles was enjoying his life, but more controversy followed in the New Year when, not for the last time, he found the offer of tabloid money too much to resist. For £500 he agreed to pose with a topless model for the *Daily Mirror*, a decision that would have disastrous consequences for all concerned. 'That thing with the topless model went a bit boss-eyed,' he admitted, 'because she had a crash when she left the shoot and was in a coma. Her boyfriend kept ringing me up to find out where she was. How he got my number I don't know, but he thought I was having an affair with her. I told him there was nothing going on – I mean, that's what she was, a topless model, so what can you expect? She was a nice girl, that model. She did her

job and we got paid. Then she drove off and I went down
the West End somewhere. Her boyfriend didn't know
where she was because she'd been in this crash; he heard
that I was down the West End with some bird so kept
ringing me. She eventually come out of the coma but it
was a serious crash and she was lucky to live.'

Already sick of his London lifestyle, his first wife Ann,
whom he'd known since he was sixteen (and she was
fifteen), moved back to Manchester when she saw the
pictures. 'I got in trouble with me wife over it as well, it
caused murders,' Bowles mumbled with a little shake of
the head. 'But she came back. That time.' Full of regret,
he put in a transfer request and was allowed to go on the
transfer list. He was also once again dropped from the
side.

As happened with all his transfer requests, however,
Bowles soon changed his mind and forgot about it, and his
chairman let him get on with it. Jim Gregory treated
Bowles like a loveable but mischievous son – even more
so than he had Rodney Marsh – and Bowles, in return,
treated Gregory something like a piggy bank. While he
was staying at one of Gregory's flats (rent free) he claims
to have sold the greenhouse from the back garden to
team-mate Dave Thomas for £100, a story Thomas vehe-
mently insisted was a figment of Bowles' imagination.
What is true is that Bowles was losing a lot of money and
constantly begged the benevolent chairman, something of
a maverick himself, for cash to cover his debts. Gregory,
who always had a soft spot for Bowles, often used to cave
in.

Elsewhere, the season was throwing up a few contro-
versies that didn't feature Stan Bowles. Billy Bremner and
four Scottish team-mates were reportedly involved in an
'incident' at a Copenhagen nightclub. Despite their denials
('There was no row in the club, no fight, and no trouble
about the bill,' Bremner claimed earnestly), they were
banned by the Scottish FA from representing their country for the rest of their careers. And at Manchester City,
Bowles' first club, Rodney Marsh was put on the transfer
list against his wishes for 'not giving one hundred per cent

to the club'. He then snubbed a move to Belgian club Anderlecht believing the language barrier would be too difficult to overcome. Fallen Manchester United legend George Best, who had been suspended from playing in any country under the jurisdiction of FIFA after he played for Detroit Express even though Fulham held his registration, made the first of his doomed comebacks at Stockport County. Later in the season he signed for Cork Celtic, who threw him out after three matches. Two other maverick footballers, Charlie George and Alan Hudson, were badly injured during the same match: Derby's George dislocated his shoulder, and Stoke's Hudson broke a bone in his foot, missing the rest of the season. Then an FA committee recommended that players should stop 'kissing and cuddling' after scoring (on the pitch, that is); if they persisted they would be under threat of being charged with 'bringing the game into disrepute'. The suggestions were later resolutely rejected.

QPR continued to play excellent football into the New Year, even prompting Tommy Docherty, manager of newly promoted Manchester United and a man who would come to have a major influence on Bowles' later career, to proclaim that if United didn't win the League he hoped it would be the London club. The entire country could not fail to be impressed by, and fearful of, QPR's potent brand of attacking football, constantly stoked by the perfect partnership of attacking midfielder Gerry Francis and Bowles in a wandering forward role.

Even during this high-flying season, Bowles did not alter his unconventional pre-match preparation: checking the afternoon's races. He would stay in the bookie's or the club lounge for as long as possible, confident that, unlike his gambling partner Don Shanks who was never as precious to Jim Gregory, he would get away with it. Managers didn't like the way he behaved, but couldn't (or wouldn't) argue. When Dave Sexton took him off at West Ham in February 1976, Bowles flicked him an angry V-sign then vowed never to speak to him again. Like Rodney Marsh and every other maverick to take the field, Bowles believed he knew best. 'That was where my strength was,' he claimed. 'I could come out of playing cards all night, or being in the bookie's for four hours, losing absolutely every penny I'd got, go out on the football pitch and perform like I was Gary Lineker.' Hardly a more inappropriate comparison could be found, but maybe that's the point. A model professional like Lineker he most certainly was not.

When the team travelled to Sheffield United on 28 February they were without an injured Gerry Francis, and drew 0–0. It was this poor result against a side featuring Tony Currie, who would later succeed Bowles in the QPR number 10 shirt, in addition to an untimely 3–2 defeat by Norwich City in April, which effectively lost QPR the League title. The season ended in a tense and ultimately acrimonious fashion. Having lost to Norwich, QPR were knocked off the top stop they had held since the beginning of March, and then had to host struggling Arsenal. With three minutes of the game remaining, QPR were 1–0 down. Then, former Gunners defender Frank McLintock popped up with an equaliser, before Bowles fell in the box to win a dubious penalty – not for the first time in his career. Gerry Francis held his nerve to net the goal from the spot and keep his team in the title race.

QPR's forty-second and last League match, on 24 April, was again at home, the visitors this time high-flying Leeds United who were just a few points behind Rangers in the table. A season's best 31,002 fans turned up to watch the match. Dave Thomas scored first, then Bowles bagged Rangers' last goal of the season, and his eleventh, in a 2–0 win which took them back to the top of the table.

And that should have been that, but with Liverpool's season disrupted by UEFA Cup fixtures, their final domestic game was postponed until 4 May. Rangers had remained undefeated at home all season and had not dropped below fifth place in the League while Liverpool had struggled in the early stages before re-establishing their supremacy. Bowles, not the most patient person at the best of times, had to sit and watch Liverpool take his title after an agonising ten-day wait. Late goals from Kevin Keegan, John Toshack and Ray Kennedy against Wolves in that last delayed match took the Merseysiders one point clear and handed them the Division One title. Wolves had been playing for survival, but Liverpool's single-mindedness proved irresistible. QPR's second place, however, had secured them a UEFA Cup place that in a few months' time would bring about Bowles' single greatest achievement as a player. Considering that in 1973 the club was in Division Two, these were giddy heights indeed.

Because of Liverpool's victory, the 1975/76 season, albeit QPR's most successful ever, was a bitter disappointment for the players. So close to winning the championship, yet so cruelly denied. 'It was the highest League position Queens Park Rangers have ever got in their history,' Gerry Francis said joylessly, 'but we really should have won it because I thought we were the best side that year in terms of flair and football and natural ability. It was a tremendous side. We had ten internationals in that team – it was only David Webb who wasn't an international and he was an excellent player for us anyway. So many times you can't remember what some of the teams were, but the names roll off your tongue. There were big clubs in the division that year but most of them never even got close to us. The biggest challenge we got as the top London club was from West Ham.'

Dave Sexton, though not an emotional sort of character (some of his players called him Stiff Neck behind his back), is still reeling from the experience. 'It was absolutely frustrating to get so close in 1976. Bloody whatsisname, the bloke who kept coming on as supersub for Liverpool [David Fairclough], always got them out of trouble. It was galling, but had a great run at the end. We were unbeaten at home all season so we couldn't have asked for a lot more. That ten-day wait was a bit nerve-racking. It's no consolation, but we must have been doing something right to be giving Liverpool a run for their money.'

Gerry Francis recalled the wait as more than 'a bit nerve-racking', blasting, 'It was outrageous. That would never happen today. All the games should be finished on the same day. We sat there as champions for nearly two weeks but not really champions, and then we had to go and watch the match at a TV studio. Wolves led for a long time, but eventually Liverpool won the game. Our whole season went up in smoke. I sat with Stan and it was a very depressing time. We jumped up when Wolves scored but slowly sank into our chairs as the game went on. We both left before the final whistle and went our different ways, really, really depressed. It was unfortunate – we were either champions or we weren't. To have that wait, then go through that game in the studio was very hard on everybody.'

Bowles insisted Queens Park Rangers were by far the best footballing side in the division that season, and sighed as he recalled having the championship snatched away. 'For the last twenty minutes Liverpool were all over them. I left before the end and said, "They're going to get three or four here, Gerry." And they did. We were twelve minutes away. Wolves were leading with about twelve minutes to go but in the end we lost the League by a point. It gives you some idea how important that season was because it's all people at QPR talk about, even now. They don't talk about Les Ferdinand, although he was a good player. They talk about the 1975/76 season, and of course getting into Europe as well.' In spite of the disappointment, not to mention all his transfer demands, Bowles signed a new six-year contract with Queens Park Rangers that June.

Emlyn Hughes, who was playing at the heart of the Liverpool defence throughout their most successful years, looks back at that season as a springboard to even greater things. It was then that the Merseysiders were becoming invincible, at home and abroad. 'It was a great time to be at Liverpool,' he enthused. 'We'd come through the changeover period of the early 1970s when Shanks had changed all the older players and we'd all bedded down. We were a very good side. A very, very good side. In thirty years' time people will look back at our record over that period, with English players. And I'm not criticising the foreign players, but we didn't have any outside influence, bringing somebody over from France or Bosnia or from bloody China or from anywhere they want to bloody bring them over. We were all English or British players, and it was such a together club. The atmosphere in the dressing room was fantastic, but it was everything about the club. Shanks started it all off and Bob Paisley took over, and there was a good team spirit.'

The record books never tell the whole story, and Bowles and his team-mates will forever be remembered as the runners-up. Bowles' QPR epitomised football as entertainment, their win-every-match approach almost taking them to the very top. They were never going to be a huge club, so the fact that they finished second rather than first makes this a better story to tell – it adds a sprinkling of sadness. The team and its star player fell just short, the plucky underdogs ultimately crushed by the mighty Liverpool. And, at the risk of taking this poetic moment too far, the maverick who nearly beat the odds.

TOP HALF OF DIVISION ONE, 1975/76

	P	W	D	L	F	A	Pts
Liverpool	42	23	14	5	66	31	60
Queens Park Rangers	**42**	**24**	**11**	**7**	**67**	**33**	**59**
Manchester United	42	23	10	9	68	42	58
Derby County	42	21	11	10	75	58	53
Leeds United	42	21	9	12	65	46	51
Ipswich Town	42	16	14	12	54	48	46
Leicester City	42	13	19	10	48	41	45
Manchester City	42	16	11	15	54	46	43
Tottenham Hotspur	42	14	15	13	63	63	43
Norwich City	42	16	10	16	58	58	42
Everton	42	15	12	15	60	66	42

Late on in that famous season, Bowles' marriage finally collapsed for good when Ann, who had just about forgiven him for the topless model incident, found out about his relationship with a young actress he'd met at the White City dog track, Jane Hayden.

Tact was never Bowles' forte. His actions often annoyed team-mates as well as wives, though the consensus remains that his was a wonderful talent. Former QPR right winger Dave Thomas is, in contrast to Bowles, a sensible man – a PE teacher, occasional commentator and keen gardener these days. In fact, Thomas couldn't be further away from Bowles in terms of personality. An excellent player in his own right, with eight England caps, he is down-to-earth, open and, by maverick standards (even though he did wear his socks down around his ankles, shunning shin-pads), rather dull. So when he says that Stan Bowles was 'the top striker of the era', there is no reason to doubt him. He isn't a 'sound-bite' sort of man, and he isn't getting paid to talk Bowles up either. 'He was something else,' Thomas stated. 'He had a natural gift. He was a great player – no question about that.

'The kind of football we were playing at the time suited him. Dave Sexton had a lot to do with it – he was a fantastic coach and a super manager. With him, we played continental football, playing the ball out from the back. We were a passing side, not just a lot of good individuals but a very good team as well. The sad thing is we never won the championship and you're only ever judged on what you win. But from an entertainment point of view it was a fantastic spectacle.'

Still, Thomas is not one to eulogise for too long. He and Bowles were never exactly the best of friends. 'It's a pity that he wasn't like a Michael Owen in the modern era,' Thomas remarked. 'Owen has got a bit of a brain – a brain to have the right attitude off the pitch as well as being a wonderful footballer. Stan didn't have that really, because of his gambling. That was the biggest let-down. He used to frustrate us because he used to turn up late for training and he could get away with it. He was very close to the chairman, Jim Gregory, and had "player power", even back then. He could do no wrong. We accepted that the crowd loved him – in their world he could do no wrong, a bit like Rodney Marsh really. But Stan, in that particular era, was the top striker.'

Thomas is less forgiving about that story in *Stan the Man*, Bowles' autobiography (now out of print), which had him surreptitiously buying Jim Gregory's greenhouse for £100. 'Some things he said in that [book] were unbelievable,' he raged. 'Things about me and one or two of my team-mates. I wasn't too happy about that. I supposedly picked him up in the morning and said, "Whose is that greenhouse?" And he said, "The chairman's. If you give me £100 you can have it." One: I've never picked Stan up in my life. And two: I'd never give him £100 for a bloody greenhouse! It's an absolute load of bloody lies! But that's the way he is. People will read that and think, "Bloody hell, Dave Thomas was a bit of a bloody character." '

Rarely has the sale of a greenhouse caused such a tide of fury, but Thomas is keen to stand by his principles. Whether the exchange of cash for a small glass garden shed would ever cause anybody to think of him as a 'bit of a bloody character' is hugely questionable, but that is hardly the point. The point is that he doesn't want people to think of him as a character, just to remember him as a good footballer. If you believe Thomas' recollection of the greenhouse scandal, that would mean either that Bowles invented the story just to add spice to his own autobiography or that he actually sold it to someone else entirely.

Thomas's diatribe wasn't over. 'It's all right Stan slagging off his team-mates, saying "I was the kingpin in the team", but in fact we were all kingpins. He wasn't playing the game then and I contacted my solicitor about it. It's just not on. Not that it'll cause any major upset, but I think you've got to be honest. That was Stan, and he'll be like that for the rest of his life. I got on really well with him, but things like that really annoy me. He was a nice enough lad, but he was always controversial.'

Another team-mate, Gerry Francis, has nothing but compliments for Bowles and fond memories of playing with him. 'I've never had a relationship with another player in my whole career like I did with Stan – telepathically knowing where he was going to play the ball or where he wanted it played. He was undoubtedly the best player I ever played with, and I played with a lot of good players from my England days. During those few years at QPR, when we were going for the championship and playing in Europe, he excelled. He was such an articulate and dangerous player. He made as many goals as he scored; he certainly made a load for me. I'd play it up to

Stan and then go running past him; he'd do a little turn and knock the ball right into my path. That was his greatest period.'

In the searing heatwave of 1976, Bowles' burgeoning relationship with Jane Hayden gave his life a new sense of direction, a new challenge. Changes were afoot in the football world too, which was slowly turning into show business. Comedian Eric Morecambe had just resigned from his position on the Luton Town board, but a certain Elton John, with whom Bowles was later that year to have a brief encounter, was putting his money into Watford Football Club. The game was becoming stuffed with money, wages and transfer fees climbed inevitably towards the one-million-pound mark, and top players found themselves in the public eye more than ever. On a less glamorous note, football was also battling hooliganism, with Chelsea's thugs at the fore. British Rail's 'soccer specials' – trains to deliver football supporters around the country – were cancelled following a number of unpleasant incidents. A government working party was desperately convened to try to find some answers, with crowd control one of the main items on the agenda. Serious thought was given to issuing ID cards to officially registered fans, thereby cutting off hooligans' access to matches.

The continuing beauty of Bowles' football offered a welcome respite from the ugly scenes occurring around the country. While 1976 saw Liverpool firmly re-establishing themselves as one of the continent's leading football powers, winning the UEFA Cup as well as the League, the forthcoming 1976/77 season would give QPR their first ever chance of playing European football (although they had appealed in court unsuccessfully for the right in 1967 after winning the League Cup), and Stan Bowles, for once, took the opportunity with both hands – and, more importantly, both feet.

Rangers, in contrast to the likes of Liverpool, had absolutely no pedigree in European football. This was to be their first ever campaign on foreign shores. Knowing no other way to play, they charged headlong into the continental challenge, determined, perhaps naively, to win every game they played. Ultimately, Bowles recorded a goal tally European competition had never before witnessed from a player from the English Football League. Despite this remarkable feat, QPR, punching above their weight and missing an injured Gerry Francis, did not win the UEFA Cup – though they did come surprisingly close – while Liverpool won the European Cup, defeating Borussia Moenchengladbach in Rome.

'The European game suited our style,' said Dave Thomas. 'The continental sides had been playing like we did for years.' It certainly suited Bowles, who got off to a flying start. His first three goals came in the form of a hat-trick against part-time Norwegian side Brann Bergen during a first-leg 4–0 victory on 16 September 1976. The away leg turned out to be no more taxing, and again Bowles scored three. The existing record of nine goals, held jointly by Denis Law and Derek Dougan, was well within sight after just two matches, and the team had scored eleven goals in all.

Bowles was never a particularly prolific forward compared to the likes of Law or Jimmy Greaves, and later in his career he happily moved further back into the midfield, but this European adventure was giving him the opportunity to show off to the world, an opportunity he was by this stage in his career being regularly denied at international level. He revelled in the praise he received from his manager and from the press.

The first serious challenge in the UEFA Cup came in the very next round, when QPR met Czechoslovakian side Slovan Bratislava – a different proposition to Brann altogether. Czech champions in 1974 and 1975, and runners-up in 1976, Bratislava boasted many of the players who had represented their country in the 5–4 defeat on penalties of West Germany in the 1976 European Championship final in Belgrade the previous June. QPR, as always, had nothing to lose, and the game in Czechoslovakia finished 3–3, Bowles getting two of the goals. Although the Czechs were supposedly poor travellers, the second leg a fortnight later gave QPR a few unwelcome surprises. The fact that goalkeeper Phil Parkes was voted man of the match tells its own story; QPR did not get things all their own way. Nevertheless, another seven goals were scored: five for QPR and two for Bratislava. The team had scored nineteen goals in their first four European matches ever – not a bad way to start! Bowles' memories of the two-leg tie stretch as far as 'It was even colder [in Bratislava] than Carlisle!' but the home leg is mostly remembered for his record-equalling strike, alongside three goals from Don Givens and one from Dave Clement.

Going into the third-round match against Cologne on 25 November, Bowles was under pressure after an X-rated tackle on Middlesbrough defender Willie Maddren, who accused him of purposefully going over the top of the ball. Bowles was upset at the accusation, insisting, 'I know I don't kick opponents, my team-mates know I don't, and I just want Don Revie to know I don't' – rare evidence that Bowles cared about his reputation and international career. Dave Sexton backed him up. 'Stan is not a violent bloke. I will not discipline him.' (A first time for everything!) Incidentally, after this unpleasant incident with Maddren, though not necessarily as a direct result, English referees were given their very own 'supremo' to oversee standards.

The clash with Cologne came just a week after Bowles and England failed to beat Italy in Rome in an important World Cup qualifying game, so the forward was eager to show England manager Revie what he could really do. The doyen of football journalists, Brian Glanville, noted in the build-up to the match that players like Bowles – players who were willing to take opponents on – did not get the same treatment on the continent as they did in domestic football, going on to praise not only Bowles' 'astonishing footwork, swerve and balance' but also his 'resilience and determination'. To answer any remaining critics, Bowles scored a sensational volley against the Germans to cap a fine performance in a remarkable 3–0 home win. He latched on to a hopeful, stabbed poke through from Givens, took the gentlest of touches to kill the ball, slipped it between two defenders in a flash and then curled it around a young Harald Schumacher and into the back of the net. 'That's the record!' shouted commentator Barry Davies, as if it were inevitable. The second leg on 8 December was more taxing, a Don Masson strike securing Rangers' progress on away goals even though Cologne scored three in front of 50,000 German fans.

Off the field, Bowles was facing another test of his character: it was revealed he had not been keeping up maintenance payments to his estranged wife Ann. He was in fact hundreds of pounds behind and facing a month-long jail sentence. But Bowles was broke – completely broke. He owed money not only to Ann but also to a selection of local bookies and to Queens Park Rangers, who'd forwarded him several months' wages. He was one of the most admired footballers in Europe, yet he didn't have a penny to his name. As he recalled in his autobiography, 'The order [to pay off the arrears] came in December 1976, but I wasn't due any wages until 1978!' His whirlwind romance with the UEFA Cup was proving considerably more straightforward than his love life, especially when with Ann looking for the money she was owed and Jane eager to get married, Bowles found solace in the arms of a court clerk he had met at a previous maintenance-payments hearing and whom he remembers fondly as a fellow 'nutter'.

The quarter-final draw matched Bowles and his team with dangerous Greek side AEK Athens, who had eliminated Derby County and their goalscoring sensation Kevin Hector in the second round. Considering England's dire performances on the international scene at the time, there was much attention on English clubs in Europe and a great deal of hope placed on them. The home leg, though, came round on 3 March 1977 when domestically things were looking bad for QPR. Furthermore, England, with Bowles up front, had just a month earlier been trounced at Wembley by Holland. The restoration of pride looked doubtful.

Gerry Francis, though, was back in the side after a long time out injured, and he gave Rangers a welcome boost with two penalties, after seven and eleven minutes, to add to Bowles' eleventh goal of the campaign, just before half-time, for a 3–0 win. Bowles remembers that the AEK Athens manager was furious, believing Bowles' goal to have been offside, and this led to the QPR star receiving death threats at Loftus Road from the local Greek community. If Bowles flew to Athens in two weeks' time, the general gist of the letters warned, he'd be killed. Despite his terror of flying, these threats served only to make him more determined to go. After all, this was a great opportunity to reach a European semi-final at the first attempt.

During the second-leg match itself, the Greek fans were placated by a goal from Mavros after just eight minutes, followed by another on 65 from the same player and an equaliser on aggregate from Papioannou eight minutes from time. After extra time neither side could find a winner, so the match went to penalties. It's testimony to Bowles' courage and his love of a challenge that he volunteered to take one despite the heated atmosphere and the pressure of the death threats he had received before the game. It's testimony to his nerve that he scored it. QPR, however, were again without their other regular penalty-taker, injury-plagued Gerry Francis, and paid a heavy price, AEK winning the shoot-out 7–6 and progressing to face Juventus in the semi-final. Bowles had very much wanted 'another crack at the Italians', particularly defender Claudio Gentile who had tamed him during the recent clash with England, so he was devastated that QPR's European adventure was over, especially in such painful circumstances. Despite his carefree image and lifestyle, a passion for football burned inside Stan Bowles. He had thoroughly enjoyed matching himself against the best in Europe.

Still, QPR had done better than anyone could have imagined, and Bowles had written his very own page in the history of the English and European game. 'I got the record for the most goals, yeah – I think it was twelve. I broke the record against Cologne at Loftus Road, which was nice. It was Denis Law's and Jimmy Greaves' joint record. Denis Law, who I know well, was one of my heroes, so it was special to break his record. Jimmy Greaves I don't know so well, but he was a good player in his day as well. I've met him a few times but he seems a bit arrogant to me. He thinks he's right all the time. He thinks everything he says is right, but it don't work that way.'

It's important to point out a couple of minor discrepancies in Bowles' account here. It was not Jimmy Greaves who shared the record with Law, but Derek Dougan, the former Leicester and Wolves striker (so the rant was completely unnecessary). And though Bowles did actually score twelve goals in that European campaign, one was in the penalty shoot-out against AEK Athens and does not officially count. The official record of eleven goals stood for four years before being broken by another British player, John Wark, when Ipswich Town made it all the way to the 1981 UEFA Cup final and beat AZ67 Alkmaar of Holland to take the title.

Despite the sad end to their attempt to win the UEFA Cup, QPR's style of play, with every player joining in the attack, had proved that offensive, courageous and slick English football could produce the goods against the best teams around, even if it was your first ever European campaign. And there were some very good teams in the competition that season, not to mention some interesting results, notably Manchester United's first-round 2–1 aggregate victory over 1971, 1972 and 1973 European Cup winners Ajax, Lou Macari and Sammy McIlroy getting the goals. Also in the opening stages Derby demolished Irish side Finn Harps 12–0 in the first leg of their meeting, and 4–1 in the away leg. County's Kevin Hector bagged seven goals in the tie, and that was enough – even though he didn't get another goal in the competition – to make him joint second highest scorer alongside QPR's Don Givens. Manchester City beat Juventus 1–0 at home thanks to a Brian Kidd goal, but lost 2–0 in Turin. In the second round

Juve faced City's red rivals, again losing 1–0 in Manchester before securing a 3–0 win at home and, inspired by Zoff, Tardelli and Bettega, going on to win the competition, just squeezing past Atlético Bilbao, who'd beaten the likes of Barcelona and AC Milan to get that far.

Gerry Francis, who missed much of the season through injury and could only watch the UEFA Cup exit from afar, believes that things could have been very different. 'We were suited to European football, and we only lost on penalties to AEK Athens. It was unfortunate because I was missing from the away game after we'd beaten them 3–0 at home. I'd scored two goals and Stan got the other. We were all set to play Juventus in the semi-final, but had to play Arsenal on the Saturday; I scored the winning goal there, but in doing so I was stretchered off and missed the return against Athens. I was the penalty-taker at the time. If we'd beaten Athens and Juventus,' he fantasised, 'I think we'd have gone on to win the competition.'

1976/77 UEFA CUP CAMPAIGN

First round
16 September: QPR 4 Brann Bergen 0
30 September: Brann Bergen 0 QPR 7

Second round
21 October: Slovan Bratislava 3 QPR 3
4 November: QPR 5 Slovan Bratislava 2

Third round
25 November: QPR 3 Cologne 0
8 December: Cologne 3 QPR 1

Quarter-final
3 March: QPR 3 AEK Athens 0
17 March: AEK Athens 3 QPR 0 (7–6 pens)

On the domestic front, QPR fans had to settle for a lowly fourteenth place come May 1977, just four points away from a relegation place, while Liverpool again finished on top. Bowles managed just four League goals, two in the League Cup and one in the FA Cup. Don Givens, the other reliable source of goals, added only ten League and two Cup goals to his UEFA Cup tally.

BOTTOM HALF OF DIVISION ONE, 1976/77

	P	W	D	L	F	A	Pts
Middlesbrough	42	14	13	15	40	45	41
Birmingham City	42	13	12	17	63	61	38
Queens Park Rangers	**42**	**13**	**12**	**17**	**47**	**52**	**38**
Derby County	42	9	19	14	50	55	37
Norwich City	42	14	9	19	47	64	37
West Ham United	42	11	14	17	46	65	36
Bristol City	42	11	13	18	38	48	35
Coventry City	42	10	15	17	48	59	35
Sunderland	42	11	12	19	46	54	34
Stoke City	42	10	14	18	28	51	34
Tottenham Hotspur	42	12	9	21	48	72	33

Two seasons of success, at home and then in Europe, could have been the foundation for much more if the club had managed to keep the team together, or even to strengthen it, but one by one QPR's players began to attract the attention of traditionally bigger, richer clubs, and were lured away. 'It was just a shame that the momentum wasn't carried on,' Francis said. 'Because it wasn't a big club it couldn't keep the nucleus of the team. We could have had a dynasty, a decade of being a top side. Once you start selling it's very hard to keep the top players together. Stanley had a great scoring record that season. I think he would have moved away from QPR sooner if it hadn't been for the fact that he was very happy in the environment there. He got on very well with Jim Gregory and, like me, got to love Queens Park Rangers.

'QPR are a selling club, and if you make a world record bid, they are going to sell. Phil Parkes went for £550,000, which was a record for a goalkeeper then. Nothing's changed now. There are big clubs getting 40,000 people in a week and there's QPR getting maybe 15,000. It goes back to the roots and how the clubs were established – whether they started off as a Second, Third or Fourth Division club. Teams like the Tottenhams, Arsenals and Chelseas are all established top-flight clubs from their origins. That's always been the case. Just because you're the biggest club it doesn't mean that you've got the best team, but it does give you the resources to keep your best players.'

Events at Queens Park Rangers over the next couple of years certainly bore out Francis' somewhat negative view, bringing to an end a woefully brief but wonderfully bright golden era. Bowles was the main creative force in that greatest of all Queens Park Rangers sides, a clinical finisher, deadly from any angle, playing behind Irish international Don Givens. On the left of midfield was Dave Thomas, on the right Gerry Francis. Providing stability and no lack of vision or skill in the centre of midfield were Scottish international Don Masson and either Mike Leach or John Hollins. The first-choice centre-backs were Frank McLintock and Dave Webb, flanked on the left by Ian Gillard and on the right by Dave Clement, who kept Don Shanks out of the side. In goal, Phil Parkes was a gargantuan force. The balance and mixture of the side was virtually perfect. All that was missing was a bit of luck.

QPR striker Don Givens saw that the players were now beginning to realise Bowles' special treatment at the club was symptomatic of a small-club mentality. 'I'm sure that Stan got looked after in lots of ways better than most of the other players,' he complained. 'All the players were aware of what was going on, and in the long run it's probably the reason why the team broke up very quickly. I was there for six seasons and there were lots of things going on. At the end of the day you know that you're playing for a very good side, but you're not at a great club. That's the way I felt and that's why I wanted to get out. I think if you spoke to some of the others who left at the same time they'd say the same thing.'

Suddenly there was an avalanche of players looking elsewhere, allowing themselves to be tempted by big-money offers and the prospect of playing for genuinely big clubs. 'It was not just that Stan was getting a few quid,'

Givens expanded, 'but the whole attitude of that kind of situation. Different people reacted differently to Stan. Personally I've always thought that if I go in and discuss my contract, come back out and find out that Joe Bloggs sitting beside me is getting fifty quid a week more than me, then that's my problem, not his. I should be able to discuss my own contract and be happy with it. If someone's abusing the situation at a club to my detriment, then they're causing a problem, but if Stan's getting a few quid because he's in trouble, huh, that's not my problem. However, it was something that set a trend at the club and snowballed a little bit into other areas, and then in the end you do begin to think that maybe you're not quite being appreciated and you're not at such a great club after all.'

Bowles, ignoring any unrest and accusations of unfairness among team-mates, had been living with Don Shanks until they were finally evicted for not paying – or rather not being able to pay – the rent. The pair could often be seen driving around in an out-of-service ambulance which, Bowles claimed, helped them get to the bookie's a lot quicker than any other mode of transport because it still had its siren.

Bowles had had a somewhat less amusing experience in an ambulance with Shanks, however, when he broke his leg during a League match away to Bristol City in March 1977, the Saturday following QPR's heartbreak defeat at the hands of AEK Athens. In a typical fit of rage, Bowles chased after an opponent with just two minutes left on the clock; his foot caught in a muddy patch and he broke his leg in two places, as well as dislocating his ankle. He was carried to the sidelines, his injuries sponged down by some medical staff who were way out of their depth, and a blanket placed over his legs. When the final whistle blew, Bowles' team-mates trooped off, leaving their star player 'among a herd of Bristol City supporters who were swearing and spitting at me as they walked past'. QPR chairman Jim Gregory insisted that Bowles should go to his own personal physician for the operation rather than anybody in Bristol, so Shanks accompanied his friend to London in an ambulance.

Depending on which version of the tale you believe, Shanks either asked the ambulance driver to stop so that they could all get out for something to eat at the services, leaving a delirious Bowles in the back, or he made the driver wait while he rang through a bet for a dog he fancied at the White City track. Whatever really happened, when Bowles woke up he was in Charing Cross hospital in a bed next to Peter Sellers, and, as he tells it, he lived in the lap of luxury, chatting on the phone, drinking champagne and, of course, placing the odd bet. The steel plates inserted in Bowles' leg are still there to this day, after Jim Gregory talked him into delaying the operation to have them removed. It was an ignominious end to an eventful season.

The next one, 1977/78, was to start in even more colourful fashion. A pre-season tour to Belgium should have been Bowles' opportunity to get himself back to full fitness after recovering from his operation, but after scoring on his return to the side, against fellow tourists Derby County, in an event QPR went on to win, Bowles and Shanks had a bit too much to drink in a bar owned by a joint friend before returning to the team hotel. When the staff at the hotel refused to serve them, Shanks had the bright idea of collapsing on the floor as if having some kind of fit. 'Quick, get him a drink!' shouted Bowles, fully aware of the ruse. The waiter brought over a brandy, only for Shanks to stand up and polish it off in one gulp. The pair then merrily ambled off to their room to sleep it off.

Within minutes, however, the Belgian police, together with their dogs, were knocking on their door threatening to shoot it down if they didn't get out of bed. The two players were taken to a police station where, according to Bowles' recollection of the evening, they were set upon by policemen with truncheons. Then one officer removed Bowles' shoes and socks and started to bend his toes backwards, all apparently without telling the footballers what they had been arrested for. After a night in the cells, it was finally explained to them that the waiter at the hotel had rung for an ambulance just after fetching Shanks his medicinal brandy, and that not using an ambulance when it's been called out was considered a serious offence in Belgium. On their return to Britain, of course, Bowles and Shanks sold their story to the press, earning themselves a few extra quid.

Bowles endured numerous run-ins with the authorities throughout his career. On another occasion police searched his house after some jewellery and travellers' cheques had been stolen from Heathrow airport. Gerry Francis recalled another occasion, before Bowles' wife Ann left him, when they were (surprisingly) enjoying a quiet evening in together. 'We were playing at Arsenal and we'd trained at Ruislip. We went back to his house for dinner with his first wife Ann and the kids and then we had to get on the coach and go to Arsenal. We were sitting down, watching the telly and having a bit of dinner, and there was a knock on the door. Ann opened the door and it was the bailiffs. They took the telly, the settees we were sitting on and everything. Stan was doing his nut, going mad. Something hadn't been paid! Nothing affected his playing career. He was the only player I know who could have all these things going on at home – problems with his wife, problems with money – and just put it out of his mind. He played in a way that suited him, and just shut everything else out.'

There would soon be a lot more to shut out as the upheaval at Queens Park Rangers continued. Dave Sexton left to manage Manchester United before the start of the 1977/78 season, and things started to gradually tail off for Bowles. Sexton was replaced by former Rangers player Frank Sibley, who struggled to maintain the momentum of the last two seasons. Dave Thomas was sold to Everton, and before Christmas Dave Webb and Don Masson had both jumped ship too, to Leicester and Derby respectively, as well as David Needham, who went to Nottingham Forest. The arrival of Leighton James from Derby was not enough to halt the inevitable slump. Domestically, goals were even harder to come by than in the previous season, Bowles topping the charts on a lowly nine as QPR finished in nineteenth position, just outside the relegation zone.

BOTTOM HALF OF DIVISION ONE, 1977/78

	P	W	D	L	F	A	Pts
Derby County	42	14	13	15	54	59	41
Norwich City	42	11	18	13	52	66	40
Middlesbrough	42	12	15	15	42	54	39
Wolverhampton Wanderers	42	12	12	18	51	64	36
Chelsea	42	11	14	17	46	69	36
Bristol City	42	11	13	18	49	53	35
Ipswich Town	42	11	13	18	47	61	35
Queens Park Rangers	42	9	15	18	47	64	33
West Ham United	42	12	8	22	52	69	32
Newcastle United	42	6	10	26	42	78	22
Leicester City	42	5	12	25	26	70	22

In the summer of 1978 Sibley resigned. Alec Stock took over as caretaker manager until August, when Steve Burtenshaw was appointed. He quickly signed Glenn Roeder and sold Don Givens and Leighton James. In February 1979 giant goalkeeper Phil Parkes was allowed to leave for West Ham United, and relegation began to look more than just a possibility. With Bowles simply not scoring, a young Clive Allen was given his debut, but his contribution was not enough to drag Rangers from the mire. Chairman Jim Gregory took drastic action and sacked Burtenshaw, then surprised everyone with his announcement of the man to replace him: Tommy Docherty. The Doc had already been in charge at Loftus Road for 28 days in 1969. The move was a strange one and cruelly timed as the team still had one game of the season left to play. Docherty couldn't inspire them and they lost 4–0. Twentieth position in the 1978/79 table ensured relegation, and six interesting years in the First Division came to a shuddering halt.

BOTTOM HALF OF DIVISION ONE, 1978/79

	P	W	D	L	F	A	Pts
Middlesbrough	42	15	10	17	57	50	40
Bristol City	42	15	10	17	47	51	40
Southampton	42	12	16	14	47	53	40

Manchester City	42	13	13	16	58	56	39
Norwich City	42	7	23	12	51	57	37
Bolton Wanderers	42	12	11	19	54	75	35
Wolverhampton Wanderers	42	13	8	21	44	68	34
Derby County	42	10	11	21	44	71	31
Queens Park Rangers	**42**	**6**	**13**	**23**	**45**	**73**	**25**
Birmingham City	42	6	10	26	37	64	22
Chelsea	42	5	10	27	44	92	20

With Tommy Docherty's arrival, Bowles' days at Loftus Road were numbered. QPR were deteriorating, players were leaving and there was no money to bring in replacements. Bowles had already made a stand, refusing to travel to Holland on a pre-season tour; then he handed in a transfer request to Jim Gregory. This time there was a difference: it was his first, and last, serious request. Gregory (reluctantly) and Docherty (less so, though he did once call Bowles, apparently without irony, 'a model professional' and the 'best player I've seen') agreed.

Bowles recalled that his time at QPR came to a natural but hurtful conclusion, with the once super-cool London club falling from grace and not altogether unwilling to see him depart. There was an enquiry about his services. 'Tampa Bay Rowdies came in for me when Rodney Marsh was the manager! It worked out at about £1,200 a week with a flat and a car, but I don't drive anyway so a car wouldn't have been any good to me. I like America, but I didn't fancy going and living there. I've been associated with west London, even though I'm from Manchester, for the last thirty years now.' In fact, Gordon Jago was still the manager of the Rowdies at the time; Marsh, along with George Best, was playing in the doomed North American Soccer League. Nevertheless, Bowles did not want to be away from his beloved west London and, much as he'd done when Hamburg tried to lure him to Germany, he rejected their overtures. Crossing the Atlantic to get to the White City dog track would have been a bit much, even for Stan Bowles.

But Bowles' star was slipping fast at Loftus Road, and the fans were looking forward to having a new hero. Sure enough, Tony Currie was signed from Leeds to be the new star of the Division Two show, and he proved something of a revelation in Bowles' number 10 shirt. 'Getting the number 10 shirt just seemed automatic, really,' Currie said with a shrug. 'There was no talking about it, I just took it over. I think my first game was against Fulham, and I don't know if Stan was dropped and I took the shirt. I just don't remember. I had the number 10 shirt at Sheffield United and Leeds. It was my number, and of course number 10 is *the* shirt. I mean, Pele, Maradona, innit?'

'Tony was fantastic. You run out of superlatives for these players,' Dave Thomas remarked. 'The number 10 shirt at QPR is legendary, and Tony Currie filled it admirably in the same way that Simon Stainrod did later. They [Marsh, Bowles, Currie, Stainrod] were the four players that really deserved it. Currie was right up there with Marsh and Bowles in terms of showmanship and ability and fitting that famous shirt. The only difference is that Currie didn't play nearly enough for us. He was a wonderful player – he had as many tricks as Bowles or Marsh. If you say that Bowles and Marsh were Man Utd and Liverpool, then Currie was Aston Villa or Leeds. Slightly behind those two, but still spoken of in reverential terms and with a great deal of affection.'

Currie, who had in fact signed schoolboy forms with QPR at the age of fourteen after playing as a defender for his school side, hadn't wanted to leave Leeds United, but 'family problems' – his wife was unhappy up north – forced his hand. A move to another First Division side – he only found out later that Arsenal had wanted him – was blocked by Leeds so the player plumped for a club on its way down. 'I settled very well straight away,' he remembered, 'because they were a good bunch of lads. And if the crowd take to you straight away, which they did, then that's 60 or 70 per cent of settling in. The dressing room was a great place to be. Bloody hell, with Ian Gillard, Bowlesy, Don Shanks and Martyn Busby! Buzzer, he was the biggest joker of the lot.

'It was a crossover period for the club. I joined in 1979 and Stan was in and out of the side. I think he ended up in the number 7 shirt. It was a joy to briefly play with him because he was on the same wavelength as me, but I don't know what sort of relationship Tommy Doc and Stan had. I'd have had him in the side, but he didn't get on with Tommy Docherty and that's why he was unhappy. But people are never happy when they're not playing all the time. He was still the star. The fans loved him because he was still there even when all the 1976 side had split up. I certainly didn't take any star rating off him. He just wasn't in the team. We all knew he'd be leaving and it was a shame. But I suppose he could be a bit moody, Stan.'

Currie's time at QPR was spoilt by injury, however. In fact, when he signed his contract at the club he was on crutches, having damaged his ankle in his last game for Leeds. It took him two months to get into the side, then later on in his Rangers career, in the early 1980s, manager Terry Venables laid the now-infamous 'astroturf' pitch which, in Currie's words, was 'Bloody rock hard! It was like playing on concrete.' It wasn't until 1983 that Rangers got back to anything like the level of success they had almost become accustomed to. After winning the Second Division that year, ten points clear of Wolverhampton Wanderers, they returned to the top flight for the 1983/84 season and finished in fifth place. In 1986, safely dithering in mid-table, they reached the League Cup final by beating Liverpool in the semi-final, only to be trounced 3–0 by Oxford United, themselves enjoying a brief foray into top-flight football. A fifth place again in 1988 and 1993 (in the inaugural Premier League season) was followed in 1996 by relegation, a desperate blow from which the club has resolutely failed to recover, even getting relegated to Division Two at the end of the 2000/01 season.

4 Marsh and the Mavericks – the Golden Era

The regrets are all part of the legend, part of being a maverick.

FRANK WORTHINGTON

The *Oxford English Reference Dictionary* describes a maverick as 'an unbranded calf' and, infinitely more fitting in the context of this book, 'an unorthodox or independent-minded person'. No mention of talent or success, then; certainly no mention of football. Football, however, has virtually claimed the maverick as its own. You don't get maverick badminton players or hurdlers.

The mavericks of the 1970s were phenomenally talented footballers who, through various forms of bad behaviour, never reached the heights they should have reached. Alcohol, gambling, women and attitude were usually involved. But who were the major players, and what does it take to become a maverick?

For the sake of brevity, George Best, it is probably safe to say, was the best of them all. He had everything – lightning pace, vision, strength, balance and mesmerising footwork. But 'best' is a vague word and the term 'maverick' needs to be defined further. Non-conformists and entertainers, the handful of players known collectively as the mavericks – Best, Bowles, Marsh, Currie, Osgood, Hudson, Worthington, George – were the most talented players of their time. Their talent was equalled only by their refusal to bow to authority. A bubbling mix of pride and genius elevated them to cult status, particularly as they played during a time when the England national team was huffing and puffing but not blowing any houses down. Yet a series of England managers threw the mavericks only scraps to feed on, struggling to find a way of incorporating their individual talents into formations or systems, or simply not trusting the players to put on an England shirt responsibly. Still, the only one of the controversial group who did not wear an England shirt even once was Northern Ireland superstar George Best.

In maverick terms, Best's off-field career is peerless. He did more disappearing acts than anyone else, he had more fights, he certainly had more Miss Worlds, he ended up in prison and he quit top-flight football at the age of 27. Best set a standard few could hope to match. The only thing that could possibly count against him when establishing the ultimate definition of a maverick is the fact that he was named European Footballer of the Year and won the European Cup in 1968, whereas players such as Stan Bowles and Frank Worthington, despite their wonderful talent, won virtually nothing. Part of the essence of being a maverick is throwing away opportunities for success.

For example, Alan Hudson fell out with England manager Alf Ramsey and was banned from international football for three years. Then he fell out with Ramsey's successor, Don Revie, telling him he was too busy to play against Brazil in April 1978. 'I just don't like people telling other people what to do,' he once said. While playing for Arsenal he was sent home from a tour for partying a little too hard, and later walked out on the club. After football and a selection of doomed business enterprises, he was declared bankrupt. There are similar strands running through the careers of each of the mavericks' lives; many of football's great characters were never too far apart. Hudson was once set up by a newspaper, along with Bowles and Worthington, to drink champagne with a few girls (provided by the paper) in a hotel room before going on stage to speak at a show.

One reason why players like Bowles are still loved to this day is their ability to laugh things off, to make a joke in the face of difficulty. Bowles' manager during his season at Crewe, Ernie Tagg, insisted his former player was like Stan Laurel, of Laurel and Hardy fame: always with a grin on his face, letting nothing trouble him. Bowles, forever at war with a consensus, has little time for the tag. 'I don't think I was a bad boy,' he maintained with a shrug. 'The only f***ing maverick I've seen was an old cowboy series called *Maverick*. I don't know how it's defined in the dictionary – a bit of a rogue, someone who just doesn't care about anything or something like that. I wasn't really like that. It was just a term they made up and it stuck.' Still, his lifestyle and charisma meant he was always in the newspapers, always in demand, and at one point his fan club was said to be second in size only to George Best's. As Frank Worthington observed with a smile, 'In the 1970s there was an abundance of characters and lots of great individual players. Nobody epitomised that as much as Bowlesy. That QPR side was brilliant and Bowles was the icing on the cake. He could turn the game with one piece of magic.'

Stories become expanded and distorted over the years, but the hunger for gory detail is as strong as ever. The 1970s witnessed the beginnings of bad boys in football, and in the midst of an increasingly fertile and promiscuous youth culture the decade happily courted controversy. They were undoubtedly the maverick years, and now, as football has turned quickly into big business – on the back, it must be said, of the public interest the mavericks stirred – it seems as though it were a century ago.

Worthington, who in a varied twenty-year career played for Huddersfield, Leicester, Bolton, Birmingham, Leeds, Sunderland, Southampton, Brighton, Tranmere, Preston and Stockport, can be included in the list of great 1970s mavericks, probably at the top along with Best and Bowles. Looking back on the era, he hardly recognises it as the same game that is being played today. 'People have a fascination for the era,' he explained. 'It's about players who were individually gifted and could turn a game with one piece of brilliance, like Bowlesy, Marshy, Alan Hudson and myself. That's exactly what the fans want to see – somebody who can do something different with a football. Now it's all a little bit more predictable and you know exactly what players are going to do.

'Like Beckham, for example. A lot of people try to compare him to George Best, who was an absolute genius, an all-round genius. Beckham is one-dimensional, even though he's brilliant at what he does. One moment of magic that will stick out is a set-piece – and he has wonderful technique when scoring like that – and his fantastic service. But he can't go past players, leave two or three defenders trailing in his wake, on their backsides, with a bit of mesmerising magic – he does it with one simple pass or a cross. It's a wonderful skill, but you can't compare it with Georgie Best. Ryan Giggs is the nearest thing to a George Best, but Best had that bit extra that lit up any stadium. He was a phenomenon.'

For anyone who never saw Bowles play in the flesh it's difficult to visualise how good he was, especially as he rarely gets any publicity for his football these days. Don Givens, Bowles' strike partner at Queens Park Rangers, offered his opinion. 'I can see a lot of similarity between Stan and Dennis Bergkamp. I saw Bergkamp in training a lot at Arsenal when I was coaching the under-19s there. They have totally different lifestyles, but as footballers that would probably be the kind of player Stan would be today, with a lot of intelligence on the pitch. Stan was half-blind – he couldn't see somebody 25 yards away. If we were out having a drink, he'd wave back to somebody who was waving at him and then turn to me and say, "Who was that?" But on the pitch, jeez, he could see everything, he had that great vision.'

It is a valid comparison, particularly with the added ingredient of an absolute hatred of flying. On the pitch, Bowles had the ability to control a game, like Bergkamp, using perfectly accurate passing and a rare vision in attack. Bowles also had the ability, like David Ginola, to drift past opponents, though he utilised his dribbling skills less often. And in the same way Ginola at his best is singled out for rough treatment from opposition defenders, so Bowles suffered more than his fair share of bruising tackles, such was the desperation to stop him.

Ginola is also a good example of how a player can be both good and bad for a club. He has been one of the very few top players in recent years to keep the ball inches from his feet when charging at players at full speed and have the arrogance and skill to believe that he can get past them, whoever gets in his way. When it comes off, it is football's most beautiful sight, but what has Ginola won in the game? He can hardly be called a maverick, but he is the nearest equivalent – in terms of talent, disenchantment and what-could-have-beens – the Premiership has seen. Even great players like Eric Cantona and Ryan Giggs passed the ball to a team-mate in a better position, but Ginola's great strength – in this context, at least – is to go for glory. Managers have criticised him but never changed him. When he's trusted, he can win games, but a one-man show doesn't win titles.

This theory was proved at Liverpool during the 1970s, and their results speak for themselves. Former England defender Emlyn Hughes insisted that his Liverpool side, possibly the greatest side of them all, thrived because there were no mavericks in the side. They relied on consistent excellence rather than one man's magic tricks. 'It was important that we won. It might sound not very nice in terms of football, but it was not important that you showed everybody how good you were,' Hughes said animatedly, 'that you could flick the ball over your head and bounce it on your bum, and flick it down on seven knees. Nobody was interested in all that – we were interested in winning trophies, which is what football is all about. That's what we did, and nobody has ever done it better than we did. This Manchester United side over the last ten years has been superb, but they've not been able to win abroad [consistently]. We won six European trophies in nine years.'

Because of this ideal of having a workmanlike but skilled and effective team, English football stimulated a need for mavericks, and further strengthened the maverick players' desire to entertain. Like Liverpool, Nottingham Forest grabbed European success with a defensive and uninspired line-up, and when Bowles joined them in 1979 he could not get into the side. People wonder why the England national side has not been successful for three decades. Well, part of the reason at least is that genuine talent has blatantly not been encouraged in the English game.

That said, the mavericks were often their own worst enemies, and in each case there is great cause for regret, though few would admit to it. Frank Worthington is open about how his maverick lifestyle and attitude spoilt his career. 'The one regret I have,' he said sadly, 'is when I came back from an England under-23 tour but I'd been living in the fast lane. Bill Shankly was ready to sign me at Liverpool for a record amount of money at the time. The last thing I'd done at the medical was the blood pressure, and the fact it was too high was just a sign of the way I'd been living my life. That cost me what would have been a wonderful move to Liverpool, because on the international stage me and Keegan were brilliant together – we complemented each other. It would have been fantastic.' Shankly told Worthington to relax on holiday and get his blood pressure down, but one three-in-a-bed incident with two Swedish women and a famous affair with a fearsome lady from the Belgian town of Knokke later, Worthington failed his medical again. 'Given my time again I would have heeded the warning and got my feet up with a good book. Lots of early nights, no threesomes and definitely no Knokkers,' Worthington later admitted. 'But of course the regrets are all part of the legend, part of being a maverick.'

'People look back and wish there was a few of those characters around now,' said Givens. 'While nobody wanted to lose, winning didn't seem as vitally important then. The League has got so much bigger over the years and those kind of players have been phased out because manager's jobs are on the line a lot more. Stan was not going to work his nuts off for you! He would never give you ninety minutes of non-stop running. Managers today surround themselves with people they know will work 100 per cent for them. So even if things go wrong they can say they've given it their best. That's why those players are just not encouraged. Football is a little too manufac-tured. But then, at the top of the Premiership we're seeing the influence of the foreign players who bring special things to the game, like Zola and Bergkamp.'

Today, the world's most skilful players – Rivaldo, Figo, Zidane, Totti, Del Piero, Owen, Henry, and countless others – are given such adulation, are so cherished and pampered, their pockets filled with gold, that it seems certain they will go on to great things, winning World Cups and Champions League medals. It's like a conveyor belt. Even the opposition defenders are not allowed to get too close, just in case they spoil things. Today's stars have their egos boosted until they become larger than life – and it seems, on reflection, that they have an easy time of it. The top stars of the 1970s risked, at best, a broken ankle every time they ventured out on to the pitch. That said, it's often easy to complain about rich and famous strikers, but the game has moved on at a ferocious pace. Players are fitter today, and more are technically excellent – a product of youth systems and professional commitment all around the country.

There is, however, a dearth of personality, so observers try to reintroduce some trace of maverick behaviour, television and newspapers highlighting each and every incident in the hope of uncovering a new bad boy. Is Roy Keane a maverick because he gets sent off a lot and eyeballs referees? No, for a number of simple reasons. One: he's an engine-room midfielder, albeit of wonderful talent, and mavericks should ideally be dazzling wingers or magical forwards. Two: he's won so much in the game that there's little room for disappointment and regret. Three: he's boring. He's never married Miss Ecuador an hour after meeting her, for example; he's never gone missing for a month without explanation; he just hasn't got that unique 1970s charisma. Or long hair.

It's difficult, too, to classify people like Gazza or Cantona as mavericks. Their antics are too fresh in the memory, too recent and too ugly. It seems that the term cannot be used to describe somebody playing here and now, it's become solely 'retro', to use a slightly tired word. The mavericks have a 1970s gloss to them, an air of legend. Who knows what current players journalists and authors will be writing about as rebels or mavericks in thirty years' time?

The gloss is not entirely undeserved, as the decade was one of creativity and breaking the mould. For many people, football was not about professional commitment or nurturing talent, it was about pure, explosive skill and the players who could provide it. The zeitgeist knocked down the gates of Lilleshall, the nation's military-style training centre, and let the madmen in to play. 'It was a free spirit sort of thing,' Worthington cheerfully confirmed. 'I don't think we've seen anything like it since. Rock 'n' roll and football went hand in glove. It was phenomenal. The money and the profile weren't around then like they are now, but it was an explosion of talent in football and in music. We all used to go and see shows and all the live entertainment and it was a very, very exciting time to be involved with football. Not just English football, but right across British football. There were a lot of brilliant individual players having a good time, enjoying ourselves and enjoying the phenomena around us. Fantastic.'

This exciting cultural atmosphere was felt by everyone, and many people latched on to it, as Brian Little, the former Hull City manager and once one of England's best young forwards whose career was prematurely ended by injury in the late 1970s, confirmed. 'Some of the things that went on in those days you might be well and truly in trouble over [now]. It was just lads being lads, and being allowed to do that. Playing in the period when we did was great – it was more of a laugh than today, we had more fun. There's a different mentality around the game today, in all areas. I look back at that period when I was young and playing – if you weren't going to win the League by February and you weren't in danger of being relegated, then the game was relaxed and enjoyable. Now, it's from day one of the season right to the last weekend. You're on edge, and people expect you to do things.

'The way Stan Bowles played the game was very seventies,' he added. 'The profile wasn't as great as it is today, but some people seemed to enjoy the limelight.

Stan certainly seemed to enjoy it. He had unbelievable ability, he was technically gifted, and, like the whole seventies period, was able to play with a little bit of a smile on his face. And occasionally let his temper flare a bit. He was up there with George Best without a doubt.'

Fun was the key word for the youth of that colourful era, who had grown up on Elvis Presley, the Beatles and the Rolling Stones. Drawing a succinct comparison, Frank Worthington complained about today's television programmes, such as *Popstars* and *Pop Idol*, which set out to manufacture pop singers and groups. 'There's no originality any more. Bowles epitomised the time we were living in. He was one of the great original players.'

At every party, however, there is a disgruntled neighbour banging on the wall. As well as the maverick genius, the 1970s had to contend with the hatchet men. The latter existed solely to stop the former. One reason, of course, why neither Bowles nor Marsh nor any of their maverick contemporaries excelled as they should have done was that opposing teams were so terrified of their skill they would keep most of the players behind the ball in an effort to withstand the onslaught. Marsh eventually tired of this treatment and moved to Tampa Bay Rowdies with a parting shot about leaving behind a grey country, a grey game and grey people. As former QPR defender Dave Webb said in Rob Steen's *The Mavericks*, 'Ossie [Peter Osgood], Rodney [Marsh] and Bowles were always the ones who got the worst of it [unfair tackling] because they were dribblers, but as an all-round talent, Bowles was the best of the lot. Rodney and Ossie were the type who needed the ball given to them. Bowles could do even more. He was the most marvellous individual talent I ever played with.' As Little recalled, with a slight wince, 'Even when I played I knew that if I'd had a good game the week before, and the opposition manager had seen it, then the first tackle would chop me in half. And they were allowed to get away with it, whereas today it just can't happen. Today, forwards want the ball to their feet, they want to jink around in the box. I'd like to play now – it's set up for goals to be scored.'

So football in the 1970s was more violent, with teams happy to kill off a game if they were satisfied with the result, and equally happy just to try to take out the opposition's star player. Bowles and his generation of entertainers had to rely on their wits and skills alone if they were to survive, let alone prosper. But prosper they did.

In *The Mavericks*, Frank McLintock, another former Rangers defender, suggested a reason why Bowles frustrated defenders. 'To him, everyone else was a mug. In a one-against-one situation, like Jimmy Greaves, you would always fancy Stan. And he would always pass at just the right time too. The main difference between him and Rodney was that Stan's main aim was to win.'

Opinion is divided about whether Bowles was 'better' than Rodney Marsh, whose time at Queens Park Rangers began in 1966 and ended, with relegation, in 1972. The argument has simmered for years, particularly among QPR fans. Football is about opinions, and Marsh and Bowles, two of the most charismatic and controversial players ever, arouse more varied opinion in observers than most. A comparison between Bowles and Best or Bowles and Osgood would not be as relevant as one between Bowles and Marsh because these two players have a strong link, effectively swapping clubs in the early 1970s. They were also similar as players, both of them remembered and revered for their brilliance as crowd entertainers.

So it's difficult to separate them once and for all – to reach a final, irrefutable verdict on the question that has been aired and debated in every pub in west London and far beyond for many years. There are numerous comparisons to make, among them the fact that Bowles and QPR missed out on the League title to Liverpool by one point in 1976, and Marsh and Manchester City (along with Liverpool and Leeds United) missed out to Derby by the same margin in 1972. The argument that follows from that is that having such a self-confident, even selfish, player within your ranks might entertain the fans but won't win you any silverware. As Marsh once admitted, 'They [City] f**ked up by signing me. I didn't play badly, I just upset the rhythm of the team.'

Don Givens has no problems with the difficult task of choosing who was the best out of the select group of top players. 'I'd put Bowles second only to George Best. I saw Rodney play but never played with him. When you play with people regularly you appreciate them and realise their faults a bit more. But I always thought that Stan was more efficient than Rodney, who played to the crowd a little bit more. But then if I'd played with Rodney for six years maybe I'd appreciate him a bit more.

'Stan was the kind of player people wanted to see. Now, all these years on, we're seeing less and less of that kind of player but a great percentage of the supporters are only interested in seeing something a bit different, something special that they can remember and go back and talk about in the pub. And because of the type of player he was, Stan produced those moments more than anybody else. He was always going to be very popular with the supporters.'

Frank Worthington is similarly keen to offer his thoughts when trying to establish a list of the best mavericks, but is less sure that Bowles deserves to finish above Marsh. 'Who was the best of the mavericks? Besides myself? Ha ha! You cannot separate the mavericks of the seventies.' He paused, then contradicted himself. 'Rodney Marsh had something different that separated him from everybody. The fans absolutely adored him at QPR and Manchester City and he was a fantastic player. Because of his total individuality he became a spanner in the works of City's well-oiled machine. That's not taking anything away from Marsh – it's just that he was so gifted that the people around him couldn't read exactly what he was trying to do. It was Manchester City that had to adjust to Rodney Marsh, not the other way around. From a fan's point of view, if you were going to see any one gifted individual player you would say Rodney Marsh. But to go and see a player of talent that harnessed itself and linked its way into the team, you've got to choose Bowlesy because he was magnificent. The way he operated with

Gerry Francis, Don Givens and Dave Thomas – absolutely brilliant side to watch.'

And that, it seems, is the sole difference between the players. In training they could probably match each other trick for trick, but on the pitch, when results mattered, Bowles used to think of the team first while Marsh was 100 per cent an entertainer. This difference affects each player's popularity in different ways, depending on who you speak to.

Bowles is more enthusiastic in his opinions of Rodney Marsh than he is when trying to characterise himself. He is tired of the old question of whether he was better than Marsh but has on many occasions offered his answer in no uncertain terms. 'People have the argument all the time – who was better? But Marsh never done it consistently at the top grade. He went to Manchester City when they were clear at the top and they lost it. Although they did like him in Manchester, they liked the way he played. Every time I meet him all he talks about is himself and money. You know, when he's had a drink or whatever. "When I done this or that . . ." Shut up, Rodney, for f**k's sake!'

Bowles has always been more vocal in his personal dislike for Marsh, who declined to be involved with this book, than vice versa. Bowles' bile doesn't seem to stem from jealousy, although Marsh's profile in the football world has remained comparatively higher; rather, it is because on the rare occasions Bowles is interviewed he is always asked about Marsh. And he has never been one to hold back with his opinions. Marsh, meanwhile, has hardly ever displayed maverick behaviour in his response to the question, even going so far as to be quite complimentary about Bowles in his autobiography.

Through the years Bowles has made some extremely unsubtle comments about Rodney Marsh, some of them quite painful to read. Writing his column for the Zoo betting website in August 2001, he offered a 'verdict' on the question of which of them was better: 'If Rod Marsh was a better footballer than me, then Anna Nicole Smith married Howard Marshall for his looks and he fancied her for her brain,' he stormed. 'It galls me to see Marsh on the telly every f***ing day. Believe me, he was a good footballer, but in my class? I think not.'

And that wasn't the end of this particularly fierce attack. After apparently being informed by a reader that Marsh had claimed to be 'a far better player' because he played more games for England, the tirade, though occasionally amusing, went over the top. 'Marsh wasn't the most popular player in the game. He was all right, I suppose – when he was asleep. If I could afford Sky I'd cancel it on the strength of that comment [above], which has infuriated me. Marsh had been doing a bit of the flash stuff before I arrived [at QPR] and so expectations were high. I was Marsh's replacement, he'd just been sold to Manchester City for £200,000. Rod settled in well, immediately costing City the title! Only QPR fans can truly say if I was better than Marsh. He was skilful, admittedly, but he couldn't tackle a fish and chip dinner. He was known as the Marshmallow Man in the game.

'In all honesty I like Rod really, but fancy him saying he was better than me, far f***ing better than me! Marshie is very lucky I'm not taking this matter further. I've always hung out with the wrong lot.'

And that's where things get a little embarrassing, Bowles referring to the villains he claims to know so well. Trying a bit too hard to make himself sound like 'the guv'nor'. Maybe it's all a joke, or maybe Bowles has been so close to controversy most of his life he can no longer survive without it.

In trying to distinguish between Bowles and Marsh, it is essential to examine their QPR careers. After he signed on 9 September 1972 for £112,000, Bowles watched his first game from the stands. The team drew 1–1 away to Burnley – their eighteenth match without defeat. Manager Gordon Jago promised that his new player would feature in the next game, but nobody could have predicted the impact he would have. Just two minutes into that next game, against Nottingham Forest, he set up Don Givens for the first goal; then, just before half-time, he scored the second en route to a rousing 3–0 victory. Though attendances were down all over the country because of the increasing threat of hooliganism, the Loftus Road faithful had a new hero. They had hungered for a new Rodney Marsh, and Bowles' dream debut while fearlessly wearing Marsh's hallowed number 10 shirt, turned him from an uncertainty, maybe even a risk or a liability, into every fan's favourite. QPR were unbeaten since selling Marsh to Manchester City, but the supporters had become accustomed to having a genius in attack. Bowles took over the reins with aplomb. As he once commented, 'I joined Rangers as just another 23-year-old; that is, another 23-year-old who had been kissed lavishly from head to toe by the great footballing God in the sky!'

After drawing with Bristol City, Rangers lost their 'unbeaten' tag after a 4–1 defeat at the hands of Hull at the end of September. Nevertheless, Bowles seemed, for once, to be taking his opportunity to shine, despite the difficult circumstances. Having been named as Marsh's heir he carried on living up to all the expectations, even though it was no easy thing to do.

BOWLES' QPR RECORD

Season	Division	FA Cup	League Cup	Total games*	Total goals*
1972/73	2	R5	R2	39	18
1973/74	1	R6	R4	51	22
1974/75	1	R5	R3	40	12
1975/76	1	R3	R4	43	12
1976/77	1	R4	SF	39	19
1977/78	1	R5	R3	48	9
1978/79	1	R3	R4	34	1
Totals				294	93
Averages	1	R4	R4	42	13

*Includes European games

Marsh's achievements at Loftus Road shouldn't be underestimated. He played a massive role in establishing Rangers as a side to be feared. Back in 1966 Fulham got rid of him because Johnny Haynes, Britain's first £100-a-week footballer, thought he was a bit of a show-off, causing manager Vic Buckingham to take the misinformed step of asking him not to dribble so much. Understandably, Marsh refused, and QPR manager Alec Stock snapped him up for just £15,000. He was only 22 years old, and while his large physique offered no clue to the dazzling talent he possessed, it quickly became clear that Fulham had made a big mistake.

The first highlight of Marsh's QPR career was scoring the team's second goal in a 3–2 win over West Bromwich Albion in the 1967 League Cup final, despite Rangers being in the Third Division. They had beaten Colchester, Aldershot, Swansea, Leicester, Carlisle and Birmingham to reach the final. Then he led QPR into the Second and First Divisions in consecutive seasons – no mean feat for a club, and their first ever crack at top-flight football. But with no trace of the wild ranting of Bowles, in his autobiography Marsh made an effort to sound humble about his contributions in the late 1960s: 'Everybody seems to think I was the star of that Rangers team, but it's not true, not the way I see it. Les [Allen] was – no doubt about it. Rangers would have won nothing without him. He was the player who made everything work.'

MARSH'S QPR RECORD

Season	Division	FA Cup	League Cup	Total games	Total goals
1965/66	3	R3	R1	16	8
1966/67	3	R3	Winners	53	44
1967/68	2	R3	R4	26	14
1968/69	1	R3	R2	22	4
1969/70	2	R6	R5	47	21
1970/71	2	R3	R2	42	23
1971/72	2	R3	R4	36	20
Totals				242	134
Averages	2	R3	R4	35	19

MARSH'S CAREER

Club	Date joined	Games	Goals
Fulham	October 1962	68	22
QPR	March 1966	242	134

Manchester City	March 1972	150	47
Tampa Bay Rowdies	January 1976	23	12
Fulham	August 1976	22	6
Tampa Bay Rowdies	1977	87	41
Totals		592	262

Goals:games ratio of 1:2.25

For someone with such a reputation for being outspoken – and, in his playing days, difficult to handle – Marsh is surprisingly in favour of the 'old school' approach to running football clubs. While as a player he was more than content to spout his opinions on managers and teammates, he is keen for clubs to maintain a balanced hierarchy of power, with players and fans at the bottom. As he once told Jimmy Hill on the Sky Sports website, 'If you're not careful football will implode in this country. At the moment it's back to front. Player power picks the manager. If the fans don't like the team they sack the chairman.' It was always the case in the 1970s that the order of power at football clubs was very distinctly defined, with the players at the bottom, even the star players. That is why the 'difficult' players moved clubs so often.

Perhaps Marsh's successful relationship with QPR chairman Jim Gregory, one later mirrored by Bowles', is at the root of his pragmatism – a word seldom bandied about when the mavericks are in town. After all, the ease with which he acknowledges the paternal need for a traditional and cast-iron club system goes against a number of his other personal experiences with the powers-that-be. Maturity has brought a serene wisdom to Rodney Marsh; he is well read, eloquent and authoritative. Somehow, it seems as though he's letting the mavericks down.

During his playing days, however, Marsh was the ultimate showman. Glen Matlock, one of the original members of the Sex Pistols, remembered one incident that sums up the maverick in Marsh. 'Marsh put the ball down on the penalty spot and we all expected him to score. But just before he did the run-up he adjusted his boot. We couldn't work out what he was doing, but as he's run at the ball and dummied to kick it, his boot has flown off. The keeper has dived for it, caught the boot, and as he's gone down Marsh has put the ball in the back of the net with his other shoe!'

The supporters loved this type of mischievous arrogance, and his incredible skill, at least while he was at Loftus Road; opinion since his years in the blue and white hooped shirt has altered dramatically. QPR fan Dave Thomas insisted, 'If you conducted a poll of a hundred QPR fans, Stan would wipe the board with Rodney Marsh. He would come out as number one, and rightly so. That's not just because of what he did on the field but because of his attitude to QPR ever since. Fans love players who love the club, and despite all the clubs he's played for his heart and his affections are with QPR. Stan is there, he's one of us, and Rodney Marsh is no longer one of us.'

'Marsh was a bit different because he was in the lower divisions as a QPR player,' explained Steve Russell, who has been watching Rangers since 1960. 'But Bowles even did it in Europe and was a better all-round player than Marsh, who used to take too many players on. Bowles was more of a team player. He scored goals and he would take on defenders but he would also lay the ball off. He had a great effect on the team. He never used to hold on to the ball for too long. He had a good football brain.'

Gerry Francis, the QPR midfielder who had realised his side needed someone who could provide fresh impetus and sparkle, recalled Bowles' early days at the club and put them into perspective. 'All fans love a hero, particularly a goalscorer. They'd had Rodney at QPR through the 1960s and they'd won the League Cup as a Third Division side, the first one at Wembley. They got to the First Division and I played a game as an apprentice at that time. Having got there, they found they were a bit short, just not good enough, and went straight down. Rodney left. We had a little period when we needed a replacement, someone who could come in and get a few goals, and Stan fitted the bill. He was quite happy to take the number 10 shirt – "I'll have that!" – and not only did we get back to the First Division and stay there, we took it by storm and nearly won it! He took over that mantle very, very well.'

Having played with him for many years, and also with Marsh as a youngster between 1969 and 1972, Francis remains openly in the Bowles camp. 'People wonder about Rodney Marsh and Stan Bowles, but to me Stan was the better player because he was a winner. You can be an artist and play tricks but not be the person you need to be to make a winning team. Stan played at the highest level for a long time while Rodney did near enough all of his work for QPR in the lower levels. He had one year in the First Division and scored very few goals in a side that was relegated. Rodney was an entertainer – if he nutmegged someone it was a big thing for him. But Stan wanted to score goals and win games.'

Clear proof that Francis is not Marsh's biggest fan came in November 1994 when he resigned as QPR manager in protest at club owner Richard Thompson's plan to appoint Marsh as chief executive or Director of Football. 'Gerry Francis hates him!' is Bowles' typically forthright conclusion. 'No one really found out whose decision it was to try and get Marsh in at QPR, but because Gerry doesn't like him he was convinced he was behind it all. He banned Rodney from the ground and I don't think he's been back since, as far as I know. When Gerry was there Rodney wasn't allowed upstairs or anything like that. Gerry never liked him, going back to when he was about seventeen, and he wasn't a bad judge as it happens. Rodney has his little say and he thinks he's the only one that can say it because he's on Sky every week, and all that. I don't worry about it.'

'It all came to the fore in the early 1990s when we had Richard Thompson as chairman whom we felt was not running the club well,' Russell recalled morosely. 'His chairmanship was one of sell, sell, sell. We were on the brink of seeing a very successful side with the right couple of signings, but instead he sold off Les Ferdinand and a lot of our top players. We finished eighth, narrowly avoiding relegation. What I mean by that is we were in an elevated position but could see the dark clouds on the horizon. Twelve months later we were relegated. That was synonymous with the Thompson era.

'At that time Marsh backed the chairman, and the fans believed that he was telling them that they did not understand their own club. They also saw it as an opportunity for Marsh, no longer a regular on match days, to promote himself. In response, they produced a poster with a quote from Bowles: "Of all the clubs I've played for, QPR will always be my team." ' While the fans saw it all in black and white, the club had apparently been holding talks with Marsh about him returning as Director of Football, a position that could have effectively replaced the then manager Gerry Francis.

'There was one famous incident,' Russell continued, 'at the height of the tensions between the board and Gerry Francis when Rodney Marsh was seen at a game for the first time in ages – whereas Stan Bowles walks down South Africa Road to games, emphasising that he is a man of the people. Marsh was photographed in the directors' box wearing what was obviously a QPR scarf that had just been bought from the club shop. It was like a Christmas jumper, it was that new. It was such a crass photo opportunity that it fooled no one. In fact, it only made people more alienated towards Marsh and his views. He wasn't right to back Thompson. There's nothing more patronising than listening to someone who thinks they've got all the answers, and that's what Rodney Marsh did.'

Marsh has irritated many QPR fans because of this, but the reason he has a lot to say is because he's paid to do that by television companies, who want his face on the screen because he is a legend. His talents will always live on even when arguments and bitterness have been forgotten. In terms of longevity, then, Marsh has the edge on Bowles. Executives love to invite colourful former professional footballers on to their programmes not solely for the sake of nostalgia, but because there is an absence of genuine originality in the modern game. Characters like Marsh and Bowles have been squeezed out in favour of more reliable, occasionally less English, players. 'Clubs don't encourage individuals,' Frank Worthington complained, 'but then any club that could find another Eric Cantona would be over the moon.' Brian Little agreed. 'Society's changed, football's changed, everything's changed about it. Football is a very different game today, more business than entertainment, and it is clear that the sport has driven out any chance of allowing such maverick behaviour to happen any more.' Football is simultaneously trying to relive maverick exploits and ensuring that they never happen again.

A player, though, can usually be idolised only at one club, and Marsh transferred to Manchester City, who already had heroes like Colin Bell and Mike Summerbee. What's more, events subsequent to Marsh's playing career have affected the way fans think of him at QPR. Those who grew up in west London claiming Marsh's name whenever they played football with friends, teenagers who once shook his hand and then refused to wash for a fortnight, even younger sisters who could name only one footballer – their brother's hero Rodney Marsh whom he wouldn't stop going on about – found themselves disappointed at the player who made the QPR number 10 shirt legendary. 'You don't want your heroes to be mortal, and unfortunately he's upset a lot of QPR fans with ill-founded and ill-informed comments,' Thomas complained. 'A few years ago Marsh said – and some people might say it was prophetic – that QPR were heading down to the Conference if they weren't careful. That angered a lot of fans, who thought, "What right have you got to say that?" The fact that we've plummeted down now almost proves he was right, but people were offended that he spoke out because it was perceived as slagging off the club.'

The same fans still have posters of Stan Bowles up on their walls – his charisma and affection for QPR have endured. Bowles would never bad-mouth the club, never throw the fans' loyalty and adoration back in their faces. Not that Marsh ever intended to offend anyone at QPR – he was just offering an opinion, as he often does. But in building the perfect caricature of a maverick, a man of the people with a rebellious streak, enduring devotion is a key ingredient. The myth that built up around Rodney Marsh has eroded – cause for QPR fans to hold the myth of Stan Bowles even closer to their hearts.

The major criticism of Marsh's game, despite the comedy, the virtuoso performances and the spectacular goals, was that he would rather take four players on (and probably beat them) than pass to his team-mates. Following that 1968 promotion to Division One, fan Dave Thomas soon came to realise that his side was not going to stay there for long. 'We were totally ill-equipped for the division. We finished with a record low number of points – eighteen – and only won four games. It was a torrid time, and Marsh didn't do it at the highest level. He went on to Man City, where he did manage to do it at the highest level, and he's held in very high regard there. He's now a Maine Road legend. That doesn't make him twice as good as Stan Bowles, it makes him only half as good. I have no hesitation in saying that Stan Bowles is the greatest QPR player of all time. By a long, long way.'

The point is maybe that Bowles had a better understanding of when to pass and when to perform his magic, or at least a stronger will to win games. In maverick terms, Marsh went for glory, while Bowles – somewhat incredibly, considering his lifestyle – was more sensible. On the international scene, Marsh was given four more games to prove himself than Bowles but it was an opportunity he simply failed to take advantage of. As with Manchester City, it was difficult to fit the one-man-band into England's orchestra. Ultimately, the likes of Marsh and Bowles provided a fantastic spectacle, but their cavalier football, reckless lifestyles, addictive personalities and clashes with authority proved to be their downfall.

The days of Stan Bowles are long gone. The cheeky smile has all but died in English football today, with players like Gazza struggling to carry the flag. The mavericks' era was a one-off and will probably never be repeated, even though it produced some of the most popular characters in the history of the game. What would football fans give for just a glimpse of a Rodney Marsh or a George Best today? Then again, the possible repercussions of Stan Bowles earning £50,000 a week don't even bear thinking about!

5 From Hero to Rehab: Manchester City to Carlisle, 1967–72

Take it from me, with the company he's keeping, you'll find him in an alley one day with his throat cut.

SAM BARNES, CREWE BOOKMAKER

'Stan could have been something big at Manchester City if he'd just waited for his chance,' lamented Tony Book, City's most successful captain of all time. 'He was there, he was amongst it, and it was just a question of being patient and waiting for his time to come. That is the difficult thing for that kind of talent – they want to go and strut their stuff, don't they?'

Book was signed from Plymouth Argyle for £17,000 in July 1966 by Joe Mercer on the advice of his assistant manager Malcolm Allison, who'd managed the 30-year-old full-back at Bath and Plymouth. Just two years prior to joining City he had been a part-time bricklayer. His signing laid the foundations for a decade of success at the club. Book became universally known as 'The Skipper', helping City to the 1968 League title, the 1969 FA Cup, and the League Cup and European Cup Winners' Cup in 1970. Throughout those high-flying days at Maine Road, Bowles was no more than a bit-part player, obviously talented beyond his tender years but never allowed a prolonged run in the first team. 'He was a lad coming through the ranks when I joined,' said Book. 'Manchester City have always tried to bring a few local lads through and I think there were five or six in the team at that time. He was trying his best to get in the team. He wanted to be amongst it as much as anybody. I know that he used to get really disappointed at times when he was left out and that got to him in the end. He went missing once or twice. Those kinds of things didn't augur well for him because Joe Mercer expected everybody to play their part.'

Bowles, who'd been the sort of youth who put fireworks through people's letterboxes and got chased through the streets by the police, was playing out another role, however, outside football. His youthful enthusiasm for gambling and his villainous connections offered him a part in a financially rewarding sideshow at a time when he should have been focusing on becoming the star attraction at Maine Road. In an era when First Division footballers were earning about £35 or £40 a week and relying on win bonuses and large gate receipts, an enterprising teenaged Bowles had decided that other sources of income should be investigated. 'I've been associating with gamblers and gambling people all my life so I just fell into it,' he said. 'Plus, I liked it. I was never any good at it, but I liked it.'

It's not an apology, as many involved with football today would like to think, just an explanation. Though today's game has altered so that top footballers are forced to be role models for children all over the world, the likes of Paul Merson and Tony Adams thrust in front of the cameras to confront their demons for the nation, Bowles comes from an era when gambling and drinking were almost as much a part of the game as training. He did, however, allow his career at his first club to crumble before his eyes, particularly in his early years when there were aspects of his life that were simply more important than football. Always wanting to make money to take to the betting shop, and too young and inexperienced to realise that there was plenty to be made by playing top-flight football, he worked for a network of villains in Manchester known as the Quality Street Gang, running bets across the city.

Bowles is proud of his relationship with the gang, mentioning it at every opportunity, and, though never involved in any serious criminal activity, he clearly enjoys the reflected 'status' the connection lends him. Even today, he has the appearance of a wide-eyed teenager when talking about the lifestyle he has known all his adult life. 'I think it was [retired Deputy Chief Constable of Greater Manchester Police] John Stalker who said the Quality Street Gang was a myth. It wasn't a myth at all. Whatever was going on in Manchester at that time, they knew about. It was a big network, and still is now really. But it's not so much the older ones, the ones who I knew and am still in touch with today, it's like their offspring.' Bowles' association with these 'unsavoury characters' stretches back to his teenage years. 'A lot of us grew up together so we just took it from there,' he recalled. 'I was getting more money working for them than I was from playing football.'

Football writer with the *Manchester Evening News* Paul Hince has known Bowles for many years. Both Manchester-born, Hince was involved in many facets of Bowles' early career and many comparisons can be made between the two men. 'We both come from strictly working-class areas in Manchester,' he explained. 'Stan's from Collyhurst and I'm from Gorton. We both played a lot of junior soccer. I used to play four times every weekend and Stan did as well. We were both selected for the Manchester and District Sunday League representative side, which was a big honour. I was a right winger and Stan was all left foot, but for some reason I played outside left and he played outside right – that's just how it worked out.'

The two talented young footballers might have come from similar backgrounds but they had differing attitudes to life and football. Bowles had never harboured any professional ambition in all his young life other than to make money and have fun, but his old friend had a much more pragmatic approach. Despite his promise as a youngster on the Manchester football scene, Hince decided that he should serve an apprenticeship in journalism – his first love – before trying his hand in the sport. 'I went into journalism straight from school and worked on a local paper. I signed what were called indentures, which means you sign up to a three-year apprenticeship. I served my time because in those days if you broke your indentures you couldn't get back into your career. Stan got snapped up straight from school by City, but I didn't play until I was nineteen.'

Hince never really wanted to be a footballer and had to be convinced by City manager Joe Mercer, who tempted him with the warning that if he turned down the opportunity he would grow bitter and, in years to come, would always regret the decision. A lot of pressure to succeed, then, Hince's signing evidence, if any were required, that success in football is something even the most grounded individual cannot help but dream of. Bowles, perhaps, knew all along that he had the natural talent to succeed and did not need another profession to fall back on if things did not work out at City. He wasn't dreaming, he *was* the dream.

When Hince eventually did sign for Manchester City Bowles had already been there for a year or so working to break into the first team. The club had a very famous and revered scout named Harry Godwin who had spotted many of the side that went on to win the championship in 1968. When he went to the Bowles' prefab house in Collyhurst with a professional contract tucked under his arm after watching Bowles play for a local side called Broadhurst Lads, there were immediate signs that dealings with City's newest player were not going to be straightforward.

Hince laughed as he recounted the tale, once told to him by Godwin. 'Stan wasn't highly educated and neither was his family. Stan's brother was crawling around under the kitchen table with nothing on from the waist down and had his hand in Harry Godwin's pocket to see if he could pinch anything! Harry and Stan went through this form for the club. Name, age, education, the usual questions, and then Harry asked what denomination Stan was. He looked puzzled and replied [cue thick Mancunian accent], "What does that mean, Mr Godwin?" So Harry told him it meant what religion he was. Stan's mother was sat over by the fire – I think she might have been having a drink of gin – and Stan asked, "Here, ma, am I one of them Catholics or one of them Protestants?" And his mother scratched her head and said, "Oh, I don't know, Stan. We'd better wait till your dad gets home and we'll ask him." ' This resembles a scene from a 1960s sitcom and, like much of Bowles' life, makes for an entertaining story. In later years the Maine Road management also had high hopes for Stephen, Bowles' inquisitive younger brother, who was potentially an even better player, but he did not develop as hoped and never made the grade. He was probably put off by all the stories about his brother.

'Manchester City signed me straight from school at about sixteen years old,' Bowles said, casting his mind back almost forty years. 'Then I signed as an apprentice when I was seventeen and full forms at eighteen. I made my debut when I was eighteen as well, which was unusual because they normally liked to wait till you were about twenty.' This debut, on 13 September 1967 during a mid-week League Cup game against Leicester, was one of the most spectacular City fans had ever witnessed. A young Bowles – too young yet to be Stan the Man – came on in the second half in place of Neil Young who had been suffering from flu, and promptly scored two goals. And the following match, a League game against Sheffield United that Saturday, proved that the new hero was not a one-trick pony: Bowles scored two more goals.

The then Manchester City assistant manager Malcolm Allison told author Ian Penney that he remembered the young local lad as 'a skilful left-sided player with a good instinct for goals. This proved the case when he scored four times in his first one and a half games for us. Off the field was another matter for Stan, however, and we clashed on more than one occasion.'

Despite the drama of this entrance, Bowles seemed unfazed. His priorities lay elsewhere. 'All of a sudden there was a new kid on the block,' he remarked casually. 'But that didn't last very long because I was still mixing with those same kids. I used to run the bets from pub to pub. I'd take the bets from one side of town to the other and fetch the money back or whatever. I'd be paid at the end of the week. I was getting about £150, cash in hand, and we're talking about the late sixties, so that was quite a lot of money. I used to get about twenty quid for playing football. So you can see the difference. Football was sort of secondary. I was pretty good at it, though.'

Still, since signing schoolboy forms, Bowles had worked hard to get himself into the first team, a point that should be remembered by the many who assume he was lazy because of his phenomenal talent. Following his call-up to the City first team, and a pay rise to £20 a week, Bowles bought himself a new suit to celebrate. Typical of any teenager, no thought was given to saving rather than spending his earnings. He was suddenly a first-team player, or so he thought, and was determined to enjoy the experience.

In an era when newspapers were less prone to hyping new stars, journalists were reluctant to get carried away following Bowles' excellent debut for City. In 45 minutes of League Cup action he'd scored twice and almost got his hat-trick in a convincing 4–0 win. However, when he bagged two more against Sheffield United it was difficult not to feel excited about the eighteen-year-old's future. 'His first games were special,' agreed Tony Book, 'but like all the really talented people I've played with and worked with over the years, he had a little something different about him. Stan loved to gamble. Not that it affected his football, but he'd go anywhere to gamble.'

Sure enough, just seventeen days after his debut he was in trouble. The Manchester derby often brings out the worst in players, and Bowles, never one to run from a confrontation when involved in a match despite his slight frame, ended up fighting with United's Brian Kidd. The two had known each other for years. At the age of eleven Bowles had played alongside Kidd for the Manchester North Area side and Manchester Boys, winning the Manchester Evening News Cup. It was this unseemly incident, in a typically niggly match, that gave Bowles the first inkling that publicity, particularly bad publicity, paid well. City manager Joe Mercer wanted the two players to make up publicly, and a lucrative photo shoot for the papers was arranged. Kidd was not overly enthusiastic, but Bowles wanted the cash. Every cloud has a silver lining.

In the 1967/68 season, when Manchester City won the Division One title ahead of Manchester United, Liverpool and Leeds, Bowles made just four League appearances in addition to that League Cup fixture. His tally of four goals was impressive, but Neil Young scored 21, Mike Summerbee 20, and Colin Bell and Francis Lee bagged 17 each. Bowles just couldn't get a look-in. Indeed, the next season, 1968/69, he started just one League match and came off the bench during two more games (one League, one League Cup), failing to score at all. Bowles didn't play for a single minute during City's run in the FA Cup, which eventually saw them lift the trophy at Wembley after beating Leicester City 1–0.

'He started to build up a reputation at that time as a bit of a wild child,' Paul Hince recalled, 'which he wasn't. He was actually very quiet and shy. I used to take him into town and we'd pick up my girlfriend from work and go for a cup of coffee. Stan used to walk five paces behind us he was so shy. But even then he had this problem with his gambling, and Maine Road was the place to be if you liked a bet. There were three or four Scottish players who were gambling mad. Literally. They'd gamble on a fly walking up a wall, they'd bet on who would walk through the door next! Anything. I used to see Stan on the team coach playing cards and every penny he'd got on him had gone before we'd got outside Maine Road! He's always had that streak, that was his weakness.'

After two years of relative peace and quiet – leisure time not necessarily wisely used – and a handful of first-team appearances, Bowles' career at Maine Road exploded into chaos. He just had too much time on his hands and felt too much frustration at not getting in the side for every match. Something had to give. Maybe the root of the problem was the ill-defined roles at the club of Joe Mercer and Malcolm Allison. Both men seemed to want to be in charge of team affairs, the latter striving to wrest power from his colleague to prove he could be the boss in his own right. Bowles suddenly found himself caught in the middle. Allison was certainly not opposed to players with reputations as trouble-makers, having convinced Mercer to sign winger Tony Coleman from Doncaster Rovers earlier that year. Coleman became a regular drinking partner of Bowles and also went on to play more than a hundred times for City. The flamboyant Allison also frequented Manchester's hottest clubs, even earning the nickname Champagne Charlie, and Bowles once complained that everywhere he went he would hear that Allison had been there before him, publicly criticising him. Bowles, who loved the nightclub scene, found this intensely irritating and embarrassing.

In July 1969, a few months after marrying his first wife, Ann, who was now heavily pregnant, Bowles decided to stay away from a short training camp in Southport. When Allison returned, he found Bowles in a nightclub and flew into a wild temper, even though Bowles tried to explain that Mercer had given him permission to stay away. Allison was insistent that those decisions were his and his alone to make and, according to the player's own recollection, threw a punch at Bowles. The fist was narrowly avoided, then Bowles threw a punch of his own, which landed. At that point the fight was split up by the reserve-team coach, Johnny Hart. Considering that it was a match-up of David and Goliath proportions (the young Collyhurst lad was once thought too slight to play professional football), Bowles was probably extremely grateful for the intervention. Even in a time when footballers were 'real men', punching your manager in the face was considered unacceptable. 'Two incidents in nightclubs ended with blows being thrown,' Allison later admitted. The second incident wasn't far around the corner.

At the time the nation was getting teary-eyed at Prince Charles' investiture at Caernarfon Castle. There he stood, side by side with his smiling mother, balancing a big, wonky crown on his slender head and an XL sheepskin shawl on his shoulders. The newspapers, in the days before everyone decided to poke fun at the royal family, went overboard in their adulation and pride. There was even less room for sports coverage than usual. They were hardly, then, going to report on a brash but skilful young football wannabe who had had a scrap with his boss. Still,

Bowles' time at the club was, in retrospect, over from the moment he aimed his blow at Allison.

He didn't help himself at all when, just a few weeks later, he did hit the headlines by missing a flight to Amsterdam for a pre-season friendly, then going AWOL for a while. 'We had a friendly against Ajax – remember Ajax? – who were a really good side then,' Bowles recalled, smiling again. 'I never turned up at the airport and my excuse was I got there and the plane had gone. But unbeknown to me it had been delayed for four hours! That was the final straw.' Bowles makes the headline-making incident sound like an everyday occurrence with his deadpan delivery. 'I didn't like flying at all then,' he continued. 'In actual fact, since then I've flown all over the world, but then I was petrified of it. I was getting ready in the morning to go to the airport and I just panicked. The only thing I could think of was to go round to my mate's house and for him to keep me out of the way. They couldn't find me, and they even had the police out looking for me because of my connections. But it wasn't like that – I was just hiding in a house not far from where I lived.'

Hince explained that there was already some bad feeling between Bowles and the club before that famous no-show. 'He'd already had a fallout with City about his contract because he didn't think they were offering enough when he came to sign a new one. And then he failed to turn up for this friendly match against Ajax. What he didn't know was that the plane was delayed so long he could have walked there and still been on time! They even had the police looking for him! He fell out of favour after that and City got tired of him.' Hince took a more serious view of the incident than Bowles, exasperated by his friend's behaviour. 'At Maine Road, although he wasn't getting rat-arsed and he was never a violent person, he was skipping training when he felt like it, and a young player out to impress doesn't miss a game against a big European side. Especially as he was going to play, he wasn't just in the squad. He wasn't a prima donna, but he wasn't very professional. He wasn't dedicated.'

Only in later years would Bowles be able to add 'dedication' to a curriculum vitae that already included 'breathtaking talent' and 'no shortage of confidence'. As a young footballer he made the mistake of assuming that his skill would force others to accept him as he was, but Manchester City was a big and successful club that didn't like being taken advantage of.

'Not for the first or last time, he'd overslept,' said Allison, a man who prided himself on commanding respect. 'Realising he couldn't get to the airport on time for the flight he never even bothered to try and get there. When the flight was delayed by four hours it gave me and Joe [Mercer] ample time to try and track him down, but it was all to no avail. Stan was hiding in a friend's wardrobe. To say I wasn't delighted with his behaviour would be an understatement!'

Shortly after the Ajax episode (the game itself finished 3–3), Bowles and Allison clashed for a second time, in the Cabaret Club in Manchester. Tony Coleman had invited Bowles out for the night and Allison thought it an irresponsible gesture. The City assistant manager charged over to tell Coleman so, and a fiery Bowles replied, in so many words, that he should keep his nose out of it. Allison was outraged at what he saw as impertinence and threw a punch. Again Bowles reciprocated. Coleman, as Bowles remembers it, then smashed a glass on a table, but just as all hell was about to break loose the bar's owner interrupted and calmed them down. 'The Cabaret Club was run by one of the Quality Street Gang,' Bowles said, adopting the dramatic expression of a seasoned storyteller, 'and was the major club at the time in Manchester – it's closed now. Allison come in and said to us, "This is all you want to do – hang around with these people." So my mate Tony Coleman, who was the first-team left winger by the way, chinned him! Tony was a bit of a handful and Malcolm was about six foot four!'

The newspapers never quite got the whole story at the time. They knew that Bowles had gone missing prior to the flight to Amsterdam to play Ajax but reported that Mercer and Allison had forgiven their young star. Few people knew the whole truth about the chaos behind the scenes that was leading Bowles inexorably to the Maine Road exit.

Tony Book laughed at the memory of Bowles' numerous indiscretions. 'He and Allison would have their little "get-togethers", and I know that Joe Mercer used to get to him now and again as well. He set himself up for it. He was one of those people – he wasn't going to be put on. The "mavericks" were talented people but they always had a little thing about them and they just did the wrong thing at times. They think it's better for themselves but maybe it's not. That's the way they are, and it's all part of why they've got that talent. There were no mavericks regularly playing in the City side at that particular time, but the most talented players at Maine Road in that era were Stan and Rodney [Marsh]. The others were ball-winners who wanted to win. People like Stan, although deep down they want to be winners, they don't worry too much about that as long as they are strutting their ability. They're happy with that. Whereas a lot of the others, they wanted the team to do well, not only individually but collectively.'

Book also remembered that Bowles was desperate to be part of the first team and had difficulties coping with rejection. Bowles had clashed with Allison, but it was essentially Mercer's desire to pick the same players for every game that hurt. When Tony Book joined, Mercer had promised him 'I'll always pick my best team', and he resolutely stuck to that, much to Bowles' obvious irritation. So long as the team was doing well, Bowles would not get his chance to break through. His youthful assumption that he was good enough, in the days before squad rotation, was in direct opposition to the club's loyalty to the first eleven. Although a few signings were made during Bowles' four seasons at Maine Road, the successful trophy-winning side did indeed remain effectively unchanged throughout his time at the club.

'Stan was an inside forward, or whatever you want to call him,' Book explained, 'and at City they already had Belly [Colin Bell], Youngy [Neil Young], Frannie [Francis

Lee] and [Mike] Summerbee. So there were some very talented players already there and it was difficult to break into the side, unless somebody got an injury. Especially because we were going so well and winning trophies. It was a very settled side at that time. Over the seasons we didn't get too many injuries – that was one of the things at that particular time. When we won the championship we used fourteen, maybe fifteen players. That's the way it was in them days – you knew that the first eleven was basically playing most of the games.' Book suffered an Achilles tendon injury at the start of the 1968/69 season that kept him out for 25 matches, but come the end of that same season he was lifting the FA Cup and was named joint Footballer of the Year with Derby's Dave Mackay. No matter how long the first-choice players were injured, the management would always keep faith and put them directly back in the side when they returned to fitness. 'There were some great names there,' Book continued, 'so the team basically picked itself. That was a big part of our success: picking the same team that started the week before. I don't think there is anything Stan could have done about it because he was only a kid and our success came along at that time. He didn't have a sniff, like.'

When he did get a chance, though, he was usually sharp enough to take it, in spite of an apparently lackadaisical approach to his fitness. Paul Hince recalled meal-times *chez* Bowles: 'I went to his house before a big match against Spurs once, and Ann called us into the kitchen when our dinner was ready. We had steak pudding, chips, peas and a big loaf of bread. I said to him, "You're not eating all that, are you? You'll be playing soon!" And he said, "Oh, no, no, no. Don't worry." And in the match he was absolutely brilliant.'

And he did get a few chances as he developed his physical strength and all-round game, though his four years at City were hardly as productive as they could have been.

Spectacularly going from unknown teenager to revel-ation to problem child and then to yesterday's news, Bowles would regularly miss training and sometimes simply not turn up for matches ('I was doing other work, and then in the end it was the all-night drinking and all that'). It wasn't so much that Bowles didn't want to be at Maine Road, more that he was incapable of thoroughly applying himself in the face of so much competition. 'I only played about nineteen or twenty games for Manchester City in total over a period of four years,' he said, matter-of-factly. 'I wasn't taking it seriously at that time. I eventually got sacked from Manchester City because Joe Mercer and Malcolm Allison had just had enough.'

Focusing on the positive side of those four years, Book remembered, with a sense of wonder, the rare occasions when Bowles was allowed out on to the pitch to do his thing. 'He was on a par with the very best. What a talent – he was exceptional! He scored goals for fun. I used to love to see him play. He made it look easy because he was a naturally talented boy. It came easy to him. When he was given a chance you could see that he had a special talent. It was just a matter of time before the potential was fulfilled. It wasn't until he got out of Man City and started playing lower League football that that happened. There's a lot of players who've done that and you've got to admire him for that. I always said to young players when I was coaching at Maine Road, "Go away and prove me wrong, because if you do I'll be the first to shake your hand." '

Over the last few weeks of his City career, Book and the rest of the squad could clearly see that the restless and irresponsible Bowles was itching to get away. He wanted regular football, that's all he needed. Players can either be patient in the reserve side, waiting for their chance at a decent run in the side to come, or go elsewhere to prove their old club wrong. During his final full season at Maine Road, 1969/70, Bowles had played eleven games in the League plus another as a sub and one more in the League Cup, but without notching up a single goal. With Lee, Bell and Young still scoring for fun, Bowles was not needed. Neither was he particularly liked or appreciated, so in the summer of 1970 Mercer and Allison told him that his services, such as they were, were no longer required.

* * *

Bowles' old friend Paul Hince, whose own full-time football career had proved short-lived, had returned from playing for Charlton Athletic, was establishing himself as a freelance football journalist and setting up office in the centre of town. One day, without warning, Bowles walked in to tell him that City had given him the boot but that he had received an offer from Bury. The manager at Bury, Hince noted with some concern, was Colin MacDonald – a man known as a real tyrant and somebody Bowles would never get on with if his life (or rather, his career) depended on it.

A few miles to the north of Manchester, in between Bolton and Rochdale, sat Bury Football Club. Having become accustomed to Division Two football for a decade or so, Bury now found themselves stuck in Division Three. A brief return to the second flight ended in instant relegation in 1969, and the club needed a spark to ignite the planned explosion back up again. Stan Bowles could have been that spark. His time at Bury was certainly explosive, but he lasted just three weeks.

Despite the fact that he had been sacked by City, Bowles was still regarded as a top young player. MacDonald insisted on playing him as an outside right, and Bowles was unhappy with the way the team played and what was expected of him personally. In fact, he hated it. 'I went to Bury,' he recalled, 'but I got sacked from there as well. Similar kind of thing – I didn't turn up for training. The final straw was when I turned up in a cab and didn't have any money and I said, "Well, take it out of my wages." The manager – I forget his name now, Colin something; he was the England goalkeeper at one time, but I didn't like him anyway – said he wouldn't pay it. So I said, "I'm going home then." So I jumped back in the cab and went home and got sacked the next day. Three weeks I think I was there. I didn't enjoy it.'

Bowles had been skipping training from the moment he arrived at Bury, but this was the clinching moment. He had turned up for a match early in September three-quarters of an hour late, all the players and the manager sitting on the coach waiting for him. When he finally showed up, Bowles casually climbed out of his taxi, argued with MacDonald in front of the rest of the squad and, it seemed, hammered the final nail into his own coffin. Bury steadily slipped towards the bottom of the table and were relegated to Division Four at the end of the season.

For a while it seemed nobody would touch him with a bargepole, then he went to see Hince again. 'So he came to my office, and it was very reminiscent of the [first] meeting. Because of my work I was in touch with many of the clubs in the area on a daily basis, and he asked me if there was any club I could suggest. I was playing part-time at Crewe, so I phoned the Crewe manager Ernie Tagg and explained that Stan needed a bit of handling and a bit of straightening out – but that if he could get him playing he was available on a free transfer and Ernie would be getting a top-class player. Stan was desperate, he was really on his uppers. Ernie said, "OK, put him on the next train to Crewe and I'll meet him at the station." So I told Stan to get his arse to Piccadilly station and go and meet Ernie. He said, "I haven't got enough money for the train fare, can you lend me some?" I thought, "F***ing hell, Stan", but I rang up British Rail to see how much it would be and lent him the five and sixpence for the ticket to Crewe. Then he said, "What if I nod off and go past the station? I'll have to get another ticket to get back!" "Don't nod off, then!" I replied. "Simple as that." '

Tagg met him at Crewe station as planned, and the first thing he said to Bowles was, 'I understand you're on your uppers, Stan.' Then he gave him a few quid. Of course, from that moment Bowles was eating out of his hand, and he eagerly signed. Before Bowles had arrived Tagg had told Hince not to give him any more money, cleverly surmising that Bowles would be depressed, alone and broke when he turned up – the perfect frame of mind for Tagg to use to his advantage. 'I pulled out a fiver and tucked it into his jacket pocket,' Tagg recalled, 'saying, "That's for you, Stan, whether you sign with us or not." That put a smile on his face. He was a bit lackadaisical at first, hardly answering my questions. He seemed to pick up a bit when he realised I wasn't pulling his leg, because

I think he'd got to that stage when he thought nobody wanted him.'

Having met Bowles, Tagg then rang Joe Mercer at Manchester City to find out more about the player Hince was recommending. 'I didn't know much about Stan, I'd never even heard of him! I was signing him blind, really. Mercer gave him a good reference football-wise, which was all I was interested in. Then Joe said, "But he's the only player who can miss a plane by four hours!" Joe was level-headed, and he thought that nobody was going to cure Stan.'

For his part, Bowles had realised that if he wanted to continue playing football, a move to Crewe was his only option. 'I'd been sacked by Manchester City and Bury, and Crewe said, "We'll give you a week's trial." On the third day they signed me up on a two-year contract. But I couldn't believe they were getting paid for playing football – that's how bad they were!' But being sacked by two clubs in two months is more than just bad luck in anyone's book, and Bowles was somewhat fortunate that anyone was willing to trust him.

There was so much baggage that came with the special talent, as Hince stated. 'He had gambling debts and was always skint, always asking for advances on his wages, and his then wife would be ringing saying, "We've got no money." Clubs couldn't handle it.' Bowles' behaviour was self-defeating, arrogant and insulting at times, though compared to some of today's lurid newspaper stories – players beating people up and urinating in bars – quite mild. Bowles drank very little at that point in his life. He was, however, a ferocious gambler. 'Unfortunately,' Hince said with a laugh, 'there was a bookie's right opposite the main entrance at Crewe, so on pay-day he was straight in there. There was many a time when Stan would come out of training at midday with his pay packet and then go home to Ann and the kids two hours later without a penny. It caused all sorts of trouble. What Crewe did was give Stan a tenner in cash and give the rest of his pay packet to Tommy Doyle, an odd-job man at the club, who'd take it straight to Ann. Stan seemed quite happy with that.'

Tagg was open from the start, insisting that if Bowles was incapable of knuckling down at Crewe, one of the worst clubs in the League, then his career would be over. Bowles, always impressed by straight talking from managers if he could fathom the truth in what they were saying, acknowledged that he would have to start trying harder. 'You couldn't believe he had so much ability but didn't appreciate it – he was wasting it,' Tagg observed. 'If he'd stayed with his mates in Manchester he wouldn't have lasted ten minutes, and he knew when he came to me that that was his last chance. But he didn't realise that he had to put anything into the game to get anything out of it. I thought that the only way to manage him properly was to keep him away from the racecourses. I decided to play ball with him, but if somebody had signed him and expected him to play straight away they'd have been very disappointed and he would have gone.'

Tagg was the only man in the world willing to take a chance on the problematic young striker. He owned a pub in the area and would occasionally not turn up for training if there was an important darts match to preside over, and it was in this pressure-free environment that Bowles, initially unimpressed with Crewe Alexandra, rediscovered his love of football. Hince certainly recognised the change in him at that critical stage in his career. 'At Crewe he never stepped over the line even though he still had gambling problems. After being sacked by two clubs, that really could have been the end of the road. The penny dropped, and he played out of his skin.' Modern footballers sign themselves into clinics for rehabilitation from drug or alcohol problems or depressions, but Bowles began a self-imposed course at Crewe.

Bowles' arrival in the Fourth Division hardly caused a storm of interest, but Crewe fans soon started to take notice. His debut was away to Darlington on 28 September in front of 3,255 fans, a game Crewe won 1–0, the goal coming from midfielder Kevin McHale. Five days later Bowles made his home debut, this time in front of 2,804 supporters (the biggest gate for a while), with Stockport County the visitors. Crewe lost 2–3 but Bowles did net his

bove Bowles in a
*C*arlisle United shirt,
*N*ovember 1971: deter-
*m*ined to resurrect his
*y*oung but eventful
*c*areer (© Empics)

Right In his trademark
*o*vercoat, Bowles is
*g*lum after a court
*a*ppearance in January
*1*973. He and Don
*S*hanks were later
*c*leared of driving a
*v*an used in an armed
*r*obbery (© Empics)

Left Bowles reaches the heights after his first England call-up i[n] March 1974, with a little help from QPR team-mate Frank McLintock
(© Empics)

Right More foul play: Birmingham City resor[t] to sinister tactics to stop Bowles, who late[r] perfected the artistic crash landing
(© Empics)

Right Making it look easy: Bowles is delighted after scoring his only goal for England, against Wales in May 1974
(© Sporting Pictures)

bove Bowles' magical left foot could carve open defences, as it does here
gainst Manchester United in September 1975 (© Empics)

Left Never one to shy away from the cameras, Bowles has his snap taken by QPR team-mate John Hollir (© Empics)

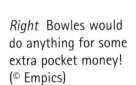

Right Bowles would do anything for some extra pocket money! (© Empics)

ight Looking
ocussed, but Bowles'
ppearance on the
BC's *Superstars*
rogramme turned
to a shambles
© Sporting Pictures)

elow One for the
hoto album: Bowles
ith Dennis Tueart,
Mick Channon, Kevin
eegan and Emlyn
ughes while training
ith England in 1976
© Empics)

Above Bowles found i
hard work against
Italy's deadly defender
Claudio Gentile in
November 1976
(© Empics)

Left In his final
England game, Bowles
typically glides past his
opponent, Holland's
Johan Neeskens, in
February 1977
(© Empics)

bove Even the likes
f Liverpool's Alan
ansen found Bowles'
kills more than a
andful (© Empics)

ight One of Bowles'
reat strengths was
ever giving the ball
way, as demonstrated
gainst Arsenal's David
rice in September
978 (© Empics)

Above Even the advertising hoardings were on Bowles' side as he faced Ajax in Nottingham Forest's 1980 European Cup semi-final (© Empics)

Left Bowles looks uncertain in his Orient shirt, August 1981, and the smile soon left his face (© Empics)

first goal for the club, the first of 18 in 51 appearances. Next came wins over Southend United, Workington, Hartlepool and Scunthorpe United, where Kevin Keegan was emerging, before Oldham Athletic ended the run.

Off the field, as always, things did not flow so promisingly. Bowles' gambling was as damaging as ever, and he was still mixing with the same type of people he'd known all his life. 'A few weeks after we'd signed him,' Tagg recalled, 'his wife turns up and is knocking on my window, saying, "He's brought no wages home!" I had to give her a few quid for the children's sake. Later, after Crewe decided to split his wages, half for him and half for her, she came back and was smiling. She said, "You don't have to split his wages any more. He's not going out – he's staying in at night." I took her word for it, paid Stan his full wages like she told me to, and a few weeks later she was back again. "He's doing it again – he's not bringing any money home!" That's the sort of trick we had to put up with. He couldn't stop gambling.'

In that 1970/71 season Crewe reached the second round of the FA Cup, losing there 1–0 to Chester, but were eliminated from the League Cup in the first round by Tranmere Rovers. They did, however, reach the quarterfinal of the Watney's Cup and the semi-final of the Cheshire Premier Cup. The glory did not end there, though, as the club were runners-up in the Ford Sporting League, pocketing £30,000. Crewe really were just about the worst side in the country but they had managed to capture and harness the talents of Stan Bowles, who, despite his track record, had been good enough to play at Manchester City, the club that the year before had won the First Division championship. He stuck out like a sore thumb in Division Four. It was too easy for him.

Supporters appreciated what he achieved in his short time at Crewe. Bowles had given everything, rarely having an off day, and had turned them into a side not frightened of failure. With Tagg's support he had remembered how to take charge of football matches, dictating the pace of a game. 'His mind seemed clearer and his play was improving,' said Tagg enthusiastically. 'He doubled our gates, he improved the whole team's style of play. He was the sort of bloke you'd try to help because you knew something good would come at the end of it. But eventually you couldn't do anything for him.'

It wasn't long before Tagg realised that Bowles' lifestyle could seriously damage his health. 'One day [local bookmaker] Sam [Barnes] told me, "This Stan Bowles of yours, he's with the lowest of the low. Take it from me, with the company he's keeping, you'll find him in an alley one day with his throat cut." Stan was always knocking about with these gangs. They were tricksters, trying to rob the bookies.' With this knowledge, Tagg redoubled his efforts to keep Bowles on the right path, talking to him for several hours about what he could achieve in the game if his mentality was right. Tagg was also concerned that his star player should not neglect his wife and children. At one stage he even gave Ann money from the car park money tin in his office at the ground. All this effort from Tagg was put in in the sure belief that it would be worth it, that Bowles would come good.

Crewe finished a lowly but not too disappointing fifteenth in the Fourth Division, but it was becoming clear that Bowles would soon be on his way to (slightly) bigger and better things. He had proved his commitment to football at 'The Alex', and since making his debut against Darlington had not missed a single match. Furthermore, at the beginning of 1971/72 he played in fifteen consecutive matches between August and his final game for the club on 23 October, a 0–0 draw against his despised former club Bury.

Tagg remembers a hairy moment before that game when it seemed Bowles had finally got himself in some serious trouble. 'This bloke came to my office. He was about six foot five, if not more. I opened the window to talk to him and all I could see was his belly button. I had to look up in the air to see where his head stopped. He said, "Have you got a Stanley Bowles?" So I told him, yes, I had. He said, "I'd like a word with him." This was Saturday afternoon, two and a half hours to kick-off. "There's been some watches stolen," he added, and I thought, "Oh God." Stan was seemingly in some gang. This bloke then said, "I'm afraid if I'm convinced he's in with them he'll be coming back with me." "Oh no, no," I said. "Not on a Saturday!" We only had twelve players! I told him there was no one in at the moment. He repeated, "If I'm convinced he's the man I've got to pick, he's coming with me." When he left I rang the chairman but I had no luck getting through to him. I was sitting there thinking, "What the hell am I going to do?"

'About an hour later, there was another knock on the window. It was the same man and he had another bloke with him. The other fellow was even bigger! The first bloke said to me, "You can tell Stan Bowles he's a very lucky man." It turned out they couldn't trace Stan but they had found the ringleader of the gang. "We've got the man we want," he said, "so you can keep Bowles." That was at two o'clock, and we were kicking off at three, so I went to see Stan to have a word. Even then you had to nurse him; there was no point upsetting him because he had to play. I just told him not to let me down again. And then he went out on to the field at three o'clock and played Bury on his own!'

Despite a few unpleasant incidents such as this, nobody offers more praise for Bowles than Tagg. He mourns the fact that Bowles could never shake himself out of his old ways. 'If Stan Bowles had been a level-headed man and kept the right company,' he insisted, 'then you'd have heard more about him than Georgie Best. He could have been like a Stanley Matthews, known all over the world. In fact, he was a better inside forward than Stan Matthews. If he'd had the same ideals as Matthews he could play for a World XI if they picked one.' Matthews, though, the model professional who stayed at the top of the game for many years through dedication and commitment, had ideals far removed from Bowles'. Even at Crewe, where he was striving to return to the top, Bowles would practically forget about football in between matches. Tagg remembers that he didn't need to train because he could simply turn on the style for ninety minutes every Saturday, then leave and return to his 'other' life.

During those final fifteen games for Crewe at the start of the 1971/72 season Bowles scored five goals, a one in three ratio which he maintained throughout his career. Distraught after his departure, Crewe Alexandra finished the season at the bottom of the Fourth Division. They had been briefly illuminated by Bowles' talents, then abandoned to the gloomy reality of survival without him.

'I think I'd been at Crewe for about thirteen months, or something like that,' said Bowles, remembering how his rehabilitation began to pay dividends, 'when the manager Ernie Tagg said, "Look, if you get your head together, there's a bid in for you from Carlisle. If you go up there for two years, you will definitely play for England." ' Tagg must have had a crystal ball because his predictions came true. Bowles moved on to Carlisle and began in earnest his comeback, at the age of just 22.

Crewe were not looking to offload Bowles but seemed to understand that he was a player they simply would not be able to keep. Tagg had built a reputation as a shrewd manager in the bargain end of the transfer market. He was, however, short-changed by Carlisle, who pleaded poverty and insisted they could not match Crewe's £25,000 valuation. After much bickering and bargaining, Carlisle made a £12,000 bid for Bowles that Crewe grudgingly accepted, even though the fans and management believed that if they had to sell their biggest asset at least they should make a sackful of cash from it. Carlisle rubbed salt into the fresh wound by selling Bob Hatton to Birmingham City for £80,000 just a few hours after Bowles put pen to paper on his new contract. Tagg was understandably outraged, believing that Carlisle must have known they were about to get £80,000, and refused to speak with anyone at the club again, also believing that Carlisle had made a secret agreement to sell Bowles on to QPR after a few months. 'With his ability, to sell him for £12,000 was mad, but then again, it was a surprise to be able to sell him at all! That was like a million to Crewe, but we couldn't believe it because of his reputation. Even if I had got a million pounds for him it wouldn't have been a pound too much.'

After he left Crewe for Carlisle, Bowles returned on a few occasions to visit Tagg, to show his appreciation for what the manager had done for his career. Tagg had convinced Bowles that he was capable of reaching the top of the profession. As both men accept, it was impossible to stop Bowles gambling altogether, as Tagg and Ann Bowles briefly thought had happened, but after a year in Crewe Bowles was no longer the self-destructive force he had been. All it had taken was encouragement and patience. When he realised that he was coming back as a player, he began to concentrate.

So in October 1971 Bowles moved beyond the Pennines and the Cumbrian Mountains to the club managed by no-nonsense Scot Ian MacFarlane. Carlisle United were in the Second Division and had been comfortably sitting mid-table for years. They were hoping that Bowles would add something different and give them fresh impetus in the challenge for promotion, and the club was miles from any big cities, so all in all the move represented an even bigger test for Bowles. He had proved he could perform at the foot of the League, now he had a chance to get back into more competitive football.

He made his first appearance for the club at the end of October in a vigorous match against fellow Division Two mid-tablers Oxford. He wore the number 10 shirt vacated by Bob Hatton, and it took a little while for fans to be convinced of his worthiness. He was a striking-looking £12,000 unknown from one of the nation's worst teams and was, as Carlisle fan Neil Nixon put it, 'positively alien by Cumbrian standards'. Nixon joked that when MacFarlane took Bowles off during his debut in favour of Bobby Owen he had taken off a girl and sent on a gorilla, but he would eventually succinctly summarise his feelings towards his club's newest acquisition with the following words: 'Thank f**k for Stan Bowles.'

Carlisle struggled that season, though, failing to find a system that worked. Evidence for this was the fact that in the days when a shirt number reflected a player's position on the field, Bowles would sometimes wear the number 10 shirt and sometimes 6 or 11. The only ray of hope was Stan Bowles. The enduring image of Carlisle's 1971/72 season is of the lively, quick-thinking young midfielder-cum-forward streaking through Division Two lines of defence, spraying pin-point passes to team-mates fifty yards away, his scraggly hair flapping in the wind. He scored goals regularly throughout the season, which made the loss of Bob Hatton easier to bear.

'We were in the Second Division when he came and he was the best player in it,' claimed Carlisle club historian David Steel, who still kicks himself for the fact that business commitments entailed a move to London for the season Bowles was at his club. 'That 1971/72 season was the season I saw my fewest ever Carlisle United matches, so I missed Stan! I remember seeing one of his first games, though, against Fulham. I was thinking at the time, "Who's this Stan Bowles we've bought?" And he scored our only goal that day. It all seemed to come so naturally to him. You can't teach that sort of thing.'

Bowles' poise and skill soon made him popular with fans of the Cumbrians, most of whom can now recollect having seen and nurtured one of Britain's greatest talents. Equally as soon, it became apparent that he would not be staying for long. Bowles seemed to be gearing himself up for a move to a big club. 'I went to Carlisle when I was 22 and spent a couple of years or so up there in the wilderness getting my head together a little bit,' Bowles said, overestimating the amount of time he spent in the far north of the country. 'At Carlisle we had some good Cup runs, playing Spurs and people. And I was thinking to myself, "F***ing hell, I'm miles better than some of these!" They were supposed to be really good players, all internationals. I mean, Ralph Coates was at Spurs then – I played with him later at Orient, funnily enough. He got more caps than me and was getting a lot more money than me. How he ever got *one* cap I'll never know. So I was beginning to think, "F***ing hell, I'm a lot better than this." '

Steel also recalled that Spurs match in the third round of the FA Cup. 'He scored Carlisle's goal against Tottenham. He created it out of nothing – just shimmied past a few defenders and stroked it into the net. On his day, it was all just so easy.' After a 1–1 draw at White Hart Lane, the mighty Spurs travelled to Brunton Park, where they won 3–1. Despite the loss, Bowles was the classiest player on display (in a game closely watched by QPR chairman Jim Gregory) and fortified his class with effort and passion. Carlisle fans could see just how good he was. '[His] varying shirt numbers added to the exotic mystery,' wrote Neil Nixon, 'along with Bowles' ability to ghost and glide past opposing players. The George Best comparisons were not made lightly.'

'When I went to Carlisle I started taking football more seriously,' Bowles claimed. 'I took it seriously when people told me that I could be an England player. The manager was Ian "The Big Man" MacFarlane, a big 6ft 5in Scotsman. He was even bigger than Malcolm Allison, him, and he didn't stand no messing about. I used to go back to Manchester every weekend because Carlisle was a f***ing desperate place – there was only one nightclub when I was there but it's changed a bit now – and I used to ring him up every Sunday night and say, "I can't make training tomorrow, I'm ill." And he would say, "If you're not f***ing there you're going to get a f***ing dig and you'll be f***ing sacked again." So I'd get a taxi back there, which was about £60 in them days.'

Quickly tiring of this ritual, Bowles made the decision to relax his lifestyle in order to achieve his goal of playing for England and returning to top-flight football. He placed himself in MacFarlane's hands, entrusting, for once, his career to another person's way of thinking. 'In the end I got a house up there and started settling down a bit. I took Ian MacFarlane very seriously. There were times when I didn't want to go training but he put it so forcefully I'd make the effort and do it. I can honestly say I never let him down once, and he'd tell you that. He wasn't overly strict, but once he said something you knew he meant it.' Steel remembers MacFarlane's brief tenure as manager with a smile. 'He was one of the few people who could control Stan Bowles and he even seemed to get the best out of him. He was never a man for tolerating excuses. If you were told to get in at ten o'clock in the morning, you got in at ten o'clock in the morning, or else!'

Despite MacFarlane's unique ways of dealing with his players, in the summer of 1972 he left Carlisle United, a couple of months before Bowles did. The official story is that MacFarlane's manner did not gel with the powers-that-be upstairs at the club, which suggests that he had a disagreement with the chairman or one of the directors, shouted a bit, and they reacted by sacking him, much to the surprise and dismay of everyone else. While the return of popular manager Alan Ashman was a tonic for most of the fans, MacFarlane's departure was a blow for Bowles. The big Scot was a larger-than-life character Bowles found it easy to get on with.

'Ian MacFarlane was daft, he was mad as a f***ing hatter!' joked Paul Hince fondly. 'When he was assistant manager at City [later in his career] he phoned me at the newspaper and said, "I've got a great exclusive for you! You've got to come to my house. And bring a photo-grapher." This was a week before City were going to play at Wembley. So when I turned up he grinned and said, "Well, what do you think?" I looked at him and asked, "What do I think about what?" He said, "My hat." He had a beret on or something. I said, "I'm not with you, Ian." "I've bought this for Wembley," he said. "What an exclus-ive for the *Manchester Evening News*!" But he was very good for Stan, who needed the combination of the free rein but knowing he couldn't push it too far.'

It was indeed a brief but vital stage in Bowles' career. His future development depended on self-discipline and find-ing the will to acknowledge and curb the self-destructive tendencies that had blighted his first few years in the game. MacFarlane had spotted him and trusted him, and he had repaid the manager handsomely. The entertainer in him occasionally spilled out, however. For one import-ant cup tie Bowles had a bet on with one of his Carlisle team-mates that he could get the number of nutmegs against the defender he was facing into double figures. With journalist Paul Hince in the stands keeping count,

Bowles won the bet easily. 'It was easy for him,' Hince recalled with a chuckle. 'He won it early in the second half. This was a major cup tie and all Stan was worried about was this bet.' He also still had trouble getting out of bed, and his reputation for not liking training had followed him to Carlisle. MacFarlane knew that sooner or later the call would come from Ann saying that Bowles could not possibly come to training today because he had a cold or diarrhoea or whatever. So when it did, he said, 'Right, Ann, I'll be there in a bit.' He drove to Bowles' house, tipped Stan out of bed and physically threw him out. Bowles never tried to have a lie-in again after that.

Bowles is quick to acknowledge the role of his mentors during this lowly period in his career, the men who put him on the track back to the top. The maverick had not been tamed, but at least he was willing to channel his energy in more appropriate ways.

'The most important people in my career were those early ones: Ernie Tagg at Crewe and Ian MacFarlane at Carlisle. Without them I wouldn't have made the grade. They motivated me, but they were friends as well so I trusted them. They were the most important people in my career. It was hard to come back from getting sacked twice. It was unknown in those days. But I did it. I did quite a lot of it on my own, but without those two specifically I wouldn't have done it. It helped that I liked them both as well.'

Stan Bowles' new work ethic meant that towards the end of the season a number of bigger clubs began to take an interest. Manchester City captain Tony Book, for one, could see that Bowles' move away from Maine Road had encouraged, or forced, the young maverick to try harder and commit himself to football. 'You always knew he was going to get his chance in the First Division because he had a lot going for him. He was a natural. It was just a matter of developing, but I knew he'd make a name for himself somewhere.' There was even talk in the press of him returning to start afresh at Manchester City, claims the club staunchly refuted. 'I don't think I'd have gone back there anyway,' Bowles said. 'I'd made my mind up that I wanted to go to London.' He has also claimed that City were trying to block any chances of a move to another big club by giving him bad character references.

This hunger and commitment to dragging himself back up after letting himself slip down in the first place is something of a paradox, and makes Bowles a difficult personality to pin down. When challenged, either on the pitch or off it, he would often withdraw and sulk or get angry, but when he had nobody to argue with – he could have stayed in the lower divisions for ever if he'd wanted to, and they'd have been delighted to keep him – then he came up trumps. Later in his career he dropped the baton a few more times, losing the focus that had pushed him from Crewe to Carlisle and then to Queens Park Rangers, but the move to Loftus Road in September 1972 was the impressive end result of a lot of soul-searching. The young hero, it seemed, had completed his rehab.

On 9 September the *Daily Mirror*'s Harry Miller announced his incredulity at Stan Bowles' return to stardom. 'SCRAP-HEAP' STAN COSTS £110,000 his headline roared, followed by JAGO GETS REFORMED STAR. Miller called Bowles' transfer to QPR 'one of soccer's most astonishing comebacks', adding, 'Carlisle collect the cash two years after Bowles, 23, collected his cards from Manchester City and seemed destined for the scrap-heap.' It was perhaps a little harsh to call the lower divisions the 'scrap-heap', but a couple of years earlier Bowles' career really had seemed to be as good as over. He revealed the motivation behind his return to top form and his rapid increase in value: 'Malcolm Allison, Manchester City's manager now, said I would never make it to the top. Joe Mercer said my football was all right but I couldn't change from being a tearaway. Well, I have, and I'm on my way to proving them wrong. I'm sure I'll be playing in the First Division with Rangers in the near future.' Of course, he did indeed go on to great things with QPR, and with England. Like a yo-yo he had hit the floor and bounced back up quickly. 'There was a lovely story in the *Express* when Stan later got his first England cap,' Hince recalled, 'about how far he had travelled on that five and sixpence I lent him for the train ticket to Crewe. And I'm still waiting to get it back!'

One of the ironies of Bowles' varied career is that Mercer's Manchester City didn't give him, the local boy with the magical skills, a real opportunity in the first team, but still, a few seasons later, signed a similarly wayward genius in Rodney Marsh and insisted on playing him, eventually to their own detriment. Football is indeed a fickle business. Marsh is now a Maine Road hero, while not many people even remember that Bowles used to play there! Had Bowles waited two more years, it could have been him. It must be frustrating for him to realise that he could have made it into the first team and perhaps done a better job than Marsh ever did, considering that under his belt come 1972 he'd have had a good few years' knowledge of the team, the management and the style of play. It is a cruel twist of fate in the Bowles saga, and possibly one of the reasons why he is so bitter towards Marsh.

Nevertheless, with his move to QPR Bowles was determined to put the bad days behind him, and he did, even though when he arrived at Loftus Road he was still no model professional. It's true he had learnt over the past two years to commit himself to football, but he was still just as committed to enjoying himself, and those two passions in his life meant that for the rest of his career his name would rarely be far from the back and front pages. But alongside the scrapes, he enjoyed the finest spell of his footballing career with QPR, and in September 1972 his first England cap, just as Ernie Tagg had promised, was only nineteen months away.

6 The Runaway: England, 1974–77

I'm not surprised. Nothing ever surprises me about Stan Bowles.

JOE MERCER, ENGLAND MANAGER

Stan Bowles' England career spanned three years, during which time he accumulated only five caps, mainly because of bad behaviour, bad judgement, bad tempers and an assumption by various managers that he was a bit too much of a risk. 'I had four managers with England,' Bowles summarised. 'Some say I got them all the sack! Ha-ha! Four managers out of five matches is not bad!'

As quips go this one's not bad, but not for the first time it requires a degree of salt-pinching. For a start, Bowles played under just three England managers – Alf Ramsey, Joe Mercer and Don Revie – and while it's possible that his surprisingly and infuriatingly ineffectual performances put pressure on those managers when they risked calling him into the side, it's hardly true that any of them lost their jobs over him. What is more remarkable is that Bowles is mistaken about the identity of the England managers under whom he played. So little attention did he pay to those supposedly in authority, even when those men were bestowing upon him one of the greatest honours in football, that the facts have simply faded from memory.

Like so many of his super-talented fellow footballers in the 1970s, Bowles was never allowed the time to settle into international football. Rodney Marsh was given nine games (one goal), Charlie George just one; Alan Hudson was called up twice, Frank Worthington eight times (two goals), and Peter Osgood won only four caps. Even George Best played only nine games for Northern Ireland. Their refusal to be shackled to a tactical system meant that they were replaced with more compliant players.

If there is one person who is always honest and informed in his opinions of Bowles, it is his old Manchester friend Paul Hince, the man who sent Bowles on his way back to top-flight football with a small loan to buy a train ticket to Crewe station. 'You could never see him fitting into the England set-up,' Hince openly claimed, 'because it was a bit more regimented than club football, and the management wanted to know where you were at night. He had his own routine, he didn't want to be at a boot camp for five or six days, locked up every night. That would have driven Stanley mad – and it did!' With the exception of Manchester City, Bury and Nottingham Forest, Bowles' clubs accommodated him, not the other way around. Even Carlisle's Ian MacFarlane, a strict disciplinarian, told Bowles that on the field he could do his own thing.

Bowles might not have liked discipline or organisation, but at international level there could never be different rules for different players. With twenty of the country's elite players in a hotel for a week it would be impossible to say to him, 'OK, Stan, you can go home every night.' The same applied on the pitch. Very rarely in 130 years of international football has an individual player been given a free role on the pitch, and the same is true of virtually every nation in the world, with the exception perhaps of some South American countries such as Argentina, so keen on tricks and attacking play that they are open and encouraging when it comes to individual brilliance. Even today, when players are moulded for a particular position more than ever, there is always a question mark hanging over somebody's head before a major game. Will Steve McManaman play? Can Italy find room for an ageing Roberto Baggio in their side, even if nobody has taken over his crown as the prince of Serie A? More often than not the answer is no, and managers stick to the safest options: ball-winners, wingers, a flat-back four. 'Robots, Stanley would call them,' said Hince. 'And he was never a robot.'

CAP 1, V. PORTUGAL, 3 APRIL 1974

Line-up: Parkes, Nish, Pejic, Dobson, Watson, Todd, Bowles, Channon, Macdonald (sub. Ball), Brooking, Peters

Sir Alf Ramsey, no poor judge of a player, gave Bowles his England debut in this dull goalless friendly against Portugal. In total there were six international debutants on the pitch, with QPR goalkeeper Phil Parkes also making his first appearance alongside midfielders Martin Dobson (Burnley) and Trevor Brooking (West Ham), and defenders Mike Pejic (Stoke) and Dave Watson (Sunderland).

Sir Alf was under enormous pressure at this point in his tenure as England manager following his side's failure to qualify for the 1974 World Cup. The days of Bobby Charlton, Geoff Hurst and Bobby Moore were over and Ramsey was pinning his hopes on what had been perceived as defensive sides without creativity or style in midfield. The press had long been calling for the introduction of Bowles, Marsh, Worthington, Osgood or Hudson, tiring of the likes of Nobby Stiles, Peter Storey and Alan Mullery who were meant to provide a solid foundation from which Alan Ball and Martin Peters could create match-winning opportunities. As former England defender Roy McFarland once commented, however, 'We didn't always score goals – we made the chances but they wouldn't go in. If in the 1970s we had had a Greaves or a Shearer or a Lineker, Alf wouldn't have got that criticism. After Franny Lee, nothing was solid for him up front. Franny had that temperament, that class at international level, that arrogance you need to score goals.' Most neutral observers would rather watch the mesmerising maverick players, such as Bowles, play for England than ten Alan Shearers, irrespective of results. In retrospect, perhaps Ramsey should have introduced a new generation of internationals a few years before 1974, but he stuck to his guns as critics argued that he was in a rut. Once, in a rare weak moment, he blasted at journalists, 'Where am I to find the forwards?' But it was more a question of trusting them than finding them.

Ramsey rarely made friends in the media, few among whom saw the humorous side of him, which he tended to reserve for his players. His England predecessor Walter Winterbottom acknowledged the danger in an icy public attitude, saying, 'Once the press get against you, you're nowhere.' England's most successful ever manager did bow to the pressure on occasion, however, and in April 1972 he had given the press what they wanted, bringing Rodney Marsh on against West Germany at Wembley with fifteen minutes to go in the first leg of a European Championship quarter-final. England lost 3–1. In the return leg, in Berlin two weeks later, he played Marsh from the start but then took him off in favour of Mike Summerbee. England drew 0–0, which wasn't enough to progress.

Ramsey didn't trust Marsh and his attitude to football, he didn't like mavericks. He was more accustomed to dealing with players like Charlton and Hurst, who had learnt discipline at Lilleshall and would never answer back. But, in harsh contradiction to the post-war battlers who won the 1966 World Cup, the real stars of the 1970s played with abandon and often did not take orders well. It was impossible for Ramsey to find the players to fit neatly into his tried and trusted system. Throughout the first few years of the 1970s, with Sir Alf Ramsey in charge, England could not progress. As Dave Bowler wrote in his biography of Ramsey, 'In 1966 all our world-class players, bar Jimmy Greaves, played because he believed in them. By 1972, our potential world-class players couldn't get a game because he didn't. In fairness, some, like Bowles and Hudson, wore their non-conformity like a badge of pride, determined to be awkward.' Ramsey was unwilling to try out players because the pressure to perform and qualify for the major championships was ever present, his head was in the guillotine and he simply didn't have time to waste on test-driving footballers he was certain would let him down.

Equally, the England manager was not prepared to have his authority undermined, but even so the situation became so grave that he eventually was forced to turn to

QPR's Stan Bowles as a potential saviour. Ramsey had already tested Bowles' suitability in a match between the English and Scottish leagues, which didn't count as a full international cap, on 29 March 1974, a match the English side sneaked 5–0. Bowles' performance, which included scoring the fifth goal, was thought impressive enough to warrant giving him a place in the full side. This Anglo-Scottish clash was the result of Ramsey suggesting to an FA committee – a committee, monickered the 'Future of Football', which, it transpired, was figuring out a way to sack him – that England should have three days to prepare for international friendlies, a week for competitive games and one international match each month. This was the start of the now tiresome club versus country debate. Indeed, for the friendly match against Portugal nine players were refused permission to travel by their clubs because England were not featuring in the imminent World Cup.

The match itself was hardly spectacular. The Portuguese public virtually ignored the match, with only a few thousand turning up, and it was England who started well, Bowles almost setting up Channon in the early stages. Portuguese journalists were surprised by the technical ability of the side Ramsey fielded. English football writer Brian Glanville offered the insight, 'Times may indeed be changing.' But what he gave with one hand he snatched away with the other, adding that Bowles 'had shown himself no more than a brilliant club player who cannot take the great leap forward into international football'. Damning words from an experienced and respected observer. On 4 April, the day after the Portugal game, most newspaper reports were quite restrained. Of the strikers who played in Lisbon, Malcolm Macdonald got most of the muted plaudits in the *Daily Mirror*, but then they did name him their player of the month that same day.

In the *Mirror*, Frank McGhee, a man who went on to make some fairly accurate predictions about Bowles' future, stated, 'Bowles showed all his deadly anticipation . . . looming on the scene.' He went on to register his undying support of Sir Alf Ramsey, a privilege not bestowed on many England managers since. 'The England manager's pride must be that, despite all the difficulties imposed upon him, a bunch of footballing strangers, six of them totally new to international football, came together in a foreign land and did not let either themselves, their profession or their country down.'

However, as would become apparent over the next few years, and as had been so obvious during these latter stages of Sir Alf's England reign, the nation lacked a top goalscorer. Even though Keegan and Channon scored 21 times each in 63 and 46 internationals respectively, nobody truly replaced Jimmy Greaves until Gary Lineker came along. Indeed, the following day, McGhee, having slept on his views, decided he had been a little too generous to the England players. Complaining of England's impotent performance in front of goal, he wrote, 'Stan Bowles, so exciting, impudent and demoralising in the home comfort of Shepherd's Bush, was a subdued shadow of himself.' This would be a theme common to all Bowles' appearances in his patchy and controversial international career. The individual criticism aside, Ramsey's reliance on a new-look, stylish England gave Bowles and his generation of mavericks hope for the future. The England boss had seemingly woken up to the spirit of the new decade at last, albeit a few years late.

It's not quite true to say that Bowles was overawed by the occasion, and he was certainly talented enough to be there – even to be the star turn – but he was always more at ease in his own back yard where he would without doubt be the biggest talent on show and the fans would chant his name. And, vitally, where his team-mates had learnt how to make best use of his skills – i.e. how to pass to him!

The game against Portugal was an opportunity, whether appreciated or not, to throw in some fresh faces, but Ramsey was sacked a few weeks later after 113 games in charge which included 69 wins and just 17 losses, an unparalleled eleven years of success at the helm. At first the papers reported that he had quit, but over the next few days it became apparent that the FA had forced him out after a two-month inquiry. They gave him £8,000, let him go off on a holiday to avoid the press, and then made the announcement to the nation.

In the immediate aftermath of the team's return from Lisbon, Bowles' manager at QPR, Gordon Jago, was asked to take charge of the England under-23s, supposedly to allow Ramsey time to focus on forthcoming senior international fixtures. There was much discussion in the press, however, that Jago was to be primed eventually to take over from Ramsey. The fact that Jago rejected the offer, which was made before the news broke of Ramsey's departure, would prove to be a cause for regret, not only on his part but on Bowles' too. One of the nation's finest and most popular young managers at the time, had Jago taken the under-23s job there is the possibility that he would have enjoyed an almost instant promotion to manage the senior team. And how would that have affected the international career of Bowles, a player Jago knew intimately and saw on the pitch every day? This is speculation, obviously, but Jago could well have been the man to trust Bowles and to bring the best out of him. Had everything worked out perfectly in Bowles' career he would now be remembered as one of England's greatest footballers. Then again, as has been said before, the regrets are all part of the legend.

Football was in bad shape in Britain at the time on the terraces, too, hooligans taking up as many newspaper column inches as the game itself. Meanwhile, George Best threw a champagne reception at a London hotel after being cleared of theft charges brought by the current Miss World. All he wanted to do, he said, was get back to work in his nightclub, Slack Alice. The likes of a cherub-faced Cilla Black parading her new baby Benjamin and a cigar-waving Tom Jones having his passport seized by money-hungry officials in Venezuela adorned the showbiz pages, while on the back pages, with Jago out of the picture, it was Jack Charlton and Joe Mercer who were reported to be heading the race to succeed Ramsey.

CAP 2, V. WALES, 11 MAY 1974

Line-up: Shilton, Todd, McFarland, Hughes, Nish, Pejic, Bell, Weller, Channon, Bowles, Keegan.

Mercer, who'd had the dubious privilege of (almost) managing and indeed sacking Bowles at Manchester City, took over in a seven-match-only caretaker role a week after Ramsey's unexpected departure and stuck with Bowles and the rest of Ramsey's pre-named squad for the 1974 Home Nations tournament. Frank Butler wrote in the *News of the World*, 'Mercer has brought a new freedom back to England', and Uncle Joe, who'd been steadily managing Coventry City with assistant Gordon Milne, was generally heralded as the saviour of the national game. Mercer had been delighted when one member of the 'Future of Football' committee had approached Coventry to politely enquire if he could possibly lead England in the forthcoming home internationals and in games against Argentina, East Germany, Bulgaria and Yugoslavia. Author Gary James wrote in his biography of Mercer, 'When Joe arrived at Lancaster Gate, the Belgian-born receptionist didn't recognise him. She asked, "Do you have an appointment?" Quick as a flash, Joe replied, "Yes, for seven matches!" '

The England set-up was about to become more relaxed as Mercer recognised the fact that life under Ramsey had been too stressful. The first thing Mercer said to Bowles when they met for the first time in four years at a training session was, 'I've won money on you, Stanley my boy. My son laid me odds of 6–4 you wouldn't even turn up!' 'Uncle Joe' claimed publicly that he did not have a problem with Bowles from their days together in Manchester – which, among other things, included the occasional punch-up, a dodgy alarm clock and, eventually, the boot – and Bowles insisted, 'There's nothing I really want to prove to him. I'm not looking at these games as a way of getting my own back.' Perhaps not the wisest words, as every England player should be out to prove themselves to a new England manager, especially one who could yet be offered the job on a full-time basis. Furthermore, these intended assurances were a sign that Bowles did secretly harbour a feeling that there was actually something to get his own back for.

Bowles repaid Mercer's initial faith in him with a goal in a 2–0 win over Wales in Cardiff. It was not a spectacular one, but it typified Bowles' predatory presence and speed of thought. In the thirty-fifth minute, following a hard-fought run along the right wing, Keith Weller crossed the ball low into the middle of the Welsh goalkeeper's six-yard box. Phillips dived on to the ball but spilled it, Bowles was lurking, and he scored from three yards. He had reacted the quickest to register what was, in theory, the first of many England goals, and jogged back to the halfway line beaming at his team-mates.

Bowles famously played that match wearing one Gola boot and one Adidas boot. Gola had previously approached him with an offer to wear their boots and Bowles had accepted, eagerly stuffing the readies down his sock when the Gola representative came to the England hotel before the match to deliver to a selection of players payment in a briefcase. That, though, was before he learnt that Adidas were offering more. Bowles thought he'd make a few enquiries. Too late for anyone to do anything about it, he was on the pitch, having pocketed an easy £450. It isn't recorded which boot scored the goal, but it was whichever was fortunate enough to be on his left foot at the time. 'No one told me I couldn't do it,' was Bowles' nonchalant response to the attention he received after his prank. The Gola representative, understandably, was not happy, and he rang Bowles a few days after the match to complain. The Adidas rep, however, saw the funny side of the situation and offered Bowles a permanent and exclusive boot sponsorship deal. Different people react in different ways to Stan Bowles.

The reaction to Bowles' performance of the *Daily Mirror*, Britain's best-selling daily paper at the time, is intriguing, especially considering a later incident involving one of its journalists and a hospital bed. Senior football reporter Frank McGhee's all-encompassing criticisms on the day following the Wales match are perhaps representative of Bowles' entire international career. After claiming that England should beg Alf Ramsey to come back or, failing that, give the England job to Wales manager Dave Bowen, McGhee put the boot into Bowles. 'We waited for Bowles to improve after that [opening goal] – to produce the form that makes him so impertinent, infuriating, eye-catching and effective for his club – and we went on waiting. If he couldn't shine against Wales – admittedly in the face of some intimidatory tackling – he could at this rate become one of a long line of talented players who mysteriously fail to make it at international level.' A young Kevin Keegan, who scored England's second, was also lambasted, some critics saying that the next game, against Northern Ireland, should be his last chance. Keegan, sensibly, responded with, 'I learnt a lot playing with Channon and Bowles. If you can't fit in with them, you really don't deserve to be in the side' – a comment that accepted the criticism and indirectly took all the pressure off himself. The QPR man, however, responded with claims of physical intimidation, which could easily be construed as making excuses.

That said, being punched in the face by your opponents seems a feasible reason for being distracted from your football. Bowles' second-half performance was disappointing, and he claimed that one of the Welsh defenders had purposefully hit him in the face. 'I was amazed,' Bowles complained afterwards. 'I never thought that kind of behaviour went on in international matches. When I took a right-hander in the mouth, the bloke who did it said, "There's plenty more where that came from." It knocked me out of my stride for half the game.'

CAP 3, V. NORTHERN IRELAND, 15 MAY 1974

Line-up: Shilton, Nish, Pejic, Hughes, McFarland (sub. Hunter), Todd, Keegan, Weller, Channon, Bell, Bowles (sub. Worthington)

Following Bowles' unconvincing (if productive) showing against the bullies of Wales, the Northern Ireland clash was a very big moment. But if it was a Welsh defender who deprived Bowles of half a game with his swinging fist in Cardiff, at Wembley it was not the opposition but his own manager, Joe Mercer, who dealt the damaging blow. Bowles was taken off at the start of the second half and, embarrassed and suspicious of Mercer's motives, he stormed out of the stadium, out of the England hotel and straight to the White City dog track, where he felt most at ease. 'I walked out because I was distressed,' he explained to the press later. 'I come on as sub for Stan during that match,' recalled Frank Worthington, 'and he went straight down to the dressing room, got changed, and went down to the dog track. It was only Stan who could have done that – what a character. I came on for my debut and made the winning goal.' But if the plan was to relax and hide away, nothing could have been less likely to succeed. Front-page news was just around the corner.

Bowles insisted that he had heard Mercer explain to one of the England coaches that he would take him off after a few minutes of the second half, and rather than the substitution itself it was the tone in which Mercer had spoken about it that Bowles found so upsetting. The previous England manager Alf Ramsey had rarely taken players off until the last few minutes, if at all. Bowles thought of it as Mercer's revenge for the old arguments at Manchester City – public humiliation.

Perhaps worse still, the player who replaced him against Northern Ireland, Frank Worthington, was being talked of as the next big thing for English football. *Daily Mirror* writer Frank McGhee gleefully called Worthington's introduction 'the unveiling of a newcomer of authentic talent where it is needed most in international football – in the penalty box'. Just to rub salt in the wounds, he added, 'Neither Kevin Keegan nor Stan Bowles grabbed the chance to prove they can bridge the enormous gap between stardom at club level and mere competence among the really big boys.' So not only was Bowles humiliatingly subbed in front of the cameras, he was also 'merely competent' where before he had thought himself supreme. Over the last few days Bowles had experienced a level of disdain and disgust difficult even for him to cope with.

Geoffrey Green, in *The Times*, produced an unparalleled display of literary 'mincing' in the aftermath of the game, but his sentiments were universally shared. 'One tactical change turned the illiterate into the literate,' he wrote, 'and the inarticulate into the articulate last night. It came with the substitution of Worthington for Bowles in the front line some ten minutes after the interval. Up till then England had threatened but never achieved much. Bowles, with all his clever footwork, remained a mischievous sprite, something of a jabberwocky that gyres and gimbles in the way. He went in circles, showing a pretty touch here, another there, but produced no end product. But it was the arrival of Worthington that brought a new picture to the canvas. At once the flaw was mended. Up to that moment, despite the drive of Channon and the efforts of little Keegan, the attack had been lightweight. It had worked, as it were, in shorthand. But Worthington brought not only height and weight but skill and penetration, and with that, too, a wide vision.'

While Worthington was penetrating skilfully, Bowles was fuming, on his way to the races. A few hours after the game a *Daily Mirror* reporter (Mike Ramsbottom) and photographer (Harry Prosser) tracked down Bowles at the dogs, determined to discover the truth about why he had quit. The next day, Prosser, for once on the other side of the lens, was on the newspaper's front page, his face covered in bruises. One of Bowles' mates had decided to end the unwelcome intrusion by smacking the photographer in the face, causing him – as bad luck would have it! – to tumble down a flight of stone steps. Other versions of events suggest that the photographer was actually seriously beaten up by a number of Bowles' White City friends. Bowles' long-time friend Paul Hince was outraged at the incident. 'I only ever had one row with him,' he seethed, 'and I purposefully phoned him to have the row. He'd been approached by a reporter and a photographer, and he had some of his "minders" with him – he always seems to attract these people. They beat up these two journalists. I shouted at him, "You f***ing twat! They were just doing their job. That could have been me!" It seemed to me that he was just getting above himself. That was the only time, because he's usually very amenable. He'd normally say yes to anything. He's a pussycat, Stan. I don't know what got under his skin then but it was definitely out of character.'

Bowles has since suggested that it was a mistake to quit the England team, admitting that he let Mercer down, and the fact that footballers with a fraction of his talent represented England more than he did saddens him now, but he is adamant that he never set out to be an international footballer, just a good club player. That, however, does not quite sit comfortably alongside the appraisal of the situation by Gordon Jago, who had quit as QPR manager on the Monday before the match against Northern Ireland. Jago displayed both loyalty to and sympathy for Bowles the morning after he fled the England camp. 'I've known Stan for two and a half years,' he explained, 'and I feel he needs someone to chat to. Wherever he has gone he must be a lonely man. He must have felt like the bottom dropped out of his world last night. He has always wanted to play for England at Wembley and . . . must have been bitterly disappointed. I think I might have been able to help if I could have talked it over with Stan. I know his temperament and how he would react to such a situation.' Loyalty and sympathy were essential to Bowles' career. He was offered both at club level, particularly at QPR, but neither at international level – and perhaps rightly so. His behaviour certainly proved to many people time and again that he did not deserve to represent his country.

Mercer initially refused to comment on the disciplinary action that would be taken against Bowles, but his first reaction to the striker's sudden departure sounded, simply and damningly, as though he were sick to death of his melodramatic gestures. 'I'm not surprised,' he sighed. 'Nothing ever surprises me about Stan Bowles.'

Mercer was not the only one tired of this sulking. McGhee took the time to wax lyrical about principles and responsibilities, throwing in the occasional insult for good measure. 'Stan Bowles,' he intoned, 'turned his back on something much more important to him and an England team future when he "disappeared" from that team's training headquarters on Tuesday. Bowles rejected his future at international and club level by acting the part of the spoilt child who insists on taking home the ball and the goalposts when the others won't play it his way. All right, to be pulled off a pitch in full view of fans and a television audience may be humiliating. But to be on that pitch in the first place, wearing an England shirt, should for Bowles have been an honour great enough to have more than compensated.

'I am tired of the antics of the Stan Bowleses and George Bests of the football world. In my old-fashioned way I can't help feeling that the game is more important than the players. To be fair to players such as Bowles, whose irresponsibility outweighs even his considerable ability, the players they damage most are themselves.'

Bowles' apparent lack of nous at the highest level, or rather an unwillingness or inability to take rejection on the chin, is one of the most regrettable things about his career. Was it that he didn't have enough ambition, or too much? Of course, it is all part of the real Bowles: so hugely talented that he didn't feel the need to prove himself to anybody; so temperamental, so used to having fun and so used to getting his own way that he didn't care who he upset along the way – not even England fans.

'I don't care if he's the best player in the world, he cannot be accepted back,' blasted Mercer later. 'You don't walk out on England. To do what he has done when there are others around who would give their right arms to play for England is unforgivable. There is no way you can behave like that at this level. I told him, loud and clear, he was destroying himself. I hope for his sake he got the message.' To an extent, he did, and because a player of his quality is always forgivable, he did get another chance with England, but not until the national team was desperate again, two and a half years later. He had cast himself into the wilderness, with Mercer's warning that he would never play for England again while he was in charge ringing in his ears. Knowing Bowles, he would have shrugged his shoulders and found a shop that sold the *Racing Post*.

Frank Worthington lamented the way in which few efforts were made at international level to accommodate the country's best players. Worthington – who was arguably even more successful than George Best at 'birding' and who once commented, 'My bed wasn't for sleeping . . . I was at it five nights a week, rarely with the same woman twice, and often with the odd quick one before the match' – won just eight full England caps and two at under-23 level. 'My reputation went against me at the top level,' he claimed. 'Joe Mercer encouraged individual flair, and at the top level if you don't have two or three high-class individual players who can win matches then you're not going to get anywhere, you'll be ordinary. We went off with England to Eastern Europe [in May and June 1974] and did well out there. Sadly, just after that Joe got the sack because the FA had set up Don Revie, and my international career after that was very short-lived. It was a wonderful opportunity for me and I played well, well enough to establish myself at the highest level, but a change in management and it was taken away.'

After replacing Bowles against Northern Ireland, Worthington went on to play the next seven England matches, starting six and then coming off the bench for his last cap, against Portugal on 20 November 1974. His last two games, with Joe Mercer's seven-match caretaker spell over, were under Don Revie and were both played at Wembley. Revie didn't like Worthington, who never played for his country again. It did not help the cause of the mavericks that when Worthington was replaced in Revie's first game in charge – a vital European Championship qualifier against Czechoslovakia on 30 October – the player who came on in his place, Bowles' QPR team-mate Dave Thomas, turned the game, which England won 3–0.

'Unfortunately Revie took over and he got rid of all the flair players,' Worthington complained. 'And he struggled as a result because you need the top players. You have got to have the balance right – you can only have one or two in the side. But if you don't have them at all then you're going nowhere, as it proved with Don Revie. You can't argue with what he did at Leeds because he had flair players there, but for some reason he didn't want that with England. Only Revie could explain why he didn't trust me because I thought I'd done enough under Joe Mercer to warrant a regular place in the international team. I was playing well, and Revie took that away from me. It was absolutely the same with Stan Bowles. He only got a handful of caps but he was magic. He should have been around for much, much longer. He should have won 45 caps, not just five.'

Although Bowles can try to laugh the disappointment off, make a joke of it or blame it on other people, it remains a shadow over his story, a flaw that was never mended. Perhaps he was too secure in his world. Deluded, even. A life at the White City dog track, the same people, the same routines, a life without new horizons or aims. Always willing to poke fun at himself, he admits there was a 'decadence' to the place. It was an obsession, a way of life, where Bowles would never have to stay still because a whole cross-section of society flowed through. He knew everyone and everyone knew him. That was the world to which Bowles ran to escape his annoyance at being substituted by Mercer.

After the incident with Prosser and Ramsbottom the press gave Bowles no respite, but he didn't care. He had already achieved something that many, Joe Mercer included, said he would never achieve – he'd played for his country. It didn't matter that the honour had been stained with controversy, that he had let his heart rule his head. That was just a part of life and something Bowles was accustomed to – addicted to, even. Anyway, Mercer's reign had been brief, and now Don Revie was in charge.

Revie's appointment was a surprise to absolutely nobody. He had taken Leeds United from the depths of Division Two and transformed them into one of Europe's most feared sides. Indecision at the FA HQ was as widespread then as it is today, however, and Revie was forced to ask for the job rather than being offered it. He was the only realistic candidate.

Shortly after the appointment, in September 1974, when nobody was yet sure who would be in the new England squad, Bowles was invited to attend an unusual seminar for 84 potential England players organised by Revie in Manchester. The new manager was insistent that whatever had happened between Mercer and Bowles should be forgotten, even though the *Sunday People* claimed that Bowles' inclusion affronted patriotic, decent and ordinary fans. Ignoring the unrest, Bowles attended the seminar – which was basically a publicity stunt to keep everyone happy – and even behaved himself, although he did report back to QPR late, earning a brief suspension.

Bowles did not make it into Revie's first England side for the match against Czechoslovakia, a tie which saw Gerry Francis make his international debut, as captain. Bowles had been looking forward to playing alongside his team-mate at QPR, but fate meant they kept missing each other in internationals. So Bowles had been overlooked, while the two players who supplied him at club level – Francis and Dave Thomas, who was Worthington's replacement – played important roles in Revie's first match. England did not make it to the European Championship finals, finishing second in their qualifying group a point ahead of Portugal. At least Czechoslovakia went on to win the tournament, which, to be extremely forgiving, almost vindicates Revie's decision about Bowles' non-inclusion: the Czechs were clearly the better side anyway and Bowles probably would not have been able to make the difference.

Gerry Francis rues this and a number of other missed opportunities to play at the highest level with Bowles. 'One of my biggest regrets is that though Stan played for England and I played for and captained England, we never actually played together. It was very strange because it was all around the same sort of period but never actually at the same time, either through injury or not being picked. It was a shame that our telepathic ability [at club level] was never produced for our country.'

Up front for England, Keegan, Channon and Macdonald were establishing themselves as first-choice strikers, the latter scoring a record five goals in Revie's fourth game in charge in April 1975, against Cyprus. It was Revie, by now seemingly determined not to find a place for Bowles, who called upon Alan Hudson, another somewhat 'unreliable' player, for his two caps. Hudson in turn complained that Revie's idea of strengthening team spirit by getting players to go bowling together could simply be achieved by going down the pub.

Bowles was in fact selected for the away game against Portugal on 19 November 1975 – England still at this time had the faintest mathematical chance of qualifying for the 1976 European Championship – but his fitness let him down and he did not travel to Lisbon. The match finished 1–1, Channon scoring England's goal.

In 1976, midfielder Alan Ball claimed that Don Revie picked 'yes men' instead of top-quality players. 'Some of the players picked are donkeys,' he snapped. 'Give them a lump of sugar and they run all day and play bingo all night.' Revie shot back that Ball should concentrate on his club football and start producing the goods on the pitch. One possible explanation for Revie's stubbornness is that he over-reacted to one of the legendary footballers' nights out at George Best's Slack Alice club. Partying with Elvis Presley fanatic Frank Worthington were Peter Osgood, Tony Currie, Alan Hudson and, of course, Stan Bowles. The trouble was that some of the players were meant to be at the England hotel, where Revie had set an 11 p.m. curfew. When they finally stumbled back, only four or five hours late, everybody in the hotel knew about it. The following morning, Worthington, Currie, Hudson and Bowles were approached individually by Revie and told that they had no international future. They were not the sort of players he wanted. It was a brave stance by Revie – or perhaps a foolish one – summarily to dismiss some of the nation's best footballers.

CAP 4, V. ITALY, 17 NOVEMBER 1976

Line-up: Clemence, Clement (sub. Beattie), McFarland, Hughes, Cherry, Greenhoff, Mills, Brooking, Bowles, Channon, Keegan

The criticisms of Revie's dull England mounted up. Failure to qualify for the 1976 European Championship finals added to the pressure to make it to the 1978 World Cup, and when the pressure really built Revie called upon Stan Bowles. England were in a qualifying group with Finland, Italy and Luxembourg. Desperate for a result against group favourites Italy in Rome, Revie made six changes to the side that had beaten Finland the previous month, bringing Bowles in to partner Keegan and Channon in attack.

Denis Law, the former Napoli striker who was an idol to Bowles and the man whose record tally of goals in a single European campaign Bowles was about to break with Queens Park Rangers, put his full backing behind Bowles as the man to unlock Italy's defence. 'I know it sounds a risky move to play Bowles,' he said, 'but I believe it is one that has to be taken if England are to have a chance in Italy. Bowles has the sheer talent and drive that can upset the Italians. The moment he steps out into that stadium, with the crowd chanting as only the Italians can, Bowles has to close his mind to everything but his football. No one in English football can work a ball better at close quarters. For Stan, it can be the greatest ninety minutes of his life. When you have talent, it can carry you through everything. In a game such as this, one flash of individual talent can swing everything your way. Despite all the misgivings people have about Bowles, I believe he can be the one to produce the magic.'

Words of advice sprang up from other, more unexpected sources. A Turin gynaecologist, Professor Igino Terzi, offered his own rules of engagement, abbreviated here for the sake of space. Rule one: Footballers should have sex no more than two or three times per week (depending on size!). Rule two: Sex should be brief 'so as not to overtax the brain'. Rule three: Footballers should have a long rest after 'fulfilment'. Rule four: No sex immediately after a match, or the next day. No mention of having sex before the match, then, which would have pleased the likes of Frank Worthington. QPR and England defender Dave Clement summed up the footballing world's reaction to the suggestions with an admirably brief 'Codswallop.'

Also from Turin, and to be taken considerably more seriously, were Juventus. The 'Old Lady' of Italian football had recently beaten Manchester United with some ease in Europe with a team comprising half the Italy side. This was not going to be a comfortable trip to Rome, and the pressure was on Bowles to win the game for England. 'No one has ever doubted his ability,' Revie said. 'He has played exceptionally well for his club for two seasons. Now it is up to him to play as well for England.'

After promising to change his team, Revie was attempting to get the press on his side by including Bowles. Only five of the players who had played so poorly against Finland started against Italy, but England struggled with Revie's new formation. Revie, it could be said, was panicking. What's more, he began trying to appease the England fans who had abused his side throughout much of the Finland clash at Wembley, telling them how very tolerant they were and explaining, 'We have lost our rhythm, our passing, our thinking, our positional sense, our balance – in fact, everything.' Words to inspire confidence, then, ahead of a crucial World Cup qualifying game. Also a part of the line-up to face the awesome Italians in Rome was Trevor Cherry. 'I think the boss lost his way with the press,' he remarked. 'No disrespect to Stan, but the London press wanted Stan, so that was that. It wasn't the right blend because too many of us were very similar. We were like a team of midfielders-cum-central defenders. It wasn't a good side at all.'

Bowles was keen to convince his detractors that he was a changed man, capable of keeping his head on the big stage. 'There's the spitting and shirt-pulling that you don't get in this country,' he admitted, 'but I can shrug that off. I still make a few gestures now and again but I don't let it upset me as I used to. I've learnt that the way to hit back is to hurt them where it matters – by scoring goals or helping to score them. I've been playing my best football this season and I've been doing it consistently, game after game.' Convincing words from a man who had clearly matured during his spell in the international wilderness.

The Italian manager Enzo Bearzot, who had waited to see Revie's England side before naming his own, clearly took the threat of Bowles very seriously. When he saw that the QPR forward would be playing he immediately dropped his centre-back Roberto Mozzini in favour of Claudio Gentile, explaining, 'Gentile is more mobile and faster than Mozzini, more capable of dealing with Bowles.' Cynics argued that the ironically named Gentile, an uncompromising defender to put it mildly, would 'deal with' Bowles in every sense of the word, dishing out the kind of treatment that would either make Bowles anonymous or get him sent off for protesting. 'I have seen Bowles many times,' Bearzot continued. 'He has got winning dribbling. And in his final approach and execution in shooting range, he reminds me of Jimmy Greaves.' Whether Bowles believed all the hype or not, it seemed the Italy game was yet another make-or-break moment for him.

There were a number of players missing from the squad with injury, and an altogether more serious incident was narrowly avoided when a train containing Revie and the rest of the England players brushed another train going in the opposite direction, causing all the windows to shatter but thankfully injuring nobody. Five days before kick-off Bowles himself was in bed with a heavy cold, but as Dave Webb said, 'he desperately wants to go with England to Italy'. Maybe he was too embarrassed to get out of bed after seeing that disastrous episode of *Superstars* on the BBC on the evening of 10 November. Bowles, alongside a fragrant Sue Barker raising Britain's tennis hopes and a charitable Frank Sinatra promising to keep the tickets for his UK tour cheap, was pictured in bed in the *Daily Mirror* holding a nice cup of tea and looking quite cheery. 'I desperately want to make the trip,' he was quoted as saying, 'especially after waiting so long for a recall. The only thing that will stop me is the thumbs-down from the doctors.' Don Revie spoke to Bowles on the phone and told him that if there was any way he could get out of bed then he'd be playing. The opening was there in a new-look England side, the support was there and, vitally, the determination was there. The doctor passed Bowles fit in time. Nothing, it seemed, could go wrong.

Almost inevitably against a team at home fielding the likes of Zoff, Gentile, Causio, Capello, Facchetti, Antognoni, Graziani, Tardelli and Bettega in front of 85,000 fans, England were demolished and Bowles was kept in Gentile's pocket throughout the match. Football writer John Moynihan criticised Bowles' performance, complaining that the England striker indulged in a spot of ball-juggling in the corner when the score was 2–0 to Italy. Hardly the right time for tricks! But fellow England striker Mick Channon, like Trevor Cherry, pointed to Revie's unfathomable selection policy. 'How he picked that team, the mind still boggles. I played with whoever was picked, but Rome is the hardest place in the world to play. We got a hiding and I never had a kick. It haunts me to this day.'

CAP 5, V. HOLLAND, 9 FEBRUARY 1977

Line-up: Clemence, Clement, Watson, Doyle, Greenhoff (sub. Todd), Beattie, Brooking, Madeley (sub. Pearson), Bowles, T. Francis and Keegan

Bowles' personal confidence was not dented, however, and three months later, having set his goalscoring record in the UEFA Cup for QPR, he was again touted as the man to turn England into world beaters as they prepared to face Johan Cruyff and Holland. 'Stan Bowles believes he can outshine Dutch superstar Johan Cruyff if England manager Don Revie picks him,' reported Harry Miller in the *Daily Mirror*. 'Bowles, perky as ever, said, "I've played against Cruyff and there's no denying he is one of the greats. But if I get the chance I might just do the business myself on the night."' As he played for Dave Sexton at Queens Park Rangers, who structured the London team on an attacking Dutch model, Bowles was well aware of what to expect from Holland. It was just a question of whether he would be able to produce anything similar among less attack-minded England colleagues, and, of course, whether those England colleagues would be able to resist the excellent Dutch players.

Cruyff went into the match on the back of a rare sending-off which received unprecedented publicity, many even questioning the great man's temperament. A strange turnabout, then, with Bowles the potential hero and Cruyff a 'bad boy'! It says a lot, however, that this time around the QPR man was left to talk up his own chances of greatness, his high-profile supporters dwindling, clearly anxious about backing such a tried and tested England flop.

With Mick Channon dropped, the Holland match at Wembley was a chance for Bowles to form a permanent partnership up front with new 22-year-old star Trevor Francis – later a team-mate at Nottingham Forest – who was making his international debut, but the game was another disaster. Revie, who hadn't watched the Dutch play for three years, insisted that if England worried about who was in the Holland side (likely to include Krol, Neeskens, Rep and Rensenbrink alongside Cruyff), or if they adopted damage limitation tactics such as marking the opposition's most dangerous players, then they would lose focus, become negative and get hammered. So England tried to play their own game, the end result a damaging 2–0 defeat. Holland, and Cruyff in particular, took advantage of the space they were afforded and almost recaptured the kind of football they had played at the 1974 World Cup in West Germany.

But an England victory had never been a realistic option, especially as first-choice defenders Emlyn Hughes and Roy McFarland were missing. Embarrassed by Holland's style and confidence (caretaker manager at the time Jan Zwartkruis called it 'circulation football', which sounds like a modernised but not quite as impressive version of 'total football'), England's three forward players received little or no assistance from the midfielders, who spent so much time chasing the ball that thoughts of setting up any goalscoring opportunities soon left their heads.

Cruyff was undoubtedly the star of the show, and the 90,000 fans who turned up could not help but acclaim his talent. Zwartkruis added, 'Cruyff was brilliant tonight. He was like the Scarlet Pimpernel – you saw him here, you saw him there, you saw him everywhere!' (It seems possible that he had prepared that little comment before the match had even kicked off.) In contrast, supporters would have been hard pushed to see Stan Bowles at all, so impotent was the England attacking play. The occasion almost warranted another barbed Cloughesque insult along the lines of, 'Stanley? Was he out there tonight?' Bowles was not the only culprit, though, and Revie was later honest enough to confess, 'They taught us a lesson. Our players are very despondent and battling is not enough. You have got to have craft, guile and control' – three attributes synonymous with Bowles more than any other England player on the pitch that sad evening at Wembley, which saw devastated fans jeer their inadequate, deflated heroes into the dressing room.

Revie did not hang around for long after that so he couldn't put into practice the lessons he had learnt from Holland. After months of defeat, pressure and misery, in June 1977, before the match against Brazil during an England tour of South America, he shocked the world of football by leaving the camp, claiming that he was flying to Helsinki to watch Italy face Finland. His true destination was Dubai, where he had arranged a job interview. The United Arab Emirates Football Board wanted him to work to develop football in the Emirates, and he quickly accepted their big-money offer. To rub salt into the wound, Revie announced his decision to leave on the front page of the *Daily Mail*. There were two 1978 World Cup qualifying games left to play at the time and England still had a chance of making it. Ron Greenwood, who had been out of management for three years, was appointed to pick up the pieces, but England failed to qualify for

Argentina. They finished level on points with Italy in their group, but the Italians had a superior goal difference.

So why was Bowles never the force he should have been on the world stage? Bowles' QPR team-mate Dave Thomas offered an answer. 'People will always say that he should have had more caps for England, a bit like Frank Worthington. But Stan was volatile and he had a lot of "hangers on", so-called friends. But it's always difficult to pick them out, isn't it? That's why I've got so much admiration for the likes of Michael Owen and David Beckham. They are wonderful individuals, and how they behave themselves off the pitch is a credit to themselves. Stan just couldn't do it, he didn't have that. If he didn't fancy it, he wouldn't do it. He was an individual, but he wanted to win badly. People say that he didn't bother, but that was just the individual in him.' And that's what England managers simply couldn't afford to trust.

7 Can't See the Forest for the Trees: Nottingham Forest, 1979–80

Stan didn't turn up for the European Cup final! He will regret not getting a winner's medal for the rest of his life. His own stubbornness let him down.

GARRY BIRTLES

Although Bowles is best remembered for his time at QPR, his biggest chance for glory came in late 1979 when Nottingham Forest surprisingly made a bid to take him away from the quickly disintegrating London club. It was to be both his biggest chance and his last.

Abrasive Forest manager Brian Clough, a man with a proven ability to get the best out of 'rough diamonds' like Larry Lloyd and Kenny Burns, and assistant Peter Taylor, who always decided which players Forest should buy, offered QPR £250,000. By then Bowles was just short of his thirty-first birthday, had lost some of his pace and, with his consent, had moved into a deeper midfield play-maker's role ('My passing game was second only to Glenn Hoddle and, perhaps, Tony Currie,' he once claimed). The great QPR side that had come so close to winning the League title in 1976 was all but broken up – especially when Bowles' midfield partner Gerry Francis departed for Crystal Palace in the summer of 1979 – and the club had just been relegated to Division Two, so it seemed an appropriate time for a parting of the ways. Bowles accepted Forest's big-money offer. After all, QPR, and Tommy Docherty, who was manager at the time, didn't need him any more. Currie had taken his position on the right of midfield and had even taken Bowles' number 10 shirt, so beloved of the Loftus Road faithful.

'I don't know why Tony Currie took my shirt,' Bowles insisted nonchalantly. 'The numbering system was changing, it was becoming squad numbers or something like that. But I wasn't bothered. I knew I wasn't going to be there much longer anyway because Tommy Docherty was there then. I knew I wouldn't get on with him and I knew he was looking to sell me. The fact that I was there for that bit of extra time was probably down to Jim Gregory. It wasn't down to Tommy Docherty because he's got a history of bringing in young players, people he can handle, whereas seasoned pros, he couldn't handle them. He didn't like people answering back, put it that way.'

Bowles' last game for QPR was against Wrexham on 8 December 1979. His first game for Nottingham Forest was on 22 December, away to Manchester United, two days before his birthday. Forest lost 3–0. On 5 February 1980 he found himself playing in the second leg of the European Super Cup final against Barcelona in front of 80,000 at the Nou Camp. Forest were the reigning European Cup holders, having defeated Malmö 1–0 in Munich the year before, and Barcelona had won the Cup Winners' Cup. Bowles' new side won the tie, drawing 1–1 on the night but winning 2–1 on aggregate, Kenny Burns scoring the vital equaliser in Spain. Afterwards, when captain John McGovern lifted the trophy, Bowles received the only medal of his career.

'I wasn't sure what to expect from Stan,' McGovern said. 'I expected skill, which he definitely had, but I thought that he might need to brush up on his fitness. As it turned out he never had a problem with that, he was a very fit lad. He didn't carry any weight so that helped. He fitted in exceptionally well at Forest. He wasn't with us for very long but there wasn't a problem with his character fitting in with the other players.'

Typically, though, the honeymoon period was all too brief. Bowles and Clough almost instantly began to argue, particularly about what position he should play in. Bowles said on the right, Clough said left, and Clough invariably won. If Bowles thought it had been difficult to argue his case with Docherty, then Brian Clough must have seemed an even more imposing proposition. Bowles, who claims the Forest manager believed himself to be God, was soon finding it difficult no longer to be the star of the show, to be just a bit-part player at England's top club at the time.

'I think we were all stars at Forest, but from the outside world looking in, and in the press's eyes, we were rag, tag and bobtail, we were just cobbled together,' insisted Bowles' best friend at Forest, John Robertson, now coaching at Celtic. 'But these boys were actually talented. You don't win two European Cups without being talented. I would have thought Forest would have been a good choice for Stan because we did try to play good football.' The cavalier days of Rangers' flowing football could never be relived, however, and despite what Robertson believed, Forest were a pedestrian, uninspiring side that through careful planning and resilience overachieved on an incredible scale. Though Bowles had been intrinsic to QPR's most successful years, Forest had got to the top without him and, despite spending a small fortune on him, ultimately didn't need him.

Some people saw the transfer as a mistake right from the beginning, such as long-time QPR supporter Dave Thomas. 'It was the worst possible move and no one could understand it. There was quite a bit of history between QPR and Brian Clough at that time. It came about after an FA Cup replay, when defender Kenny Burns kicked Bowles off the park. And there was a lot of bad-mouthing in the press after that game. It seemed extraordinary that Bowles should have gone to Forest and a manager like Clough. If ever there was a match that was made in hell, that was it! And so it proved. He didn't like Clough and couldn't get on with him.

'Why Clough ever wanted to buy him is a mystery,' Thomas continued. 'Clough was not the kind of manager who liked maverick players, and Stan was one of the original mavericks. It was an extraordinary move by Forest, as much as by Stan. Stan had done his time, he'd put the seasons in at Rangers and was ready for a fresh challenge. He was probably enticed by a fairly large signing-on fee. I imagine that Stan's motivation for going was purely financial. What Brian Clough's interests were will always remain a mystery. He was a regimented manager.'

But what people forget about Clough is that he rarely made the final decisions on which players the club would sign. He thought of himself as the man who would be able to get the best out of the players – through motivation, organisation and hard training – no matter who assistant Peter Taylor brought in. That said, it was undoubtedly a meeting of chalk and cheese: Clough was dry and to the point, Bowles was a bit tasty. Forest could not hide from the fact that the best players often came with an extra dose of self-belief and character. Brian Clough would tame them and, on occasion, terrify them into producing their best for him. A typical Clough forward would be disciplined, straightforward and, without being too critical, not particularly skilful, someone who wouldn't give him any disciplinary problems. He didn't want so-called 'fanny-merchants' in his side, but surely he would have classed Bowles as a maverick in terms of discipline and would have been wary about his penchant for walking out of the dressing room in his boots to put a bet on. A few of Bowles' team-mates had begun to think that QPR was not the most professional club to play for, but Forest was quite the opposite. The suspicion that Bowles was going to be more trouble than he was worth would have arisen the moment Clough found out the former QPR player was joining his club. No matter how talented, if Bowles refused to conform to Clough's rules, he would be finished.

It is understandable, though, that Taylor and Forest would want to sign Bowles. Although age was catching up with him, everyone knew what he was capable of, and though his final days at QPR had been disappointing, maybe all he needed was the adrenalin rush of playing for one of England's top clubs. John McGovern, virtually ever-present throughout Forest's glory days, explained the thought process behind the decision to bring Bowles to the City Ground. 'The initial partnership between Brian and Peter Taylor meant that Peter brought in the players.

Signing someone like Stan was a strange one, but then again Kenny Burns had already signed for Forest and he also had a reputation for being a wild character. Hardly the type you'd have thought Clough would have welcomed into the fold. But the success they had with Kenny – he turned into a superb acquisition – made them think, "If we can just get Stan to use his skill we won't get any problems with his other activities." '

The bottom line is that Forest believed Bowles would add flair, skill and goals. The situation was not unlike the rumours during 2001/02 that Sir Alex Ferguson wanted to sign Paolo Di Canio. Manchester United already possessed boundless quality in attack, but every club needs that extra flair, someone who can do things other players simply aren't capable of doing. Sometimes it's worth taking the risk. And anyway, if Bowles' move to Forest didn't work out they could simply get rid of him and bring someone else in. Countless players would have jumped at the chance to sign for the European Cup holders.

'They thought that once he got amongst the players at Forest he'd conform to the sort of discipline imposed on everyone,' McGovern continued, with no hint of humour, 'and that would allow his flair to blossom and it would be better for everyone. To be fair, Stan wasn't too much of a handful for anyone apart from himself.'

In his 1994 autobiography, Clough revealed his attitude to players who do not achieve all they can. 'There is a theory about me that says my intolerance of indiscipline and abuse of talent stems from the fact that my own playing career was cut down in my prime. I have never, knowingly, carried a chip on my shoulder about that. But it might have something to do with my attitude towards players who failed to realise how lucky they were, how privileged they were to be playing football for an extremely lucrative living. I didn't want a time-wasting, talent-wasting, trouble-making [former Liverpool and Coventry defender] Larry Lloyd plonked on my doorstep.' One could easily substitute the name 'Stan Bowles' here, but then, so disappointed was Clough with Bowles' contribution to the 1979/80 season that he very, very rarely talks about the player. In the autobiography, Bowles gets one fleeting mention in which Clough claims he and Charlie George 'did their bit before I blew them both out'. Indeed, a friend of Brian Clough, explaining why he would not be interested in contributing to this book, suggested, 'Brian hasn't got much time for Stan. He thinks he's a pillock.'

Some players were beyond even Clough's strong arm of the law, but there were other, practical reasons why Bowles couldn't gel with the side on a regular basis. As assistant manager Peter Taylor once admitted, 'We were obsessed with defence. Looking back, I think we overdid it. We didn't score as many goals as we should have, but all our triumphs were based on solid defence so there was no point changing horses. Brian and I discussed this for hours. He tended towards the more open style of play – he would, being a centre-forward. It was me, the goal-keeper, who kept reminding him of Harry Storer's words: "Build from the back." ' So in signing Bowles, Taylor had succumbed to Clough's desire for players who could invigorate their solid formation. Nevertheless, Bowles just couldn't fully break into the side.

John Robertson, Forest's top scorer during 1979/80 with nineteen goals, ruefully recalled that by the time Bowles had moved to Nottingham Forest he was no longer the player he had been two or three years previously. 'With all due respect to him he was probably a bit past his best when he came to Forest. Obviously he was a brilliant footballer, on his day one of the most talented players ever to play in Britain. I don't know if he was losing pace. Maybe it was just age because he certainly played some games when he was excellent. That can't take away from the fact that he was an extremely talented guy.' That explains why Queens Park Rangers fans felt no great anger or sadness when Bowles departed. They not only knew that he deserved another shot at glory with a bigger club but also realised his best days were behind him, as supporter Dave Thomas noted. 'He was slowing down and life was catching up with him after all sorts of shenani-gans. That doesn't diminish him in the eyes of QPR fans, though. He's still the legend.'

One Forest fan noted on his personal website, 'He could still play when he came to us but his best days, and especially his paciest days, were behind him. The theory was presumably that he would replace Archie Gemmill, a role later attempted, equally unsuccessfully, by the likes of Jurgen Roeber and Raimondo Ponte.' That said, he went on to argue that Bowles, playing alongside Trevor Francis, John Robertson, Garry Birtles and on-loan Charlie George, was 'the most potent attacking five ever to pull on Forest shirts at the same time'.

John McGovern agreed that Forest fans, of which there were surprisingly few during that season, never got the chance to see Bowles at his best. It had been just a few short seasons since Bowles had scored a record number of European goals in the UEFA Cup, but he was on the way down. 'I would have liked to have played with him when he was at his absolute peak. We never saw the best of him. I wouldn't say he wasted his ability but he never reproduced the form of his hey-day with Queens Park Rangers. He just felt more comfortable in London. It's difficult for anybody to come north and settle, just as it is for an established player in the north to move to London. It was a different lifestyle. Although, with the types of players we had at Nottingham, if he was going to settle anywhere, it would be there. There was stability and discipline within the club.' McGovern's point ignores the fact that Bowles was born and brought up in Manchester, considerably further north than Nottingham, but it's true that Bowles had become very accustomed to life in London, to the extent that he could be taken for a native Londoner, as he has been on numerous occasions.

Conditions had to be perfect for Bowles to thrive in Nottingham, and many of his Forest colleagues regret the fact that he never rediscovered the great form he had once shown for QPR. Both Bowles and Charlie George ended up leaving Forest prematurely without having had any major effect on the team. Both were willing to try, to work hard in training, but even amid a group of successful players neither was able to turn on the old magic.

Still, most professionals would have accepted the situation, knuckled down and appreciated the sudden opportunity of achieving some previously unattainable success. Bowles, though, was not most professionals, and despite the fact that people could see he was not the star he used to be, he was one of the very few who dared to argue with Clough. Life on the bench proved difficult for Bowles, but in the end he had no way out. Clough was the only star at Forest; everyone else was secondary.

'Stan never came across as having a big ego,' McGovern insisted, but the problem was not with Bowles or with Clough individually, it was only when they were together that sparks flew. 'Clough was a dictator,' McGovern added matter-of-factly. 'Some people didn't appreciate it, some people didn't like it. Clough liked his players to be very disciplined, very well behaved. He didn't want to have to worry about anything apart from their on-field form. Any off-the-field activities that brought the club into disrepute or distracted players from concentrating on their football were put down very heavily by him. And he was right. If the only problems you've got are on the field then you've got a normal manager's job. If you've got off-the-field problems then you've got more than a manager's job.' Loyalty to dictators is often long-lasting, and McGovern went on to state that Clough's record allows him to think of himself as something special. It is hard to disagree. After winning promotion in 1977, Clough's Forest won the First Division and League Cup in 1978, the European Cup and League Cup in 1979 and the European Cup again in 1980. A trophy haul to be proud of.

Forest was set up to be a club without egos – after all, beside Cloughie's there was no room for anyone else's – and matters were made worse because Bowles was not the only maverick to arrive at the newly crowned European champions' door during the 1979/80 season. Former Forest striker Garry Birtles conceded that the timing of Bowles' move to the Midlands, coinciding with Charlie George's move on loan from Southampton, was not ideal. 'There just wasn't room in the same side for Charlie and Stan. When Charlie and Stan came along, both with these extrovert personalities, it enlightened the squad. When they were together it was a joy to behold. The banter that went on between them had us in stitches all the time.' Very briefly, they made an impression on the pitch too. Bowles played nineteen League games during the 1979/80 season, compared to George's two (he had fitness problems at the time), but Robertson happily recalled just how good the Forest side were on those few occasions when Bowles and George played together. During a rare away appearance for Bowles and in George's full debut for Forest, against Leeds United on 19 January 1980, he recounted how their side went 2–1 in front through yet another Trevor Francis strike then promptly indulged in 'the best keep-ball session I've ever played in'. The scoreline remained 2–1.

So Charlie George's presence in the squad was not necessarily a barrier for Bowles; even though they could both be considered luxury players, they played in different positions. Rather, it seems that Forest's every attempt to please their new signing from QPR was thrown back in their faces. As Bowles explained, things did not go well from the moment he first arrived in Nottingham. He was aggrieved before he played his first League game.

'When I first went there I had a tax bill for £6,000,' he explained heatedly, 'and Clough f***ing paid it by cheque. In his office at the club he said to the tax collector, "Right, he owes you six grand," and just got his chequebook out. Then he took it all off my bonuses until I paid it back, but I didn't want him to. I wanted to take this bloke [the tax collector] outside and talk to him myself. I would say, "I haven't got it all but I'll give you this little bit." Fortunately at Forest we were in Europe all the time and always at the top of the League so the bonuses were very good, but I wanted to try and get out of it. If you just had a chat with them, sometimes in them days you could settle. I'd say, "I've got this much," and we would work something out. But if you write out a cheque for the full amount then of course they are going to take it. Only an idiot wouldn't.' It was probably intended to be a gesture on Clough's part, or an incentive for Bowles to make a fresh start and, in a way, wipe the slate clean. Bowles, however, read the situation differently. He felt he was being leant on, forced into a corner by a power-hungry dictator.

'When I first went to Forest,' Bowles continued, 'I was living in a hotel, but Clough wanted me to get a flat or a house. So I agreed to rent a house. All of a sudden he said to me, "You cockneys, you're all the same!" He hated cockneys, you know. I said, "Excuse me, I was born and bred in Manchester." So we didn't get off to the right start. He used to say things like that to challenge players, but that wouldn't work with me. After four or five months I was sort of banished to the reserves.' Bowles irrefutably failed the Brian Clough test, but felt it was a pointless and unpleasant one anyway. He wasn't about to be shouted into a corner. 'He was all right, Clough, when he was asleep!' Bowles added, using one of his favourite catch-phrases. 'That's not an act you see on the telly – that's how he is. Arrogant. We used to have a walk around Nottingham on a Saturday before the game. A lot of places were opened up that wouldn't be opened up for anyone else. He played on it, though. If we were in a packed pub in Nottingham he'd be the first to get served. It wouldn't happen in London because he just wouldn't get away with it.'

Bowles' controversial season-long stay in Nottingham still leaves a bitter taste in his mouth, and it will forever be remembered for the fall-out between him and the gaffer of all gaffers. Clough controlled everything at Forest, and many players had been humbled by his scathing wit and anger. No matter who the player, nobody was above the manager's wrath. He was the law, but Bowles was the ultimate law-breaker.

'Cloughie was a bit different,' Frank Worthington thought. 'He was a genius as a manager. He treated players as adults – you can't treat them as kids. If you treat people sensibly and they don't take advantage of a bit of leeway then that's fine. It's all about self-discipline. I went over the top on a couple of occasions but got found out and things went against me. You've got to learn and learn fast. You've got to play within the rules.'

Garry Birtles still works with Clough on Century Radio in Nottingham and they have always got on well, even becoming squash partners while Birtles was playing in the reserves. Although their relationship never got nasty, Birtles agreed with Worthington's assessment. 'If you stepped out of line you were in the shit. Cloughie *was* Nottingham Forest, and if anybody stepped out of line and he thought they needed punishing they would be punished in no uncertain terms. When Trevor Francis first came to the club for a million quid he was forced to make the tea for the lads and to play in the reserve team. He wasn't afraid to have a go at the biggest names and put them in their place. I think that was the key to the success of the side. There was a desire, and you knew that under Clough you'd be a winner. It wasn't about the money in those days, but you knew you'd be well paid if you were successful, and success always came with Brian Clough.'

One criticism that has occasionally been placed at Clough's door is that he took things too far, that his disciplinary actions were spiteful, erratic and somewhat childish – although it could be argued, as Birtles does, that the results Clough got demonstrate that these tactics were in fact totally necessary. He seemed to relish any opportunity to attack. Bowles was certainly not one to respond well to such unnecessary games and tests of character. He would always try to wrest some semblance of power from Clough, though never maliciously, as the following incident shows.

Forest spent a lot of time flying around for their European ties and Bowles was famed for his hatred of flying. At one team meeting, the morning after the rest of the squad had returned from some far-away land, Bowles turned up late to find Clough furious. The manager raged at the wayward player, demanding to know why he was so late. 'Well,' replied Bowles, 'I got up this morning, boss, and went straight to the airport.' His comic timing was flawless. Even Clough almost broke into a smile. Birtles recalled another incident. 'We went to Jersey once, and Stan and John Robertson went off and bought Clough this big tam o'shanter with BIGHEAD written on it. This hat was

absolutely massive. How would Cloughie react? He laughed his whatsits off! He took it in great spirits. But Brian
Clough would never be mastered at that particular point
in his career and anyone who threatened his decisions or
his way of thinking was firmly put in their place, and I
don't think Stan was someone who liked to be put in his
place.'

Things notoriously came to a head just before the 1980
European Cup final against Kevin Keegan's Hamburg in
Madrid. Bowles hadn't been included in a team to play in
John Robertson's testimonial match, so he refused to
travel to Spain with the rest of the squad. 'He's a virtual
dictator,' he said of Clough in the *Daily Mirror* before the
game. 'He bought me to help them retain the cup, yet I've
never been given a chance.' It's not true that Bowles
hadn't had a chance in the competition: he had played at
home against Dynamo Berlin on 5 March in the quarter-
final first leg (a 1–0 defeat) and in the semi-final against
Ajax at the City Ground on 9 April (a 2–0 victory). He had,
though, been dropped for both away games, half the
European fixtures he had been available for since joining
Forest, and this, it seems, was unacceptable to Bowles.
But then, as John McGovern dryly pointed out, 'If you
don't like flying and your team's in Europe then you've
got problems immediately.'

The final, held on 28 May in the Estadio Bernabéu, saw
Forest with just four subs due to Bowles' no-show at the
airport – the only time that has ever happened in a
European final – and without star striker Trevor Francis,
who had injured his Achilles tendon four weeks previously. It says a lot, perhaps, that even if Bowles had travelled
Clough would probably have chosen to play inexperienced eighteen-year-old forward Gary Mills or the versa-
tile reserve Ian Bowyer ahead of him anyway. But it was
not all doom and gloom in the build-up to the final, as
assistant manager Peter Taylor told reporters. 'We're all
right here,' he said. 'I took one look at our players this
morning and I knew they were in the mood. We'll win.'

Bowles is angry to this day. 'Walking out before the
European Cup final was the end of me,' he conceded.

'Clough wouldn't play me in John Robertson's testimonial on the Friday – and John was my best mate there – but he had promised me faithfully I'd be playing in the game. I look at the teamsheet and I'm not on it. So I thought, "F**k you. That's it. I've had enough." So I disappeared back to London. I was suspended for three weeks or something but I never played in the first team after that and we never spoke again. He used to send Jimmy Gordon, the trainer, or Peter Taylor, his assistant. And I didn't want to talk to him neither.'

'You make a decision like that and there's no way back,' McGovern said. 'If you don't turn up for *any* match there's no way back. And neither should there be, for *any* player. In today's game some players would probably get away with it because of some plc saying, "You can't get rid of him." There's too much outside influence on what a manager does now. When Brian Clough made a decision there was no referring it to the board or plcs – that was it. Full stop.'

Forest fan Chris Broughton wrote, 'What a true professional Stan was, eh? Fancy spurning the chance of figuring in a European Cup final. Most professional footballers would give their right arm for such an opportunity.' True, but it's difficult not to admire the stance Bowles was prepared to make. Of course he wanted to play in the European Cup final, but he sacrificed the chance in order to stay true to the way he felt. That kind of passion, an absolute refusal to back down, is a rarity in any sport.

Still, because of it Bowles' troubled spell at Forest was effectively over. 'It doesn't bother me,' Bowles insisted without a trace of dissemblance flickering across his face. 'I was never worried about winning medals and all that business. I suppose I was happy enough just to entertain the people in the crowd. Medals and caps never bothered me. I've sold most of my caps. My daughter's got one. Jim Gregory had one; his wife's got it now. Gary Mills got my medal in the European Cup. And he said afterwards, "Sorry about that, Stan." But I told him, "Don't worry about it, it doesn't bother me in the slightest. It's not your fault."

'I think he made a mistake with the European Cup business,' John Robertson revealed. 'He didn't go because he thought he wasn't going to play. It was such an opportunity because he could have come off the bench as a substitute, so that was an error of judgement. He'd probably tell you that himself [he didn't!]. His pride does get in the way sometimes. I would have thought he'd look back and think he could have won the European Cup. In the first leg against Ajax at home he played. Cloughie's thinking would be that away from home we'd maybe get an onslaught coming at us and he decided to go for a bit more strength in midfield. Who knows what the team would have been for the European Cup final? We never knew the team the day before a game or sometimes even an hour before.'

Garry Birtles, Forest's free-scoring first-choice striker at the time – and, incidentally, the club's top scorer in 1978/79 with 26 in total – thought Stan had tried it on again. 'Some players do that and push it to the limit. Some get away with it, but with Brian Clough you just didn't. For him to say, "Right, we're not travelling with Stan because he's not turned up," and to go to a European Cup final with four substitutes instead of five – no other gaffer would have done that. That's how strong-willed he was, and luckily we went out and won it. Stan didn't turn up for the European Cup final! I think he will regret that for the rest of his life, not being part of that and not getting a European Cup winner's medal. His own stubbornness let him down. It would have been difficult for him to get into the side but he felt that he had the talent, and I think he had the talent to warrant a place.'

As far as Clough was concerned, he claimed to have no idea why Bowles had gone AWOL, though he admitted that the player had placed his future at the club in doubt.

Forest won the final against Hamburg 1–0 playing defensive and determined, if uninspiring, football. A John Robertson goal early in the first half was the only highlight of a disappointing match crying out for some-body to perform some magic. Where was it going to come from if not from Stan Bowles? Depressingly, some may suggest, Forest became undisputed kings of Europe. The line-up in front of the ever-reliable Peter Shilton (who once stated, 'people wrote us off but we always felt we could win it') was unfamiliar because electrifying mid-fielder Archie Gemmill and Francis – probably the club's most important players – were out injured, which makes the side's achievement of joining the likes of Real Madrid, Benfica, Inter Milan, Ajax, Bayern Munich and Liverpool in the list of clubs that have won consecutive European Cups all the more impressive. While never playing the classy football of some of the top European sides – many observers had predicted Keegan's previously irresistible Hamburg would win by two or three goals – the continent could not dispute that Forest played winning football, thriving as a result of organisation and commitment. One German journalist called Forest the best side ever to win the European Cup because of where they had come from and how quickly. 'To win back to back European Cups, which even Manchester United haven't done,' McGovern insisted, keen to explain how unexpected Forest's success was, 'that was a double miracle!'

Shilton chose this match for the 1993 book *My Greatest Game*, whose fond commentary read: 'Without their play-maker (Gemmill), their star striker (Francis) and the "joker" in their pack (Bowles), Forest had little option but to funnel back, rely on counter-attacks for a breakthrough and fight for their lives. It was not going to be pretty, but who could blame them? They were defending the Euro-pean Cup.' Defending is the right word: Clough admitted after the match, 'We defended for 84 of the 90 minutes.' It worked, however, and the favourites from Germany were kept at bay despite having the lion's share of possession and scoring chances.

Amusingly, Bowles' memory is not what it used to be (unless it's always been terrible!), for after a few moments of recollection he described the goal that won Forest the European Cup in 1980 thus: 'Ah, yes. Trevor Francis scored from a John Robertson cross. I can see it now.' Francis – who had scored the winner Bowles described in the 1979 final against Swedish side Malmö – wasn't even playing in 1980, and it was Bowles' best friend at Forest, Robertson, who actually scored the winner, exchanging passes with lone striker Birtles in a rare attacking moment before driving the ball low past Hamburg keeper Rudi Kargus and in off the far post. It may be callous to point this out, but it shows that with Stan Bowles there are several sides to absolutely every story.

Bowles had talked himself out of one of the most prestigious honours in football. He'd blown his last chance at fulfilling his potential just because he disliked the manager's attitude. Clough, of course, was one of the most exacting and challenging managers in British football history; he would push his players' patience to the limit in order to establish and to increase their desire to succeed. To Bowles, however, football was not just about success, it was also about entertainment and enjoyment. In their prime, the QPR side that featured Bowles was the most attractive footballing side in the country, and he was key to their free-flowing approach. He was also accustomed to being idolised by supporters, relied upon on the pitch and wrapped in cotton wool by the club's hierarchy, who were desperate to fawn over their star. 'I think he realised that he could have achieved more,' said Birtles. 'If he'd gone to one of the bigger clubs maybe he would have. He got the chance at Forest, but obviously the clash of personalities with Cloughie stopped that.'

Bowles' emphasis on enjoyment was possibly of more use in the dressing room than it was on the pitch. If Clough brought in Bowles in order to give the team a lift, then Bowles lived up to expectations. His form might not have been the best, but he was the clear favourite when it came to jokes and one-liners. 'It's good to have different characters in the dressing room,' McGovern said. 'We were not the most lively bunch of players before Stan joined because we took our jobs very seriously and we had a serious manager. Peter Taylor used to crack a few jokes now and then, but Stan certainly cracked plenty during his time there. It helps if you've got people like that, so from that point of view he was of benefit to the side.' Birtles insisted he held nothing but fond memories of his former team-mate. 'I used to watch Stan on the training ground and he used to do that thing when he went round in a tight circle. You could never get the bloody ball off him! And he was so unassuming and such a nice fellow with it. It was difficult to dislike him. I don't think the gambling affected his career at all, it was secondary. He loved playing football and he loved gambling. One week he'd win on the football pitch and lose the next, and it was the same with gambling. That's how it went with Stan.'

Bowles' frustration at not being a first-choice player, bubbling just beneath the surface for much of the time he spent at Forest, only rarely (if somewhat publicly) spilled over. Most of the time he was a cheerful and valued member of the squad, even if internally he was struggling to remain motivated. 'There was a lot of socialising,' Birtles recalled with a smile, 'because we had Brian Clough who encouraged us to do that. We were the only team who got fined if we didn't go out on a Friday night for a drink! Stan fitted into that culture quite nicely and it was a happy bunch of players.' Clough would encourage his players to attend charity functions around the city but was always insistent that if they went, they went together in order to enhance team spirit.

The Forest squad spent a lot of time together on many such occasions, but Clough never actually organised any drinking sessions or wild nights out. Only rarely did players risk a night on the town, especially if Clough had set a curfew. 'If we won a match,' McGovern said with a low Scottish chuckle, 'we'd certainly go out and have a celebratory drink or two, the same as all the other clubs. But we won more games than any other team at that time so you could say that we had more cause to celebrate. At times you wanted to celebrate all night and all the next day, and all the next day after that, but there were too many games for you to have the perfect social life. We were constantly reminded that the time footballers celebrate was in May, when you look at where you are in the League and at how many win bonuses you've won. If you're a striker, when you look at how many goals you've scored; if you're a goalkeeper, when you look at how many clean sheets you've kept.'

In that respect, at season's end there was little to celebrate for Bowles. He scored just twice during his six months at the club – the first in his second game, at home to Aston Villa on Boxing Day 1979, the second in the next game, away to Coventry City on 29 December. That second and final goal, the third in a 3–0 victory, came after a low, driven shot from right-back Viv Anderson. The Coventry goalkeeper Les Sealey saved with his knees but the ball rebounded high in the air. With the poaching talent he had become known for, and no little athleticism, Bowles nipped between the Coventry central defenders and with a mighty vertical leap got his head to the ball. With a big grin on his face he trotted back to the half way line, warmly congratulated by Trevor Francis. But that was about as good as it got for Bowles as his un-easy relationship with Clough and lack of regular, form-building football halted the painfully brief goal rush.

Like any club in the country, the dressing room split into various groups according to their interests. Probably tired of all the professionalism around him, Bowles would have been comforted by the club's tight-knit card schools, at which vast sums of money were won and lost. 'I liked a game of cards as much as Stan did,' Birtles claimed, 'so we were in the same card school, which was interesting to say the least! It was unbelievable. We didn't earn as much money as they do now, but we'd start playing at the City Ground and we'd still be playing in the departure lounge at the airport, on the plane or on the bus to the game. It was just a non-stop three-card brag school! My last memory of Stan is seeing him being marched out of a wine bar in Nottingham by Kenny Burns because he owed him money from the cards. Kenny took him down the bank to get his money. Then Martin O'Neill came in looking for the same sort of payback, but Stan had skedaddled. Martin never got his money back! That was the last I saw of Stan as a Nottingham Forest player.'

McGovern added, 'The gamblers would stick together and other people would get on with whatever they wanted to do. That had always been the case, before Stan arrived. The manager tried to keep things under control and sensible, but at times the players had secret ways of – well, there was no money shown on the table but there was plenty of money at stake in the games. There's always ways around restrictions. People like myself would look on and think, "Phew, I would never, ever dare gamble for anywhere near that amount of money." I liked his character but I didn't like his gambling. I don't like it when people gamble and over-extend themselves, which Stan has obviously done on many occasions. But he was very lively, bubbly and easy-going. He did what he wanted to do. I liked that.'

Sticking to his resolutely forgiving view of Bowles' unerring ability not to settle down easily, Birtles continued to look back fondly to the season when the ex-QPR star arrived at the City Ground. 'My first and lasting impression was what a loveable, likeable man he was. No airs and graces, just this cockney wide boy [that mistake again!] with massive talent, and it was a privilege to play with somebody with that amount of talent. He was great in the dressing room. Some of the stories about the villainous people he knew in London – Teabag Tony, and some master forger whose name I forget! We always had some snippets of these dubious characters and everybody was enthralled listening to him.'

'I don't know how we became mates,' said John Robertson, who won 26 caps for Scotland during his Forest days, 'but Stan was obviously a legend as a footballer and I love good players. He was a good pal to me. I'll tell you a wee story. I lost my brother in April 1979 in a car crash and it affected my dad. In March 1980, just eleven months later, my father came down because it was his birthday and we went to this wine bar. Stan came along and bought him a bottle of Moët et Chandon champagne, which he kept. My dad opened it the night I scored the winning goal in the European Cup final and he died just two months after that. I'll always remember Stan buying him that champagne. We were never a champagne brigade, but that was a really nice gesture. He was like that – whatever money he had, he'd be generous with.'

There were plenty of opportunities for generosity at Forest because, as has already been mentioned, the social side of the club was busy and enjoyable. The players used to assemble at a bar called Uriah Heep's, and team spirits were always high. Bowles would be at the centre of things, assuming he hadn't gambled away all his money again. 'Stan's reputation went before him, and everyone has their weakness,' said Robertson. 'Yes, he used to gamble, but if he was winning he was a generous man. He was an outgoing guy who enjoyed his life. When he had money, he spent it. Only he can say whether he has any regrets, but Stan enjoyed his days in football. If you can look back and honestly say you enjoyed it, then what more can you ask for? That's what I think. You don't regret the things you do, you regret the things you didn't do.'

Despite the fun times, and there were plenty of them, things at Forest were alien to Stan Bowles. Clough's wild rants; being forced to play on the left of midfield; being left on the bench when he was fully fit. Bowles clearly decided that this was pressure he didn't need. His final game for Forest was at home to Everton, helping his side to a win that took them to fifth place in Division One, behind Liverpool, Manchester United, Ipswich and Arsenal. Then, with a characteristic shrug, he departed, his desire to play football at the highest level undermined by his refusal to be led and his contempt for authority. His last shot at glory, like his pistol shooting on the BBC's *Superstars*, had missed the target by some distance. This time, though, he *had* shot himself in the foot. He was out of the top flight, never to return.

In July 1980, Bowles moved back to London for good, to Second Division Leyton Orient – where, presumably, he knew he could be the star once more – for £100,000. Clough had always been resolute in his insistence that Bowles was best used at home games, and now, at last, Bowles was agreeing. It's just that Clough had been thinking 'home' meant Forest's City Ground, while Bowles was thinking of London, his spiritual home.

McGovern, the unerring professional, admitted that losing Bowles was hardly a traumatic experience. 'Obviously we became aware that he was going back to London. People always wonder if a team-mate leaving the club affects your concentration, but it doesn't because you're only thinking about justifying your own position in the side. You have to be blinkered. Players come and go – it's part and parcel of the game. It's never a surprise unless it's someone who's been a long-standing member of the side.'

After Bowles' departure, Forest remained one of the English game's big sides, notching up a few third-place finishes throughout the 1980s and early 1990s before being relegated in Clough's final year in charge, 1992/93, the Premier League's inaugural season. Third place again in the Premiership in 1995 was their last taste of top-flight success.

8 The Os and the Bees: Orient and Brentford, 1980–84

There were people at the club who thought we were signing a waster, but I was only interested in whether he could play football.

MARTIN LANGE, BRENTFORD CHAIRMAN

'I used to go and watch him play when I was at Crystal Palace and he was at QPR,' recalled former England caretaker manager Peter Taylor, remembering Bowles' glory days. 'So I saw then what an intelligent player he was. His left foot was as good as you'll see on a football field.'

Taylor, currently the Brighton and Hove Albion boss, joined Second Division Orient for a club record £150,000 in November 1980, shortly after Bowles, both of them arriving disillusioned having come from big clubs (Tottenham Hotspur in Taylor's case) who no longer wanted them. He painted a somewhat dreary picture of life at the club, which seemed to consist of an unfortunate gathering of players on their way down. 'We had a decent team, but we had a lot of players who had probably been more successful elsewhere, who were coming to the end of their careers. There wasn't much socialising as far as I was concerned. People went their separate ways, and not too many of us lived near the club.' The Orient goalkeeper at the time, Mervyn Day, confirmed this club ethos. 'Jimmy [Bloomfield, the manager] was collecting good players who, for whatever reason, hadn't maintained their standards, and he just wanted us to enjoy ourselves. Stan was a Jimmy Bloomfield type of player.'

Bowles' decision to join the small London club may have been partly made through a lack of interest from bigger clubs, but his willingness to take a step down in division demonstrates his pure love for the game. The impossible situation at Forest, as he saw it, was in direct contrast to his vision of football as a thing of beauty and fun. Therefore, though he didn't have a great deal of choice, he swallowed his pride and moved down. Under Brian Clough he had quite deliberately and publicly thrown away his last shot at European success, which was never at the top of his list of priorities anyway, so why not get back to being the star at another, more grateful club? It was meant to be a return to something like the friendly atmosphere of his spiritual home, Loftus Road. Orient were also offering a bigger basic wage than Forest and had shown their faith in Bowles by spending £100,000 on him – a club record until Taylor arrived. Mervyn Day knew Bowles would be a useful acquisition, having faced him as a QPR player. 'He was always a pain in the backside to play against because he had that ability to be playing it one way and then reverse it, or look to shoot one side, then clip it over the top of you on the other side.'

'I moved back to the big smoke that July,' Bowles once claimed, 'in order to revive a flagging career. Not mine, but that of Leyton Orient. The Os were in the Second Division and in desperate need of a flamboyant, skill-laden crowd pleaser who put arses on seats.' This was not quite how things worked out, however. Bowles only stayed at Orient for just over a year, and Taylor believes there is a simple reason: 'It might have been the difference between Orient and the last club he was at. I was the same – I didn't particularly enjoy Orient, and that's nothing against them, but I joined from Tottenham and I found the difference too big. I think that might have been the case with Stan. Forest was a big club and QPR was a very trendy club, with nice training facilities and so on. At Orient the training facilities weren't the best, and little things like that maybe affected people settling in. It was a bit of a culture shock.'

Taylor described his move to Orient as 'convenient' for getting back into first-team football after he felt he was falling out of favour at Spurs, and it was only in retrospect that he realised the problems that existed at Orient. 'It wasn't the best move I ever made because the majority of players had been good elsewhere or could've done more with their careers, me included. On our day we were a very good team, but many of us probably should have had better careers. For example, our goalkeeper Mervyn Day was once rated as one of the best young goalkeepers around. And Stan should have played for England a million times with his ability. There was too many of us who'd come from bigger clubs who found it a struggle. It wasn't Orient's fault.'

Taylor certainly found it a strain to be in a casual, even unprofessional, environment. Pervading some sections of the dressing room was a sense of anti-climax, a feeling that some players weren't taking Orient seriously. 'I found it very different when I went to Orient because people were looking at the horse racing at a quarter to two,' he explained, 'whereas at Tottenham that had never been the case.' If he thought a quarter to two was cutting it fine, what must he have thought when he saw Stan Bowles waltz in from the bookie's at a quarter to three!

At least the relaxed atmosphere allowed Bowles a freedom he hadn't enjoyed since the height of his QPR days. As Day recalled, he was as happy-go-lucky as ever, and gambling like there was no tomorrow. 'He was always drinking pink champagne at that time. He was a very charismatic person, and when he wanted to be he could be very charming. I remember one day he'd had a win on the dogs on the Thursday just before we travelled down to the West Country for a game. He gave the apprentice who was on the trip to carry the bags an absolute fortune to hold on to during the game – it must have been at least five grand! We drove back on the Saturday and he went straight to the dogs at Wembley or Wimbledon. Then on Monday he came into the dressing room and asked, "Can I borrow a tenner?" '

Not only was Bowles' magnetic personality drawing people in, his ability with the ball was still impressing too. Day also claimed that, though Bowles was no longer at the peak of his career, he could still do things with a football other players could only dream about. However, what remained most vividly in the memory of that season at Orient was his sense of style and his sense of humour. 'I'll never forget this phrase of his, which I use myself sometimes. Stan was quite a smart dresser, always wore a jacket with a pin on the lapel. He used to say, "It's not a crime to be poor, but it's a crime to look poor!" '

Every dressing room needs a few characters to keep team spirit buoyant, and in that sense Bowles could always be relied upon. 'There was no bad feeling, the spirit was fine,' Taylor insisted. 'The manager who signed us, Jimmy Bloomfield, allowed the players to express themselves. Stan was given a free rein really, and I think that was Jimmy's strength. He was very clever there because you shouldn't ever tie Stan down with the ability he had. On the field Stan was as professional as you'll get, and as good as you'll get.'

Bowles played 37 League games during that season and helped Orient reach the second round of the League Cup, where they were knocked out by Taylor's former Spurs team-mates, and the third round of the FA Cup, where Luton Town eliminated them. Six goals – the first coming in the third game of the season, a 1–1 draw at home to Blackburn, and three of which were penalties – was an unspectacular return, but Bowles, playing behind Nigerian striker John Chiedozie, also set up a few goals along the way. 'Stan made John Chiedozie,' Day claimed, 'because he put him through on goal at least eight or nine times every game. Chiedozie went to Notts County, but a lot of his play was down to the service Stan gave him.' Even so, Chiedozie managed just nine goals all season, as did fellow forward Ian Moores.

Bowles' one season at Orient, which ended in a seventeenth-place finish (out of 22, with QPR finishing eighth in the same division), despite a good start, was something of a non-event. Bowles couldn't even bring himself to have any bust-ups with Jimmy Bloomfield, who treated him with respect – a quality Bowles felt had been sorely lacking under Brian Clough. Bowles was not under any pressure so for once in his turbulent life he was

experiencing no significant difficulties, personal or financial. But cosy, friendly, hard-working and committed
Leyton Orient were neither enough of a challenge nor
sufficient fun, so before long it was time to move on
again. Even playing against his beloved QPR in Division
Two offered no emotional high. Possibly the only remarkable incidents of the entire season were the club's
decision to pioneer shirt advertising and a brief flash of
temper from Bowles during a match against Grimsby
when he picked up a bucket of water and threw it, bucket
and all, into the crowd, who'd been abusing him.

Still, Peter Taylor remembered enough of Bowles' talent
from that season to lavish a few words of praise on him,
yet another testimony to a popular and appreciated
footballer. 'His pinpoint passing was the thing I was most
impressed with. At that time he had slowed down with his
dribbling, but the ball was stuck to his left foot. He wanted
the ball and worked hard on the field to get it – that was
his strength. If you had Stan and didn't give him the ball
it was a waste of time having him in the team. He used to
get the hump and get disappointed, but that's only
because he had high standards and he wanted to be
successful. He used to enjoy life, but he was never a
problem at the football club.'

In August 1981, at the age of 32, Bowles married Jane
Hayden, 24, at the Marylebone Register Office in London.
They had met seven years earlier at a bar in White City.
Bowles had romantically spilled her drink, their eyes met
and they began to 'date'. Bowles was still married to Ann
at the time, but that soon changed. When Bowles and Jane
were out celebrating her eighteenth birthday, Jane's sister
called Bowles' flat to wish her a happy birthday. Ann
answered and figured out that her husband was with
another woman. Then, to make matters worse, Bowles
brought Jane home. Ann subsequently sold her story to
the newspapers, taking a leaf from her husband's book in
how to make best use of the press.

Marriage to Jane in 1981 made up for the disappointment of the past year at Orient and helped to settle him

in preparation for a new challenge. Peter Taylor had become so disillusioned with the game while at Orient that he quit football altogether to work for a finance company, eventually returning some time later to play for Maidstone and Exeter City, but Bowles luckily found another club that could re-ignite his passion for the game – QPR's close neighbours Brentford in the Third Division. After just seven more appearances for Orient at the start of the 1981/82 season, which included his last goal for the club in his last game, against Charlton on 11 October, Bowles made the move.

Perhaps the most settled spell of his whole career came at this, his final professional club. The fallen idol of Loftus Road quickly became a favourite with the fans and with his team-mates. Though he stayed for just a few years, the Division Three west London outfit saw him play more games than any other club except QPR.

Martin Lange, the chairman at the time, recalled his first meeting with Bowles fondly. 'When I went to sign him with [manager] Fred Callaghan there was a certain amount of trepidation on my part because I was new as the chairman – I'd only been in the chair for six weeks or so. There were people at the club who thought we were signing a waster, but I was only interested in whether he could play football. We went to meet him at a London hotel. He just kind of sauntered in and said, "I just want to play football. I'm at Orient and I can't stand the place. I hate it." He was as easy as pie to deal with on his contract. I told him what we were prepared to pay him, and he said, "Yeah, that's fine by me. I'll be down at the training ground tomorrow." It is something that just doesn't happen these days – the great players sliding down the divisions. But the great thing about him was that he was very happy at Brentford, and that came across in his football.'

Despite that trouble-free meeting, there were a few hurdles to overcome before Bowles could really find his feet. A Sunday paper had run a feature claiming that Bowles had been bankrupt and was about to become so again. Lange and Brentford won substantial damages for their new recruit after disputing the claims, and that pay-out was put towards a house for Bowles and his new wife – a gesture that, according to Lange, Bowles was unaware of. 'When I suggested he should buy this little house down the road instead of paying rent, Stan asked, "Where am I going to get the money from?" So I told him not to worry, that we had some money and it was all his. It was a bit like the old-fashioned footballers, living right next to the ground.' Then Bowles turned up at Lange's office waving a tax demand, claiming he had no idea what it was all about. 'Because he'd moved around so much it had taken a while for all the post to catch up with him,' Lange explained. 'I don't think he'd ever filled in any tax forms so it looked horrendous that he owed so much. I got an accountant to look into it and we actually got him back a bit of money from the tax authorities, so he got a double winner.' This was not the first time Bowles had been bailed out of a tax debt, but it's likely he would have been a lot happier with the way things turned out this time than when Clough had paid that large tax bill on his behalf and taken it out of his win bonuses.

Potential financial disaster avoided, life became easy for Bowles. Lange was happy to ignore any little indiscretions – after all, the gambling was hardly a secret when he signed – and Bowles was back to enjoying his football. 'It was the best thirty grand [the transfer fee] we ever spent,' Lange remarked. 'I think we got most of it back on the first gate! He was the best player ever to wear a Brentford shirt.'

Keen to repay the club's faith in him, Bowles worked harder than ever to keep himself fit and, of course, enjoyed the weaker opposition the division had to offer. 'Before a fairly routine game at Preston,' Lange recalled, 'we stayed at a hotel the night before. On the Saturday morning I looked out of my window to see Stan out in the car park on his own, limbering up. Perhaps for a man in his thirties it was necessary, but he was very committed. I know he had his gambling problems and so on, but that never impinged on his football and it never created a problem at the club. His gambling was public knowledge, but I think the supporters related to him in that sense because a lot of them liked a bet as well. At the risk of sounding a bit conceited about it, we worked out very quickly how to handle him and what his problems were. That kept him happy. It was just making sure his finances were OK, just looking after him right. We made sure that things like his mortgage were taken care of so that the money he did have to spend could go elsewhere, if you know what I mean. I remember saying to him, "Stan, if I'd have got hold of you when you were 23, you'd be a millionaire." And he looked at me and said, "No, chairman. That's not for people like me. That's for blokes like you who worry about it." Fred Callaghan knew how to handle him because he knew that Stan had this kind of disregard for coaching because of his ability. I think Fred used to make a joke of it in the dressing room, saying, "Right, the ten of you have got to do this, this and this. And Stan, you just go and do what you want." '

For a player of Bowles' fame and talent to be playing at Brentford would be like Gazza moving to Swansea City today, but it's easy to see the attraction of playing for a club like Brentford when they sort out your mortgage, give you a virtually free rein on the pitch and firmly install you as the star attraction of the team. While Bowles cheerfully went about his daily business of destroying teams single-handed, he never let his new team-mates forget the fact that he was, deservedly and irrefutably, the star of the show. Never maliciously but always full of humour and self-confidence, he would criticise other Brentford players in training for not being able to trap the ball properly or some other piece of skill he could accomplish with his eyes closed and wearing a pair of wellies.

'I always got on very well with Stan and the players loved him,' said Lange. 'They appreciated just how good he was. He used to say that he was going out to entertain his public and he had this tremendous arrogance about his own ability. But I think that was justified. If you know you're good, that's fair enough. In a very friendly way he would take the mickey out of some of the other players, but they all loved him. He could be a bit of a leg puller.'

Former Brentford team-mate and now co-presenter of Sky's *Goals on Sunday* programme Chris Kamara laughed when recalling Bowles' attitude to the lesser mortals around him. 'We used to admire him in training, the awareness he had and the ability. But he used to get frustrated. I remember during one game he made the crowd laugh when he shouted at our right-back who'd passed the ball into the crowd. Stan pretended to look through binoculars to see where it had gone! He had the crowd in stitches, and he had us in stitches on the pitch as well. He was still a character. He used to pull the corner flag out and stuff like that from time to time. But his ability rubbed off on us.' Kamara, who joined Brentford at the same time as Bowles, though overawed by the former England player's ability, relished the opportunity to play alongside him. 'Obviously I knew all about him from before he joined, but he was nothing like I imagined him to be when I met him. He was so down to earth and just one of the lads. Obviously he loved a bet, but he was no trouble. He was just great company. We had some smashing nights out at the dogs and he'd give you his last penny – if he had one!'

'The first thing I noticed about Stan was his terrific vision,' said fellow midfielder Terry Hurlock, 'and it took me a bit of time to read him because he was so far in front of most of us. But once we started to learn where he was going to put the balls it was very good, especially from the crowd's point of view.' Bowles' closest friend at the club, Hurlock was almost teary-eyed as he recalled their relationship off the pitch. 'Nothing but good times. We were out near enough every night – well, not every night, but in the summer we were out every night. Going for something to eat with the ladies, going over their house and they'd come over our house, it was a right nice little cosy thing.'

As the club became accustomed to having a top-class player on their books, life at Brentford became settled. Bowles, for the first time in three or four years, began to enjoy playing football again. Furthermore, he had another opportunity to show how good he could be. But while Bowles' time at Brentford provides ample evidence of his skills, good nature and fun-loving attitude, it also symbolises the one great regret – at least to his fans – of his eventful career. Despite having the determination to pull himself back to the top after Manchester City sacked him, Bowles' lack of ongoing ambition at the highest level and his clashes with authority meant that he finished what should have been a glittering playing career much further from 'the top' than should have been the case.

The most significant point, at least to the player himself, is that he enjoyed it. But what if – yes, another what if – he had matched his talent with the work ethic of, say, Kevin Keegan, a self-made superstar? Well, then, of course, he wouldn't have been Stan Bowles and he wouldn't have enjoyed it one bit. 'He never struck me as being ambitious,' observed Lange. 'He realised that he was gifted and always gave the impression that he was happy with what he wanted to do. He wanted to gamble and he was happy with that. And good luck to him. It's not for me or anyone to sit in judgement of him.'

There was a buoyant and enthusiastic social life at Brentford which added to Bowles' feeling of relaxation. He felt much more at home at Griffin Park than he'd done at Brisbane Road (or 'Leyton Stadium', as Orient's ground was called at the time). Chris Kamara was usually involved in the nights out, accompanying the irresistible Bowles to a selection of dubious nightspots and gambling joints in the area. 'I used to go to White City with him occasionally and we had some fabulous times. I helped him out when he needed a couple of quid. I went with Stan to this gambling school in Shepherd's Bush and watched them play cards in this unlicensed basement gambling club. There used to be massive stakes there and Stan was a good player to be fair to him – he'd either win a lot or lose a lot. If he won he was the most generous man in the world; if he lost a lot he'd just shrug his shoulders and wait for a bit of money to come in.'

Hurlock, one of Bowles' main partners in crime despite being a lot younger than the former QPR man (Brentford was Hurlock's first professional club), went along too. 'I lived right opposite Griffin Park, and Stan lived a couple of doors down from me across the road. Our wives got on together quickly and I was pairing up with him, going out in the evenings, popping out after training. He used to take me to all the gambling joints.' As Hurlock recounted, Bowles would always ensure his friends did not go short financially, giving them money for drinks if they ever ran out. Even in the twilight of his career, Bowles simply refused to save any money, the one thing about his life that today he would go back and change. 'It was a very friendly club with *plenty* of socialising,' Hurlock added with a grin. 'The players all went out a lot more then, they don't seem to do it so much know – I don't know why. It's all the f***ing foreigners I suppose. At Brentford we always used to have a day out after training, or when we had a day off the next day. We'd go drinking in the local pubs – there's one on every street corner. We'd have a couple of quiet beers in the pub. There was nothing dramatic, nothing ridiculous, nothing juicy. We just got on nicely, there was nothing to shout about.'

Bowles was probably aware that the Bees would be his last club and his last chance to play professional football. The canny Fred Callaghan let him perform, told the team to give him the ball and just let him get on with it. Bowles responded with some impressive displays, though he was never able to inspire his side to anything more than a mid-table finish in Division Three, where Brentford re-mained for a few years even after he left.

'It was a gamble for Fred and the chairman to bring in a big star like that,' Hurlock said, 'because he'd always been known to have outbursts and to be outspoken. I had heard of him when I was young and I knew he was a good player, but I hadn't followed his career. I don't know why he left Orient, I never bothered to ask him. Fred was a very easy-going manager and I suppose he handled him all right, but then again Stan didn't seem to be that hard to handle. We never seemed to have any problems with

Stan. I mean, he used to come into the changing room quite late because he'd been in the betting shop, but he done the business. There were never any outbursts going on – we just used to get on with the game. He was a great bloke, Stan, very easy to get on with. I'm still close to him. Whether he was getting his wages three months in advance I don't know, but he was always a good laugh in the changing rooms. No problem. We always used to play cards and there was no drink involved there. We used to sit there for hours without a drink, and I'd leave when it was time to leave and he'd obviously stay there a lot longer. He was not drinking a lot then, we'd just have a drink after the game.'

With maturity seemed to come a certain degree of mellowing, though never laziness, and Bowles rarely argued with anyone during his latter years as a player. There were, however, some things about his preparations that would never change. For instance, as Hurlock re-marked earlier, at Brentford he would turn up as late as possible for matches and training – a tradition begun at the very start of his career. 'Sometimes it was a problem getting him to the ground,' Kamara recalled, 'and we'd have to send one of the kids over to knock on his door. The team-talks before matches used to start at half past two or whatever, and Stan would never be there, he would be in the social club next door watching the race until five minutes before the game. He'd never go out for a warm-up with the other lads, but he'd walk out with the team at five to three. He wasn't going to change for anybody. But once you got him into a football club, that was it – you couldn't get him away from the training pitch. Until half an hour before the first race, that is, and then he'd be gone. But every day he was there till the end.'

On the pitch, Bowles was ever the show-stealing per-former. Although his pace had deserted him, his passing was still as incisive as ever. Far from taking it easy as he wound down his career, Bowles was committed to enter-tainment and took as much pleasure from giving the Brentford fans what they expected from him as he had at QPR or any of his other clubs. 'He couldn't get about as he used to,' agreed Kamara, 'but playing with him was a joy. He was playing on the right-hand side of our midfield. If he got a chance on goal he would stick it away. We had a fantastic team at Brentford in those days but we didn't have a goalscorer; we would dominate games but we couldn't finish them off. I can just remember him constantly demanding the ball was played to his feet, that was his biggest gripe. Don't give the ball away – it's precious. At other teams I've played direct football, but Stan had decided that he couldn't play that way and he didn't want to play that way. I think we should have been a little bit more direct with the side that we had because we weren't fantastic at the back if we did ever lose the ball, we didn't have somebody to score goals for us on a regular basis but we had a good midfield. I think there's no doubt he was one of the great entertainers. The crowd came to see him and they always got their money's worth with Stan.'

Bowles was proving himself something of a reformed character, never in the tabloids unless it was in the sports pages. Combining excellent football with charity work at the club and an altogether less controversial lifestyle, he finished his professional career peacefully. Further evidence of this newfound stability came when he accosted Martin Lange at the club one summer's day with a desperate look on his face. 'Stan came up to me and said, "Chairman, I'm a bit short, can you lend me a twenty?" You were always wary when Stan wanted to borrow twenty quid or something. I was thinking that he wanted it to put on a horse. But he says, "My wife's down at her mother's in Bognor and there's a bit of a party tonight so I want to go down." I thought, "Well this sounds like a bloody good story. Stan Bowles going to see the mother-in-law!" So I said, "Oh yeah, Stanley? I tell you what, I'm going down that way tonight, I'll take you." And he says, "Cheers, chairman, that'll be great!" He was telling me the truth! So I ended up on a Friday night having to take him down to Bognor! But I did stay at the party for a couple of hours so it was all worthwhile.'

The most dramatic moment of Bowles' tenure at Griffin Park came on the first day of February 1983 when, as

Chris Kamara recounts, Bowles saved the Brentford groundsman's life when a stand inexplicably caught fire and burnt down. 'The groundsman used to live in there and Stan's house backed on to that part of the stand. He went in and got this old boy out. He had smoke inhalation, but Stan got him out before the fire got to him.' However, this account, as with so many tales associated with Stan the Man at all the clubs he's played for, is not entirely factual. Although Bowles' house, 60 Braemar Road, did indeed back on to the area where the groundsman lived, it was in fact Bowles' wife Jane who rushed in to Alec Banks's aid. Banks was unhurt, as was Jane. According to a grinning Terry Hurlock, Bowles' role in the drama was rather more passive. He just happened to be walking by at three o'clock in the morning to see smoke rising from the stand, fire engines blaring and television reporters buzzing about. Swathed in his long coat, Bowles muttered, 'Just my luck the wind couldn't have been blowing the other way. If my house had burnt down I could have claimed on the insurance!' And then he carried on walking. 'It was comical at the time,' Hurlock added. 'Well, not for the poor guy who was caught in there.'

Bowles was eventually disposed of when the battle-hardened former Arsenal defender and Bowles' former QPR team-mate Frank McLintock, who'd managed Leicester during the 1977/78 season before coaching at Loftus Road for a few years, was appointed manager in Callaghan's place. Chairman Lange had his doubts about the decision to allow Bowles to depart, but he trusted the judgement of his new manager, whose three-year tenure turned out to be an average one. 'When Frank McLintock took over from Fred Callaghan in February 1984,' Kamara recalled, 'that's when Stan decided it was time to quit. He didn't think their relationship could go from being team-mates at QPR a few years before to Frank being in charge of him as manager. It was Stan's pride that wouldn't let him carry on because I think he thought Frank might not play him, and he didn't want to be around Brentford Football Club if they didn't want him.' A year later, in 1985, Lange recalled McLintock saying that he wished

Stan Bowles was still at the club, if only to take the free-kicks and corners.

Whoever first thought that Brentford's star player's time was up, McLintock or Bowles, it was clear the relationship wasn't going to work out, and Bowles had had enough of not getting on with managers. The situation was made worse by the appointment as assistant manager of John Docherty, a reserve player when Bowles was at QPR and somebody he had never got on with. Ultimately, McLintock no longer rated his former team-mate and Bowles no longer wanted to play for Brentford.

In his first season, 1981/82, Bowles played 31 League games for the Bees and scored six goals; in his second season he played 42 and scored ten; and in his final season, 1983/84, he played seven games – including his only ever League appearance as a sub – without scoring. His final game for Brentford was on 4 February 1984, his side losing at home to Gillingham 3–2.

'When he left it's like anything else in a football club,' Kamara said. 'Time moves on and people move on. Managers change and players change, and you've got to accept it. Sometimes people think "I wish he hadn't left", but ninety-nine times out of a hundred – well, a hundred times out of a hundred – the football club is bigger than whoever leaves. Certainly his presence was missed around the club, but he stayed in the area, so you could always see Stan.'

After the 'Great Fire of Brentford' in February 1983, it took months to rebuild the Braemar Road stand, which was reopened in time for the start of the 1984/85 season. Half of the enclosure had been gutted, the metal framework twisted beyond recognition, and the visitors' dressing room, the gymnasium, the laundry room and all of the playing kits had been destroyed. When the stand reopened for business in August 1984 there was, however, one less playing kit to be laundered.

Although Bowles was finished with full-time football and had gambled his way on to the dole, he wasn't finished with getting himself into trouble. The following summer, after watching Brentford finish thirteenth in the

Third Division without him, he managed to narrowly avoid yet another arrest at an illegal gambling club. In the middle of a session Bowles had popped out to order a few drinks at the pub across the road. When he reappeared he found that the police had stormed the club and were searching it with some enthusiasm, making a number of arrests.

Later, Bowles played a few games for Epping Town in the Isthmian League, but his low-key comeback with the part-timers proved extremely short-lived. Finding his side short of players, the Epping chairman pulled on a spare kit and ran on to the pitch. Before long he had punched one of the opposition players, knocking him out, and chased another into the woods at the end of the pitch. Epping Town were subsequently expelled from the league.

In 1987, Jim Gregory, Bowles' chairman at Queens Park Rangers, contacted his favourite ex-player to remind him of a promise made years before that he was due a testimonial match after seven wonderful seasons at QPR. Following a bit of organising and ringing around, a game between Brentford and QPR was arranged for 15 May at Griffin Park. Bowles played the first half for Rangers, alongside Rodney Marsh, and the second half for Brentford in a contest QPR eventually won 3–2. Gerry Francis came off the QPR bench, and George Best was also meant to be on the teamsheet but later explained to Bowles, 'Sorry, Stan, I got the days mixed up.' Bowles replied, 'Don't worry, George, I get a bit like that myself from time to time.' Before the match, in a rare moment of harmony and humour between the two, Bowles and Marsh teamed up for a photo shoot, the two of them tugging at a QPR number 10 shirt.

Financially, the testimonial match should have gone a fair way towards setting Bowles up for the rest of his life. He received around £30,000 that day and had just sold his house for another £30,000, but with so much time on his hands all of it disappeared at various dog tracks over the next few months. Despite three years of promising to stay at his side since his retirement from the game, Jane, who some thought was with Bowles just for the attention, finally decided she could take no more and walked out, never to return. With no football and no wife, Bowles life threatened to spiral out of control.

9 The Men Behind 'Stan the Man'

He wasn't a villain, he was just an ex-car dealer who knew every trick in the book. We hit it off straight away. He was my type of bloke, if you know what I mean.

STAN BOWLES ON EX-QPR CHAIRMAN JIM GREGORY

This chapter is intended to be a useful reference point, giving biographical information on those people most heavily involved with Bowles' career and an overview of Bowles' relationships with them.

JOE MERCER OBE

Mercer was awarded the OBE in 1976 for his services to football. He is remembered as a genial and hugely talented manager as well as an excellent player whose career ended sadly at the age of 39 when he suffered a broken leg while playing for Arsenal.

It was Mercer's father, also called Joe, who was the catalyst for a great career in football. Joe senior was a defender with Nottingham Forest whose top-flight career was effectively ended by the First World War and, more specifically, a chlorine gas attack during the conflict. After the war was over, Joe senior returned to his native Merseyside and his young son and began to play for and captain Tranmere Rovers, a non-League team at the time. That young son was so impressed by his father's talents that he took up football himself, practising constantly. He was snapped up by his local club Ellesmere Port, and soon attracted the attention of the region's superpowers. At the age of just fifteen, Joe junior found himself playing for his heroes – Everton.

Ten years later, in 1939, Mercer won the League title with the Toffees, and then another world war interrupted the proceedings. During that conflict Mercer was an army physical training instructor, which allowed him the opportunity to play in 27 wartime England internationals. Although he didn't want to move away from Merseyside, Mercer signed for Arsenal in 1946 and more trophies followed. Two First Division titles and an FA Cup win later, in a horrific collision with Highbury team-mate Joe Wade, Mercer broke his leg and was forced to quit.

Following that retirement in 1954, and after a fruitful but unhappy sixteen months as a grocer on the Wirral, 'Uncle' Joe became the manager of Sheffield United, who had been relegated to Division Two. Almost three years in Sheffield brought limited success, and with the crowd restless and a lack of funds at the club, in 1958 Mercer applied for and landed the vacant Aston Villa manager's job. A certain amount of 'wheeling and dealing' was required at the Midlands club, money again hard to come by, and after six years of selling his best players Mercer suffered a stroke and was relieved of his position.

Less than a year later, however, in July 1965, Mercer was back, this time at Manchester City, against medical advice and the wishes of his wife Norah. Realising that he could no longer cope with the rigours of coaching, he insisted upon the appointment of Malcolm Allison as his right-hand man. It proved to be a match made in heaven, and the pair took City to the very top.

Mercer made some astute signings, many of which kept a brash young Stan Bowles out of the team, despite his impressive debut in 1967. Francis Lee, Colin Bell and Mike Summerbee came in, as did Tony Coleman, another youngster with a reputation as a troublemaker. But after winning the First Division, League Cup and Cup Winners' Cup, Mercer was, in effect, 'moved upstairs' after a high-profile take-over battle at the club, which he thought of as a hijacking. By this time Bowles had been sacked by City after clashes with the management. Allison took over team matters and Mercer found himself virtually frozen out as a 'general manager'.

This unexpected career move deprived him of any contact with the players and so, hurt but reluctant, Mercer left Manchester City to take up a similar position at Coventry City. That seemed to be the end of Mercer as a top-level manager, but when Sir Alf Ramsey failed to get England to the 1974 World Cup, the FA contacted Mercer with an offer of becoming the caretaker manager of the national side while they found a long-term replacement. One last hurrah, then.

Mercer revitalised the England team, winning three and losing just one of his seven games in charge. As well as forgiving Bowles after their City days and giving him another chance at international level, he introduced such players as Frank Worthington to the team, his charisma and enthusiasm inspiring confidence. The FA, realising that they had accidentally appointed the right man, offered Mercer the job on a full-time basis, but he refused. It was time to say goodbye to football.

On 9 August 1990, football said goodbye to the 76-year-old Mercer, who had been suffering from Alzheimer's for a number of years.

'I got on all right with Joe Mercer,' Bowles said. 'He used to calm things down more than anything else. He was a father figure. Malcolm used to do all the coaching at City and Joe would just be in the background. He was all right, Joe.' Former City captain Tony Book agreed, adding, 'His great contribution to Manchester City was that he was a brilliant PR man, and he even used that PR when he was talking with the team. Sometimes he'd be there after training sessions and he'd put his arm around you and say, "You did well last week." Just to give you a lift. But Malcolm was the one who did all the hard work, all the coaching and everything.'

MALCOLM ALLISON

Allison had been frustrated by Joe Mercer's success in that the senior man had said, when he took the job at City, that he would stay in charge for just two years. As the seasons went by, however, and the trophies piled up, Mercer understandably wanted to stay longer. Young and ambitious, Allison was not so understanding, and cracks started to appear in their relationship in the form of arguments, disagreements and hostility.

In the annals of history, Allison will probably be remembered as Mercer's right-hand man rather than a manager in his own right, but two months into the 1971/72 season Mercer was replaced as manager by the new boardroom team. It was Allison's first, longed-for opportunity in sole control of the club. He brought in Rodney Marsh from QPR for £200,000 and threw him straight into a settled, table-topping side, much to Mercer's chagrin. 'Two hundred thousand pounds is a lot of money to spend to throw away the championship,' Mercer, feeling distant from the club in his capacity as general manager, once mocked. Within a year, Allison had quit Maine Road. The board had sold Ian Mellor without his consent and he felt that he could no longer motivate his players. Life without Mercer was more difficult than anybody had expected, even though some people think that of the two, Allison had the lion's share of power anyway, especially in the latter years.

Always a larger-than-life character, wearing a fedora hat and sheepskin coat and puffing on a whopping cigar, Allison's managerial career then took him all over the world. He won the Portuguese league and cup double with Sporting Lisbon in 1982 and also took charge of the Turkish and Kuwaiti national sides. Like many flamboyant personalities, however, Allison had a major flaw: alcohol. In May 2001, at the age of 73, he was taken to hospital after breaking his collarbone at his warden-controlled home in Cheshire. His son, Mark, told the press, 'He is very ill but he's accepted for the first time that he is an alcoholic. He still has a lot to offer soccer but he does suffer from loneliness.'

It was no wonder that 'Big Mal' and 'Stan the Man' clashed on more than one occasion at City as they were two abrasive, addictive and sometimes fiery personalities wanting different things from each other, neither willing to concede defeat. Allison was the bad cop to Mercer's good cop, lacking the geniality, experience or patience to make the effort with Bowles. 'I saw Malcolm not so long ago,' said Bowles. 'He's about 72 now and living up in Darlington. He had a bad leg and almost had to have it off.

I think that may have been through drinking. We had a few skirmishes but nothing really serious. I was probably a little bit wild then anyway. It's fair to say I've not got on with a few managers, but I get on with Malcolm now. I didn't think I was difficult to handle, but everybody else seemed to think I was. Malcolm wasn't easy to get on with himself in those days, and I think he'd admit that himself now. So it was a clash of personalities from the start.'

ERNIE TAGG

Born in Crewe, Tagg joined his hometown club as an inside forward in October 1937 before moving on to Wolverhampton Wanderers nine months later. His association with the Staffordshire club resumed when he became assistant to Ralph Ward, before being named manager himself in 1964. A pub landlord as well as Crewe manager, Tagg also drove a taxi until old age finally caught up with him. He is an honorary life vice-president at Gresty Road and, when health allows, still goes to watch Crewe play.

In 1970, Crewe were considered one of the worst teams in the League. The inspired and fortuitous signing of Bowles, who like Tagg before him left his mark despite playing for the club for just a year, turned them from the worst into not quite the worst outfit. Had Tagg not dragged Bowles from the edge of oblivion, football might have been deprived entirely of one of its great characters and entertainers.

Tagg recognises that 'there is something in Stan that shouldn't be there' but remains so impressed by his former player's talent that he also insists Bowles could today be the manager of England if he'd 'used his brain'.

IAN MACFARLANE

'The Big Man', as he was known, was indeed a big man. Six foot five and not afraid to speak his mind, MacFarlane sounds at first like Stan Bowles' worst nightmare, especially as he used to greet Bowles with a cheerful punch in the stomach and would drag him out of bed if he didn't turn up for training.

Quite the opposite was true, however. At Carlisle United, MacFarlane's first managerial job after playing for Chelsea and Leicester, Bowles prospered and completed the final stage of his football rehabilitation. MacFarlane was a straight-talking but not dictatorial Scot who gave Bowles no quarter and expected absolute commitment. Bowles responded well.

After his surprise sacking at the end of the 1971/72 season, MacFarlane went on to coach at Leicester, Yeovil, Middlesbrough, Manchester City and Sunderland before finishing his working days as a scout for Leeds United.

GORDON JAGO

Replacing Les Allen, Gordon Jago became manager of Queens Park Rangers in January 1971 when the club was struggling. After steadying the shaky defence and selling Rodney Marsh to Manchester City (March 1972) he bought Stan Bowles from Carlisle (September 1972). Jim Gregory found the money to make Bowles the club's first ever six-figure signing, and Jago's talents as a manager helped the new star player to settle in quickly.

1972 was also the year that the new Ellerslie Road stand was built at Loftus Road, just in time for First Division football. Having languished in the second tier of English football, Jago and Bowles won promotion and helped fans quickly forget about Marsh. In order to further win over supporters and fuel a sense of closeness, Jago held a fans' open day, offering them a chance to meet the players and have their photograph taken together.

Jago left QPR in October 1974 to manage American side Tampa Bay Rowdies and was replaced by Dave Sexton. He had, however, built the foundations of what was soon to become Queens Park Rangers best ever side.

JIM GREGORY

QPR winger Dave Thomas's assertion that you had to be a 'certain sort of person to handle' Stan Bowles rings truest with Jim Gregory. 'Jim Gregory liked a bit of a rogue and that suited Stan,' said Thomas. 'Stan loved Gregory and Gregory loved Stan. He had a very good relationship with the chairman. You know what Jim Gregory was like – I don't think you'd want to do business with him! I wouldn't say he was in the same mould [as Bowles] but he looked after Stan well.'

Gregory joined the board at Loftus Road in 1964 and was elected chairman in 1965. One of his first actions was to sign Rodney Marsh from Fulham for £15,000. Like Bowles, Marsh was treated like a son by Gregory. In his autobiography, Marsh recalled, 'Jim Gregory was a villain. When I say villain, I mean it in the nicest possible way. If Jim was here today, I am sure he would not mind me describing him like that, God rest his soul. A lot of people have got a different impression of him, but for me he was a top man. I was so grateful to him for rescuing my career that I gave him my first England cap. Jim Gregory was quality.'

Gerry Francis credits Gregory with the success that Rangers achieved. 'He was the one who made Queens Park Rangers. QPR before Jim Gregory was just a very average Third or Fourth Division team. Then Jim, a self-made man, came in and made it something that perhaps it would never have been. With his money, building the stands, getting the players and projecting the team forward, he made QPR what it became.'

'If you go to QPR today it's still the same as what Jim built,' Bowles agreed. 'He died about five years ago. He had the same sort of trouble as Malcolm Allison but he had both his legs off and then he just went. He wasn't a villain, he was just an ex-car dealer who knew every trick in the book. We hit it off straight away. He was my type of bloke, if you know what I mean. We had a long, ongoing relationship.'

The special bond between Bowles and Gregory was vital to the team's success – keep Stan happy and you're halfway there. 'Jim was a father figure to Stan,' Francis explained. 'They appreciated each other's personality. Stan always had a good friend there and he was happy. It's when you're happy that you play your best football.'

Funny to think now that Gregory, a year before signing Bowles, had been looking for buyers for the club but had received no offers. Without Gregory at the helm, Bowles' career at Queens Park Rangers would have been very different, and probably a lot shorter.

DAVE SEXTON

With an admiration of attacking continental football, Dave Sexton was perfect for Bowles when the former arrived from Chelsea. He allowed Bowles freedom and created an easy working environment for the turbulent player. While Jim Gregory took care of Bowles off the pitch, it was Sexton who got the best out of him on it during three glorious years together at QPR.

'Dave Sexton came in and he was absolutely fantastic with Stan,' said Dave Thomas. 'If you said something to Stan that upset him, he would just blow a fuse and walk off or go missing. From my point of view Dave Sexton was second to none, as a manager and as a person. He was a true football man and that's why we all loved him. He wasn't trying to get all he could out of the game financially. If someone said, "Bowlesy, I want you in the dressing room at 2.15" – boom! You've lost him. He'd never try for you, and if Stan didn't feel like trying he wouldn't bother one bit. Sexton respected Bowlesy, he knew how he operated, so Bowlesy respected Sexton. We all knew what Stan was like and he had to be very cleverly handled by the coaches. If you upset him then you'd never get him on your side.'

After Rangers, Sexton replaced the brash, outgoing Tommy Docherty at Manchester United, with moderate success. He took United to the FA Cup final in 1979, and the following year they missed out on the League title on the last day of the season to Liverpool. Unhappy with Sexton's perceived lack of communication with them, the fans were already restless when the manager brought Garry Birtles to the club. The striker was a complete flop at Old Trafford, so in 1981 Sexton was sacked and Big Ron was appointed, bringing with him a character similar to Docherty's but a love of attacking football similar to Sexton's.

Sexton, currently Sven Goran Eriksson's chief scout, prefers to concentrate on football and is a quiet, thoughtful man. Enquiries for interviews are respectfully turned away by the FA, yet when he starts talking it's impossible not to listen.

TERRY VENABLES

Midfielder Venables joined Queens Park Rangers in June 1969 and went on to play at the club until 1974, for much of that time as captain. It was his tactical intelligence and inventiveness in training that helped turn the side into a potent attacking force in the First Division. His ideas also hastened the development of Stan Bowles by making best use of his skill and vision. Though Bowles enjoyed a better on-field understanding with Gerry Francis and Don Givens, Venables played a vital part in making QPR a side to fear.

He moved to Crystal Palace in September 1974 in exchange for Don Rogers but, having sharpened his coaching skills further, returned to Loftus Road as manager in 1980. Under his leadership the club won promotion from Division Two in 1983 after reaching the 1982 FA Cup final.

DON SHANKS

Bowles' partner in crime, Don Shanks was a right-back who for the first five years of his career at QPR was usually kept out of the team by Dave Clement. Between 1974, after signing from Luton Town for £35,000, and 1981, however, he made 201 appearances for the club and always performed admirably when called upon. In August 1981 he was given a free transfer to Brighton and Hove Albion. Without Shanks, Bowles' career story would be considerably less amusing. In later life Shanks coached in Hong Kong, Japan, Cyprus and Nigeria.

SIR ALF RAMSEY

Sir Alf introduced Bowles to the international stage in 1974, albeit a little late to save his own job or to invigorate an England side on the wane. Ramsey, after winning the World Cup in 1966, was widely criticised for lacking the imagination to broaden his horizons and create a more entertaining England side. 'I am employed to win football matches. That's all,' he would say, refusing to give the press anecdotes or one-liners like a Malcolm Allison or a Brian Clough. Though he disliked the way football was turning into show business, Ramsey often had no option but to try out creative players like Bowles or Tony Currie.

As a player he won 32 England caps and a championship medal with Tottenham Hotspur. As a young manager, in the space of seven years he guided Ipswich Town from the lower leagues to the Division One title, then came that crowning achievement at Wembley in July 1966. Victory in the World Cup final resulted in a knighthood just five days later, but Ramsey's popularity, and public patience in his pragmatism, waned and he was replaced by Joe Mercer.

BRIAN CLOUGH

One of the very best strikers of his generation, Clough scored 204 goals in 222 appearances for Middlesbrough, finishing as Division Two's top scorer in three consecutive seasons and scoring forty or more goals every year between 1956 and 1960. In 1961 he moved to rivals Sunderland and scored 63 times in 74 games before injury curtailed his career.

After a short spell coaching at Roker Park, he became the manager of Hartlepool United, teaming up with Peter Taylor, a colleague from his Boro days. In 1968 Hartlepool were promoted from Division Four, and the Clough/ Taylor partnership moved on to Derby County. Promoted to the top flight at the first attempt, in 1969, Clough's side did extremely well to finish fourth and ninth in 1970 and 1971, and then to win the First Division in 1972 for the first time in the club's history.

After reaching the semi-final of the European Cup the following season, and despite pleas from the players, Clough resigned from Derby after an argument with the chairman, Sam Longson. He took Peter Taylor with him to Brighton, who had just been relegated to Division Three. Less than a year later he was on the road again, this time north to Leeds United, where he replaced the revered Don Revie. The Leeds players were noisily unhappy at the immediate changes Clough tried to make and, amazingly, he was sacked after just 44 days.

Nottingham Forest offered him the job of manager and he accepted in January 1975. At the end of that season Forest were sixteenth in Division Two. Two years later, Clough led the club to promotion with a third-place finish, and the following season, 1977/78, they became Division One champions. Over the next twelve years, Clough, with Taylor at his side until they fell out in 1982, won two European Cups and four League Cups with Forest, creating one of Britain's most successful ever sides and earning himself a place in history.

Outspoken and occasionally offensive, Clough was a fiery, brilliant, confrontational and clever manager, making as many enemies – not least Stan Bowles – as he did friends and admirers. 'Old Big 'Ead', as he was called, though never to his face, was a dictator, controlling every aspect of life at Forest. He would make players uncomfortable if they dared enter his office, and gave no quarter. Bowles' complaints during his season at the club would have fallen on deaf ears, as Clough had his own ideas on how to keep the trophies coming in and certainly wasn't about to let one player rock the boat.

In 2002, despite continuing concerns over his health, he is writing a column for *FourFourTwo* magazine, as controversial and scathing as ever.

PETER TAYLOR

According to Bowles, Taylor watched him play before signing him, while Clough only saw him when Forest played QPR. He added that Clough took the credit when signings worked out and Taylor took the blame when they didn't. Bowles' move definitely did not work out. Taylor tried to lighten the mood at Forest and, like Bowles, disagreed with Clough over the best position in which to play the former QPR star. Clough and Taylor fell out in 1982 and never spoke again. Taylor died in 1990.

FRANK McLINTOCK

Nine years Bowles' senior, Scottish centre-back McLintock started out at Leicester before becoming a legend at Arsenal. The Gunners sold him, perhaps prematurely, to QPR in 1973. He managed Leicester in the 1977/78 season and coached at Loftus Road before getting the manager's job at Brentford.

When Bowles found out that his former QPR team-mate was going to be his new manager at Brentford, he decided to hang up his boots. Although they had once had a scrap in training during which Bowles bit McLintock's ear before goalkeeper Phil Parkes split them up, there was no bad feeling between the pair. Bowles' decision was based more on the fact that age was catching up with him, a point that McLintock's arrival highlighted. Bowles did not want to be in a situation where he was being dropped or played in the reserves by his former club colleague, so he quit football altogether.

10 The Bad Boy: Addiction Then and Now

I blew the lot on vodka, tonic, gambling and fags. Looking back, I think I overdid it on the tonic.

STAN BOWLES

In January 2002, the *Observer* reported that top Italian clubs hire private detectives to follow any star players suspected of having a gambling, drink or drug addiction. One of Italy's top, but unnamed, players was found to be addicted to gambling, kept asking the club for money, had involved his team-mates in his addiction and was flying around the world to top casinos, carefully covering his tracks. The private eyes came from the Tomponzi Agency in Rome. Owner Miriam Tomponzi commented, 'He was like a cancer in the team,' adding, '[A young man] can be a beautiful player but a bad person.' Italian football has long used the Big Brother approach. Former Italy captain Franco Baresi, youth coach at AC Milan, once said, 'If a champion is out of line in Italy, it would be end of the road for him. All hell would break loose.'

It all depends on how you like your football. If you subscribe to the theory that football needs to learn from past mistakes and completely eradicate bad behaviour of any sort, then you are probably thankful that the days of Stan Bowles are finished. You probably also believe that video referees should be introduced, therefore eliminating any possibility of human error. Maybe you think that video evidence of every match ever played should be examined, just in case any goals that were allowed never actually crossed the line, or in case a penalty was awarded that should never have been a penalty in a million years. Then the complete history of world football could be rewritten, and everyone could sit back feeling that justice had been done.

It is impossible to turn back time, however. Human error is what makes football the most popular game in the world. It's the excitement, the anger, the delirium, the confusion. It's also about ideas and free-thinking. Ultimately, it's about heroes. The genius of Stan Bowles on a football pitch can never be taken away, even by countless tales of misbehaviour, but whether he was a hero or a villain is questionable. He was a hero to QPR fans, yes, but a villain to England fans when he walked out in 1974 and again to Forest fans before the European Cup final in 1980. He gambled on his career, and although it rarely paid off, he remains sure that it was the right thing to do. As he often says, 'That's me – take it or leave it.' Bowles still won't take any of it seriously. His addictions have cost him almost a million pounds, a number of failed marriages and, arguably, his career. He couldn't cut his losses and quit; even a big-stake gambler would have been less damaging than a constant gambler. As his old mate Don Shanks said, 'He wanted to bet all day. He just loved those places [bookies].'

Despite the constant wisecracks, Bowles' life has not been a funny one. There have been countless moments of disappointment, pain and anguish, occasionally self-imposed. Liverpool University's Professor Steve Cooper has studied compulsive behaviour and recognises in Bowles the core characteristics of someone who naturally enjoyed, and still enjoys, a perilous lifestyle. 'It's basically all about taking unnecessary risks,' he explained. 'Compulsive behaviour can be quite risky when people become addicted to gambling, or sex, or drinking, or even exercise. I would expect it to be manifest pretty early on in childhood as it's a consistent personality profile.' Similarly, Dr Roy Bailey of psychology consultants CSL Psychology and Medical Legal offered a view of compulsive behaviour that matched Bowles' profile. 'Some people form a relationship with gambling so that it's more than something they do, they've got an emotional tie to it. Research shows that in people who are compelled to do things, the pleasure centre of the brain is involved in the win/lose reaction. They get a big but temporary high which goes quite quickly, so they have to constantly try to regain that high.'

So, what begins as a hobby, often inspired by family or friends, can sometimes take a firm grip, becoming an irresistible compulsion. If that hobby is socially 'acceptable', like trainspotting or stamp collecting, then there are rarely negative repercussions, but when the compulsion is frowned upon, as heavy gambling often is, people start to question the behaviour.

According to Dr Bailey, it is difficult to claim anyone is addicted. The only evidence of addiction, he says, comes when the gambler has tried to stop but finds that he cannot. Bowles has only tried to stop gambling half-heartedly and subscribes to the belief that he cannot be changed. He has always felt that he has faced a battle with an 'Establishment' which has always looked down on him. This has probably strengthened his desire *not* to change, to prove that his way of life can work. If everyone around him insisted he had a problem, a mixture of stubbornness and compulsion made him determined to prove them wrong.

But then, 'Who's going to be the judge of who has the problem?' asks Dr Bailey. 'You have to put it into a social context. If you go to China, for example, and you're a gambler, there's no big problem. If you go to some of these famous Gulf racecourses, there's no problem. And what's the difference between someone who would gamble three or four times a year on a big race or event and someone who is driven to do it? Gambling is either frowned upon or it's not. If people like Stan Bowles ever felt imprisoned by their compulsion, then it doesn't really matter where you live.' Such is his outwardly easy-going, carefree approach to life that it is unlikely Bowles feels trapped.

It's difficult to analyse Bowles from afar. Gambling has always been linked with trying to find an escape route, usually from poverty, which is why it has always been linked with football culture. Without the benefit of a few sessions on the quack's couch, though, it is impossible to find anything Bowles would like to escape from. In his autobiography, though, he did accept that his upbringing had forced his hand and limited his career options. 'Collyhurst is one of the roughest areas of Manchester,' he wrote, 'and few people there had any hope of experiencing a normal existence. But those were the cards we were dealt, and you just had to play the best hand you could. There were only three ways out of this slum environment: become a professional footballer, a boxer or a criminal.' Bowles once confessed that he had given serious consideration to becoming a full-time criminal but admitted that he would have been no good at it, despite experience in dealing with police enquiries. It is fortunate, then, that he did eventually make it as a professional footballer.

As a young child Bowles used his obvious footballing ability to earn himself and his young friends some cash when the fair came to town. One of the attractions was an alley where participants would attempt to kick a football and knock over skittles. His friends gave him money to take their kicks for them and he would take a share of their winnings. For three days he didn't miss a skittle, and on the fourth day he was banned, the owner complaining that he was too good. It was Bowles' first taste of the highs and lows of both finance and football. Bowles' brother, who had a trial at Manchester City as a youngster but failed to make the grade, has also been involved with gambling, and in later life became a bookmaker.

What is clear is that Bowles grew up with gambling and gamblers. Rather than assume that he has some skeleton in a cupboard he is trying to escape from, it is more sensible to believe that Bowles fell into gambling and it took a hold of him. There is a split among experts in the field over whether people are born with a compulsive personality or whether they choose the route. If everyone around a person is gambling, then they will automatically assume that they themselves also will, and even should, gamble. It is the same when everyone in a person's family has gone to university; the person then feels pressure to do likewise. A belief in free will over fate is all well and good, but sometimes the surrounding culture can counteract free will.

Many of Bowles' role models while growing up in Manchester were heavily involved with gambling, and like any child he aspired to be like the adults around him. But he has never set himself up as a role model, has never gone in front of the cameras to have a little cry and explain how he gambled all his money away and drank a bottle of vodka a day and why he's very, very sorry about it. Mainly because he's not sorry, and also because there would be no point. Everybody knows what some of the players from Bowles' era got up to, and they are unequivocally pardoned. Bowles is fondly looked back on as a footballing/gambling/drinking legend, while any of today's players who accidentally make it on to the front pages are pilloried as bad role models, louts and wasters, and are made to confess. Perhaps this stems from a desperation for the country's top players not to make the same mistakes again.

Dr Bailey explained that the 'road to recovery' – known as 'the twelve steps of restitution' – includes making an inventory of all the people wronged through the course of an addiction, followed by a correction of those wrongs. Bowles has indeed taken action to improve his relationship with his children, and also his father, whom he didn't speak to for years after splitting up with Ann, but the mistakes he made in his football career are trivial compared to these in real life and should not necessarily be frowned upon too harshly. Ringing Brian Clough and apologising, for example, would probably not be one of Bowles' 'twelve steps'. The problem may be that he has never found a socially acceptable relationship that is as satisfying as the one he has with gambling. Then again, if everyone worried about being 'socially acceptable', society would be a dull place.

Seeing the fall from grace of George Best over the years has affected every football fan, no matter how amusing they find the old anecdotes. Every time Best trips up or gets a stomach bug, people think, "He's back on the booze" or even "He's going to die." He is now seen more as a recovering alcoholic than a retired football great. But, though Bowles is not in the same category as Best in terms of either fame or ill health, he is considered a 'real man' (whatever that might mean) and his exploits have turned him from footballer to legend. Lifelong QPR fan Steve Russell is blindly devoted to his hero, who honoured the Loftus Road faithful with his presence for seven glorious years. 'Nobody was concerned about his gambling or anything like that because he still did the business. He was always in the headlines for things he was supposed to have done but I don't think he ever got any criticism from the fans. Ever. There are certain players who even if they are having an off day, they never get any stick.' Psychologist Dr George Sik added, 'I think one of the reasons that Stanley Bowles' story is so interesting is because his lifestyle was so extreme and yet he was still such a talented footballer.'

Football, ever since the downfall of the mavericks in the early 1980s, has faced a crossroads and has seemingly decided to go down both routes. On the one hand, it is undeniable that without people like Bowles football would be a far less interesting place, but people like Bowles simply don't exist any more. They are driven out or worn down for the 'good of the game', and the fun is removed because of that. Now, at every club in the land, winning is more important than entertaining, and clubs have worked out how to douse the fiery 'troublemakers' before they get in the way.

Perhaps that is why the Premiership is now packed to the rafters with foreign imports. Managers, particularly England managers, never trusted the mavericks, with their drinking, gambling and womanising, and that kind of footballer was never encouraged. So homegrown players became robotic, their natural ability curbed, and the world-class players were imported from countries without a destructive drinking culture. They brought with them the skills without the baggage of temperament or person-ality. Not wishing to be unfair to players like Gianfranco Zola or Dennis Bergkamp, they are hardly front-page headline makers.

The example of Bowles' eventual decline into a self-destructive lifestyle and his admission to a psychiatric ward further strengthens modern football's commitment to driving away alcohol, bad behaviour and, to a certain extent, personality from its doorstep. 'There's a lot more awareness at clubs now and the fitness levels are much higher,' said Dr George Sik. 'Players now just couldn't drink the amount that people of Stan Bowles' generation could drink, or as often. Even back then it would take years off your playing career. If you're young and you have a lot of money there is sometimes this desire to behave in a very ostentatious, flashy way. Usually that's done with cars and clothes and not so much with a drinking lifestyle, although obviously that's not gone away yet. There's more awareness of alcohol as a compulsion, with so many recovering alcoholics like Jimmy Greaves, Frank Skinner, Tony Adams around. The bad boy image is always there being reinforced, but when young people today are asked, their role models are clean-living people like David Beckham. There's less of a hankering after those mavericks of the 1970s. A lot of young players wouldn't even remember who they were. Their influence is less pervasive than ever.' Maybe this biography is glorifying that bad-boy image to a degree, but in the 1970s the culture was a hard-partying one with footballers, musicians, actors and even journalists to the fore.

National outrage at drinking in football is understandable, but when the player in question is your best or your favourite player, the lines between right and wrong get blurred and impartiality goes out the window. 'Obviously things seem rosier looking back,' Steve Russell conceded, 'but I can't remember anyone having a go at Stan about anything. Everyone knew he was a character, but he was accepted warts and all. He was always very open about what he did and he generally performed well. I think if it started to affect him, if he'd been out drinking or whatever, then things might have been different, but it never did so there was never a problem from the fans. He did get a lot of media attention but it was nothing like recent times, that's for sure. There's probably too much attention on players today.'

The twenty-first-century football media acknowledges, even relishes, the perceived failure of stars like Bowles and is eternally either fingering openings to see if they can reveal another wayward footballer and sell more copies of their rag or lambasting somebody for getting sent off in a League Cup second-round tie against York City – to use a typically meaningless example. Paradoxically, the intensity of the modern media's gaze on football stars is so great that the players feel trapped by the attention, which sometimes forces their 'bad' or addictive sides to the surface as they let off steam. Being surrounded by wholeheartedly unsympathetic photographers and journalists means that the only way for the players to feel as if they have confessed is to face the music publicly. Have they become public property? Is it their duty to blub before the nation? Or is it possible that too much can be read into their plight?

Judge Gareth Edwards, on sentencing former Manchester United, Leeds, Everton and Chelsea star Mickey Thomas to eighteen months in jail in 1993 after he was found guilty on charges of selling fake currency to naive Wrexham trainees, stated that the Welsh midfielder had failed in his 'duty' as a 'distinguished international sportsman'. This indicates that, despite the fact that Thomas never signed a contract containing the clause 'I will behave impeccably for the rest of my life', the judge thought his fame made the crime even less forgivable.

Voicing some anti-maverick leanings, former QPR winger Dave Thomas explained his opinion of how footballers should behave. 'When you're a professional footballer, you're not only representing your club on the field, you're also representing football and yourself off it. You've got to be a role model. If you want to go and get pissed up one night, don't go down to your local pub and start smashing someone, get your friends at home, draw the curtains and do what the hell you like. But the press, they want that, don't they? Because it sells newspapers. Bowlesy was a reporter's dream. If he wasn't getting the publicity from playing football, they create other public-ity. I didn't socialise with him. There were "dodgy" characters that a lot of the players wouldn't mix with. I was just the opposite of what Stan is. Just the opposite. With all Stan's habits he'd call me a bit of a boring bastard, really. He probably respected my lifestyle.'

Life under the microscope is full of pressures that can only be completely understood if they have been experienced. In 2001, Julie Burchill, pondering among other things the beauty of Mr and Mrs Beckham, wrote, 'The weird, sad thing about English football is that only when the players were paid pocket money did they seem like real men; the minute they got a man's wage they became Lads. Think of the heart-breakingly named George Best, so addicted to the bottomless bottle that he would apparently rather die than stop suckling at its toxic teat, or Stan Bowles, heavy-duty gambler who by 1983 was downing a bottle of vodka and eighty cigarettes a day, his body not so much his temple as his mangy old lock-up.' Burchill's point is that Beckham, perhaps more so than any other player in the modern game, has not fallen victim to the temptations that still surround football. 'As David Beckham was learning to kick a ball,' she wrote, 'this first generation of pop footballers were falling like skittles.'

Over the last few years Beckham and his cheerful wife Victoria have been abused and despised even more than they have been adored. His last-gasp goal against Greece to earn England automatic qualification to the 2002 World Cup, however, was his final exoneration, and he is now a hero. A paragon of hard work and extraordinary talent, the Manchester United star was hated, on the surface at least, for getting sent off at France 98, but also, it seems, just for being too good-looking, too charming, too lucky, too rich, too showy and too skilful. Now fans have realised their mistake and accepted that the man is also too English to hate for ever. It is surprising that while the goonish Gazza has maintained his place in England fans' hearts around the country, despite his dubious antics on and off the field, Beckham, clearly a better, more reliable and less injury-prone hero, is only now getting the plaudits he deserves. It seemed as though the media and the supporters were testing Beckham to see if they could break him, to turn the frightening, precocious talent into a wasted one, to create another Bowles or Best. That would make everybody feel better about themselves, wouldn't it? But the player, with incredible strength and grace, won. 'Golden Balls' Beckham is not necessarily symbolic of all footballers these days – there are plenty who still waste their talent as well as their cash – but he is a walking, talking (sometimes) manual on how to reach the top and stay there.

The existence of a book such as *The Lad Done Bad*, which proudly chronicles 'sex, sleaze and scandal in English football', not to mention the book currently in your hands, shows that the public is indeed still obsessed with misbehaviour. *The Lad Done Bad* says of George Best's lasting contribution to the sport, 'Best's ultimately self-destructive genius forced football to grow up and adapt, sometimes painfully, to the voracious media interest in its protagonists. His antics established a gloriously troublesome tradition hundreds of wayward geniuses (and not-so-geniuses) since have sought to uphold, albeit few with quite the same verve and vigour. George Best broke the mould of the professional footballer, and refashioned it forever in his own unique image. In many ways the spectacular rise and disastrous fall from grace of Georgie-boy, soccer's first superstar, was also the making of the modern game itself.'

In Beckham, though, football can be seen to have truly 'grown up'. Best and his numerous heirs responded to media attention, criticism, boredom or dissatisfaction through rebellion; Beckham has risen above it. He hasn't even seemed to be biting his lip. He has simply done his own thing and has maybe become an even bigger superstar than Best. In the 'maverick era' football superstars were still quite a novelty. It was because of Best, Bowles and the rest of the motley crew that the media began to get so interested, beginning a potentially disastrous and vicious circle that reached an embarrassing and painful nadir with the reaction to Beckham's red card against Argentina in 1998, and which has now reached its zenith with his ascension to the Football Throne.

Like Beckham, Bowles has certainly never been public property. Nor Best. Nor Frank Worthington. Nor Alan Hudson, Tony Currie, Peter Osgood and Rodney Marsh. Nor any of the bad-boy generation. Though he has admitted to having a problem with his addiction, Bowles has never made public any regrets, never groaned about decisions he's made, never blamed pressure. He knows it's all his own fault, doesn't expect salvation and doesn't ask for it. Consequently, however, he doesn't really deserve it.

The life of a footballer has changed drastically over the years, from the strict, disciplined, indoctrinated Lilleshall days of Bobby Charlton through the wild, rebellious antics of Stan Bowles to the suffocating media scrutiny surrounding modern-day megastars. Some of these lab rats cannot cope with the intense pressure, and explode. In 1998, after Paul Gascoigne had been admitted to a drying-out clinic, a report on the links between football and alcohol on the BBC Online Network said, 'Alcohol has always played a central role in the game. Reports of the problems that players have suffered are becoming more and more frequent. But why is it that so many supreme sporting stars of the past and present have struggled with such a destructive social problem? The life of a professional footballer, where fame and adulation are thrust on impressionable young men, carries with it particular pressures. Top players are given enormous amounts of money and, apart from a few hours of training every day, there is little to fill their time. This combination of excessive wealth and boredom can prove a dangerous mix.'

Even with this analysis in mind it is impossible to pigeonhole Stan Bowles. He was not paid 'enormous' amounts of money, though it was more than the average working person in the 1970s, and anyway, his risk-taking tendencies surfaced long before wealth, fame or adulation became realities. His lifestyle was never a reaction to external influences, it was just the way he was.

Addictions to drink and gambling are often the result of the report's 'dangerous mix' though, especially, according to psychologist Professor Carey Cooper, when British clubs do so little to prevent it. '[Players] are not cosseted, helped or supported in that regard by clubs, whereas if you go to other countries like Italy, a lot of the clubs treat the kids as part of the family.' 'Managers and coaches have been known to encourage drinking sessions in a bid to instil a collective spirit that they hope will transfer to the pitch,' the BBC report continued. 'And even when they disapprove of such activities they still seem to accept it as an intrinsic part of the game. Footballers operate in a macho world where heavy drinking has always been accepted, if not glorified.'

As former Aston Villa striker Brian Little pointed out, the social scene in the 1970s was very, very different. 'When I played, [Villa manager] Ron Saunders encouraged everybody to have a beer before matches to try and get the spirit together. You wouldn't feed your players beer today!' Little also laughed about the fact that his best feed of the week was his pre-match meal at the club – steak and toast. Dr George Sik added, 'Until recently there were managers who would encourage, even enforce, a drinking culture to aid team bonding. That's probably gone now, with the continental influx, and also for economic reasons if players can last a few more seasons it's worth so much financially.'

Legend Frank Worthington, who laughed off the suggestion that managers encouraged drinking sessions as a team-bonding strategy, said, 'Stan got a lot of publicity in the seventies but not always for the right reasons. Losing another few hundred quid down the dogs or whatever. It was just one of those traps that he fell into. Certain other players have fallen as well – Peter Shilton did it, for example. We all like a bet here and there, but when it takes over your life like it did with Stan then it's not healthy.' Worthington also questioned the term 'bad behaviour' and insisted that gambling, drinking or womanising was all part of the job of entertainer. 'What's wrong with that? As long as you know where to draw the line. That's what the 1970s era was all about – enjoying yourself. Nowadays players can't enjoy themselves because of the media coverage. Any minor discretion is highlighted in the next day's newspapers. From that perspective we were very fortunate. But the money in the game today probably compensates for that. They've got to be very careful. We had a little bit more rope and we could get away with things. They haven't got anything like what we had.' Give a footballer a length of rope today and he'd probably hang himself, or the media would do it for him.

The 'macho' side of football is undeniable, so should supporters expect anything else? Footballers are put on a pedestal, and it's easy to forget that despite their privileged lifestyles they generally come from the same type of background as the fans at the ground or those watching on TV. After all, most people are quite competitive, and most people drink too much now and again. Who hasn't tried to convince a friend to stay for another pint before last orders down the pub? Taken the mick if they order a half?

But the relationship between players and the newspapers, tabloids and broadsheets, has altered and expanded over the decades. Ian Ridley of the *Observer* has carved himself a particular niche in terms of reporting on the lives of the addicted footballer. Not only has he listened to Tony Adams and Paul Merson bare all, he got his hat-trick with Gazza in September 2001. Adams' inclusion in this list just goes to show that it is not only the creative players who fall into the 'dark' side. His revelations were ground-breaking within football, and meant that more and more people began to appreciate the very real dangers faced by professional footballers, even going so far as to sympathise with them. The entertainment game was not, it seemed, all about glamour, money and good football. Adams' *Addiction* is one of the best-selling football books of recent times, suggesting either that observers are more interested in the struggles of therapy and recovery than addiction itself, or that they simply wanted to read all about his drunken exploits.

Frank Worthington mourns the decline of Paul Merson, whose addictions were revealed in front of millions of television viewers. 'The profile goes with the territory, and the profile is huge. You're up there to be shot at. It's fine – I haven't got a problem with it. I thought Paul Merson was a brilliant player, but he just let things get on top of him. He got in with the wrong people, and as a football player you can never do something like that. It was a huge mistake.'

Embattled Leeds United manager David O'Leary, in the aftermath of the Ian Bowyer/Jonathan Woodgate scandal of 2001, argued in his programme notes, 'It's no excuse to say that they are just doing what thousands of other young men do. The other young men don't have the privileges footballers have. If they want to earn big money, enjoy the fancy cars and the first-class lifestyle, they must accept there is a price to pay.'

O'Leary also criticised them in the *Sunday People*, fuming, 'British players should ask themselves why it is you never see foreign players getting drunk, abusing their bodies and hogging the headlines for misbehaviour. They can enjoy themselves with a glass of wine or two. British players have to get legless. It is part of the British way of life and not exclusive to footballers, but Joe Public doesn't earn £20,000 a week. Of course players are targets, I know that. It comes with the territory, and they should know it too.'

The main similarity between 'then and now' is the obsession with seeing famous people humbled, and also with misbehaviour in any form. As David Lacey wrote in the *Guardian*, 'Footballers in the dock attract as much public attention as pop stars, screen idols and the better-known politicians. There is an understandable fascination in seeing men who can earn millions from kicking a ball defending charges of kicking another human being for nothing.'

It is a perverse fascination and an apparently cruel need for humiliation that fuels a love of scandal. Indeed, at the end of Jonathan Woodgate's trial, the judge, Mr Justice Henriques, said, 'It is right that you are no longer confident and brash', seemingly indicating that footballers not only have to stick to the law but can and should have their personalities clipped and moulded to order because of their fortunate position.

Further expressing the need to completely enter the footballer's world and mind, Bill Bradshaw wrote an intriguing, intimate and ultimately absurd piece in the *Observer* about Woodgate's teenage years, even mentioning the barmaid's hairstyle at the Leeds defender's favourite Teesside pub. Bradshaw did, however, highlight a few worthy points. Woodgate, he wrote, was sucked into a drinking culture and, as he became more successful, got 'a reputation for "flashing the cash", acting "the big I am" on nights out'. Woodgate also apparently used to burn twenty-pound notes for fun and was banned from a local student union for causing trouble. So now we all know. What good does this information do anyone? None. If anything, it does more harm.

Lacey observed that if reputations count when selecting an England team – both Bowyer and Woodgate were considered off limits by the FA during their trial – then finding eleven suitable players might be tricky. 'In living memory,' he wrote, 'the national side has included, at various times, a wife-beater, more than one alcoholic, a suspected rapist and several gambling addicts. It has also been captained by a former guest of Her Majesty.' Football tries to give an impression of being a perfectly sleek and glamorous business, but it is and always has been too unwieldy to fully control. There will always be someone to let the side down.

'Christmas doesn't exist if you are a footballer,' O'Leary said after revealing that Leeds had employed a sports science manager to remind players of the dangers of alcohol abuse. The law has been laid down for the future of English football: take your job seriously or find a new one. Still, over the Christmas 2001 period football's never entirely wholesome name was dragged through the mud once again as newspapers reported on a festive West Ham party collapsing into drunken anarchy, with sordid tales of an unnamed player urinating on a West End bar, while at other clubs players were also drinking themselves silly. The *Daily Mail* summed up the mood in the media on one double-page spread announcing FOOTBALL'S SHAME; DRUNK STARS HEADING FOR THE GUTTER ALONG WITH THEIR GAME; WE'RE AT AN ALL-TIME LOW; and DISGRACE OF THE BOOZE BROTHERS.

The impression the newspaper created that football had reached an all-time low is difficult to qualify, however, as the interest in footballers' normally mundane private lives has never been so high. It's not just that footballers operate in a macho world, it's that they have a few thousand quid to spare, and in some cases not a great deal of imagination. Some top footballers choose to live out the tempting dream of being a George Best or a Stan Bowles – a maverick who can wow the crowds, throw some money around and then throw a party for all his mates. The difference between the generations is that Bowles and the other mavericks were unique, they were originals.

Under pressure, Bowles was in bed with the tabloids who could make or break him (and they paid him for his troubles), while footballers now have to run away from them. Today's popular culture, reflecting an ever-increasing social insecurity, requires appetites to be constantly sated, in many cases appeasing the need to read about others' misfortune. Footballers, as youthful millionaires placed on cheap flat-pack pedestals, are easy targets, against their wishes but sometimes because of their own actions. Footballers who stray will never again be thought of as flawed diamonds. That was then, this is now. The changing years have hammered in the final nail in the coffin of the maverick.

Occasionally, newspapers try to invent a new Stan Bowles, perhaps blaring that Patrick Vieira is a disgrace for getting sent off, or that Robbie Savage is, well, a disgrace for getting sent off. But it doesn't really work any more. The tabloids are running out of rich seams to mine, and football is running out of characters. Stan Bowles has carved himself a comfortable niche as the ultimate gambling football legend, with plenty of walk-outs and arguments to look back on. There will never be another footballer like him.

Perhaps as a reaction to football's desire finally to relinquish itself of the 'bad boys' tag, an absurd twist came about at the start of 2002 in the form of an ITV series called *Footballers' Wives*. This added a new, slightly weird weapon to the ongoing war for 'ownership' of footballers. Seemingly believing that there was not enough dirt under the fingernails of the game already, the series actually *invented* new footballers to spy on. Just as in *Hello!* magazine, viewers could see inside the characters' homes, have a front-row seat at their weddings, watch them get drunk, fight, cry and get themselves on tabloid front pages. Audiences were shocked and appalled. And couldn't turn off. Now it's not the footballers who are addicted, it's everyone else!

11 Stan the Old Man: Life After Football, 1984–2002

People always say I'm an icon, but what does that mean? I need to check that in the f***ing dictionary!

STAN BOWLES

'There's 37 pubs in Brentford,' says Bowles knowledgeably, introducing the area where he's lived for the last twenty years and evoking memories of a comment from Chris Kamara, who remarked, 'There's a pub on every corner and he's been in them all!' 'It's only a village,' Bowles goes on. 'It finishes at the bottom of the road down there [points right] and at the bottom of the road down there [points left]. You wouldn't believe it – you can walk through it in ten minutes and it's f***ing full of pubs!' It doesn't sound like the most sensible place to live for someone who used to drink a bottle of vodka a day and ended up in a local hospital's psychiatric ward.

But Bowles, 54 on 24 December 2002, loves the area, and everyone in the area seems to love him. Sitting in one of his many locals after the barmaid offered a friendly welcome, with a dripping Alsatian scratching at the back door to come in from the rain, Bowles sometimes seems like his mind is elsewhere. He is mostly attentive and chatty, but eye contact is minimal as he cocks his head slightly and gazes at the slowly filling ashtray on the table. On more than one occasion his conversation drifts off a little and he sits in smoky silence waiting to be jolted into action with another question. It is reminiscent of Ernie Tagg's first meeting with Bowles, at Crewe train station, when Bowles was disillusioned with football and scarcely answered Tagg's questions. He doesn't seem depressed, though, and is often animated and chatty, but with his short attention span he doesn't seem to relish the chance to relive his life story.

Life after football has been no simpler for Bowles than it was when he was training (almost) every day and playing (almost) every Saturday. Although he might argue that a simple life is all he's ever led, gambling and drinking his way through whatever challenges he faced, fate has always thrown a spanner in the works to derail the rollercoaster. If you 'play life a day at a time', as Bowles has always done, some days are going to be worse than others.

After his second wife Jane left in the late 1980s, with Bowles collecting unemployment benefits, drinking constantly and chain-smoking, his life hit rock bottom. 'I got put in hospital because I was drinking so heavily,' he confesses. 'I was on about a bottle of vodka a day and all that. I came to my senses a bit because for five days I was in the psychiatric ward.' He laughs. 'They were all f***ing nutters in there! I said to the bird [the nurse], "What am I doing in here?" And she answered, "You want to have a look at yourself. That's why you're in here." ' Life at the West Middlesex Hospital was indeed strange. In the bed to his left, Bowles remembers, was a man who would only speak in French, while on his right was a patient who called him Eric, even waking him during the night to say, 'Come on, Eric, we've got a train to catch!' 'I had to go in there,' Bowles continues, 'because I was in a pub just down the road from here and I had a major panic attack. I thought I was having a heart attack. It's not actual pain you feel, but your heart races. Say there's just two of us sat here at the table now, it would feel like there's fifty people here. It's enough to do your bloody head in, I'm telling you. You can't keep still. It turned out to be delirium tremens – DTs. Which are alcohol-induced. That was about 1987, a while after I finished at Brentford.'

Without exception, his former team-mates were surprised at the news of Bowles' condition, having never considered him to be a particularly heavy drinker. 'I was very shocked to see him go into hospital,' said former Brentford midfielder Chris Kamara solemnly, 'because he wasn't a hard drinker and I never thought he'd become an alcoholic. That was only when I knew him, so he must have changed. Today we talk about the drinking culture in football but in those days we didn't look at it like that. It was just a case of when the game was finished on Saturday that was it – we'd all go out together.'

At this point in the conversation Bowles doesn't hide the traces of regret etched into his naturally bright features. His words have been slowing down – hardly likely to be a consequence of the three pints he's consumed so far – and he's been staring at the ashtray with particular attentiveness. Not for the first time, his mobile phone rings, a welcome distraction. 'There goes that f***ing phone again,' he says with half a smile, and walks off.

His gambling reached its zenith during the 1970s, his drinking peaked during the 1980s, and ever since then he has been sorting himself out. He doesn't drink as much now, he certainly doesn't bet as much now, he doesn't take Valium any more and he's cut down from smoking eighty cigarettes a day to twenty. 'I didn't start smoking till I was about 31, 32,' he reveals unexpectedly, sitting back down. 'And I didn't even start drinking till I was about 22. I didn't like the taste of it.' And then the irresistible one-liner: 'I've made up for it now, mind!'

Despite this willingness to live up to certain expectations, Bowles is solemn when looking back at how alcohol affected him as his playing career drew to a close. 'I had been drinking heavily at Brentford. I wasn't really bothered any more because I knew I was going to finish with football. It was just a matter of time. I didn't get sacked or anything, I just walked in one day, when Frank McLintock was the manager, and I said, "That's it, Frank, I've had enough." I just walked out, and that was that. I did go back there once but I was basically sick of playing. It became like a job, and that's how it gets after a while, after I'd been playing for seventeen years.'

It seems strange that Bowles' version of his final days at Brentford differs so much from that of Martin Lange, then the club's chairman, who recalled McLintock wanting an ageing Bowles to leave. Maybe Bowles doesn't want to remember his final club as somewhere he was quietly asked to leave, or maybe Lange, like any other club chairman in the history of the game, prefers to believe that Bowles didn't walk out on Lange's club of his own volition. Whatever the truth of the matter, it was a long time ago, and the old memory plays tricks. The truth, as ever, is probably somewhere in between.

But Bowles had made no provision for life once his career was over, had no plan of action. Once he was released from the West Middlesex Hospital he wandered aimlessly, sleeping on friends' sofas or even living on the streets. As he freely admits, he was not in the best shape during that troubled period of his life. He played a few games with the George Best Newhaven Select XI – a travelling circus of ex-players organising charity matches – but beyond that there was little to connect him to the football world he once belonged to.

Alcohol abuse was ruining his body, but he somehow pulled himself through with a determination not usually associated with a 'maverick'. It's reminiscent of his efforts to get his career back on track after Ernie Tagg gave him the chance to play at Crewe Alexandra. Getting back up from the blows he deals himself seems to be a common theme in Bowles' life. Not that he's tee-total and innocent as a cherub these days. He maintains the look of a geezer-cum-gangster, striding through his environment like he owns the place.

Paul Hince, Bowles' friend from Manchester, commented on the fact that it's difficult to pinpoint exactly how Bowles makes his money these days. 'When I ask him what he's doing at the moment, all I can get out of him is, "A bit of this, a bit of the other, a bit of ducking and diving." I think he works on his local market sometimes. He's turning into Del Boy. A diamond geezer!' Hince still sees Bowles occasionally. 'When he had his long white hair he looked really weird, like a middle-aged hippy! He rang me up when he was writing his autobiography because he said that I've got a better memory about his early years than he has! He turned up at my office with two men who were helping him write it, and they looked like they were straight off the market in Deptford. Broken noses, cauliflower ears. After we've had a chat I take him downstairs and buy him a cup of coffee and he brings out this huge wad of notes that would have choked an elephant. "Right, me old son," he says, talking like Del Boy, "how much do you want?" It was typical Stan. He must have had a thousand pounds there.'

From the mid-1990s onwards, things seemed to get better for Bowles, offers of work coming from various angles. His efforts at staying within the loving arms of the football fraternity, however, even when invited by admired former colleagues, have never worked out. During the mid-1990s Dave Webb, then managing Brentford, contacted Bowles and offered him a coaching job. 'Coaching at Brentford went on for a season and a bit,' says Bowles. 'Me and Dave played together at QPR so he just gave me this little job one day a week, taking the forwards. I worked with some good players: Bob Taylor, Nicky Forster, Carl Asaba, Marcus Bent. They're all still playing well now. I wouldn't want to get into full-time coaching, though. It's a 24-hours-a-day job. I want a job for about two hours a day! If there was a coaching job at QPR, I wouldn't be interested. I did do a little bit of work for Gerry [Francis] when he was there, but say there's forty kids in training, there's about ten or more coaches! They've all got their coaching badges, and I haven't got one, so they are all trying to tell me what to do. About two weeks I lasted there. There's not many people who can tell me what to do. I'll listen and take it on board, then use it to my advantage. But I wouldn't tell them that.'

Also during this period of his life, Bowles met wife number three, Diane, and they married in 1994, Bowles 'adopting' two stepchildren, Zoe and Tommy. Unfortunately he recently split up with Diane – who found another man and moved to Newcastle – and, as is his way, he spent about nine months in Manchester letting things sort themselves out. 'I was having continuous arguments with her so I went back to Manchester for a while,' Bowles says with a shrug. 'We just had a major row and enough was enough. I'm with another girl now anyway.' Bowles grins, and admits that wedding number four might not be too far away. 'Oh yes, I like a wife.' Despite those bright blue eyes, there is a hardness behind Bowles' gaze. Always insistent that nothing bothers him, there is no trace of anxiety or upset over the divorce, finalised in March 2002. 'It shouldn't take him too long to find another one, I wouldn't have thought!' confirmed long-time companion and former Brentford team-mate Terry Hurlock. Paul Hince added, 'He likes churches and weddings. He's a serial husband!'

For all his habits, Bowles was never a womaniser, although at the height of his fame, when he was playing for QPR and England, female admirers were like moths around a flame. Still, it would be a brave move for any woman to marry Bowles, even a mellowing version of Bowles, now in his fifties. 'Loveable rogue' is a phrase often bandied about, and when it comes to Bowles the 'rogue' seems to outweigh the 'loveable'. Impossible to live with he may be, but he's also apparently difficult to live without. 'I got on famously with my first two wives,' he explains. 'My second wife, Jane, rang me up this morning. In fact she rings me every day. And my first wife, Ann, I still see her. She's got a couple of pubs in Manchester. And all me kids are in Manchester.'

Bowles had three children with Ann – Andrea, Carl and Tracey, although Andrea is apparently not too keen on Dad. When Bowles married Jane Hayden in 1981 there was a painful story in the newspapers – MY MEAN DAD BY STAN BOWLES' DAUGHTER – in which Andrea claimed she didn't even get an invitation to the wedding, a story Bowles puts down to his daughter's inexperience with the tabloids. She had asked the *Sun* for photos of the event, and the paper screamed, 'Playboy soccer star Stan Bowles snubbed his biggest fan on his wedding day ... his daughter Andrea.' While Bowles accepts that he let his children down on more than one occasion, rarely visiting them in Manchester for instance, the bitterness has faded with maturity.

Still living in Manchester, and still working for the *Evening News*, Paul Hince is pleased to say that Bowles does visit his home town now and again. 'He does come up and see them. There's no animosity any more. His son was celebrating his sixteenth birthday and of course he'd never seen his dad play. So Ann asked me if there was anybody I knew who could get him a video of Stan scoring as a present. I phoned up Brian Barwick, who used to produce *Match of the Day* on the BBC and is now producing *The Premiership* on ITV. He was the head of BBC Sport. It must have taken him hours but he cut together every goal they could find Stan scoring on television – Crewe, Carlisle, England, everything. He didn't charge me, he just said, "Wish the lad a happy birthday." ' Memories of Stan Bowles can drive the hardest of men to great acts of charity.

To anyone who grew up with Bowles it is something of a surprise that he stayed in London, as his Manchester connections have always been so strong. The lure of the capital city's bright lights convinced him that the Big Smoke is definitely the place to be, a conclusion he came to many years ago. Bowles is still in touch with many of his old friends from Manchester, though, and he met up with first wife Ann during his nine-month self-imposed exile from Diane. 'When we were married, Ann just didn't like being away from home so she took the kids back to Manchester and there was nothing I could do about that. I stayed on and we got divorced. I think the football and the lifestyle was more important to me than the marriage at the time because I signed a four-year contract with QPR, so there was no way I could leave. I could not afford another mistake. And I knew there was money to be got.'

That last comment is essentially the story of Bowles' life. He was driven by the ambition to prove people wrong, to show Malcolm Allison that one day he would play for England. His private life was in tatters, his wife and children desperately unhappy in London, but more important than any of that, Stan Bowles needed money and he needed football.

Bowles no longer needs the huge flood of cash to fuel his gambling habits, however, and a few pints of lager is cheaper than a bottle or so of vodka a day. Typically, he makes enough money to survive and have some fun. He has taken a road well travelled by former footballers: writing columns, after-dinner speaking and the like. He has previously teamed up with Peter Osgood, Ron Harris and Charlie George to entertain the masses with a colourful after-dinner routine.

When an associate of his enters the pub, Bowles bellows, 'Hey! You got my stuff?' The man shakes his head and chuckles. 'F***ing bollocks you are!' Bowles shouts, then complains, 'He's promised me two pairs of kids' trainers for the last four f***ing weeks.' He doesn't bother to explain why he needs kids' trainers, and it seems rude to enquire. The old man later wanders around the pub, when Bowles has departed, selling a jacket to a teenage girl and promising her father to get him some trousers in the same style for Christmas.

'Now he's finished there's not a lot he can do apart from keep busy,' observed Hurlock. 'He's not a greedy drinker, Stan. He'd sit there and chat and that lager will last him all night. I don't know if he's drinking too much – I suppose he is, because he's always in the pub when I speak to him! He's always chopping and changing with his interests but he is in the f***ing betting shop every five minutes as well, so nothing's changed too much there either!'

In recent years Bowles worked with the Zoo betting website, writing about his colourful career in an absurdly over-the-top manner, almost creating a caricature of himself. The self-deprecating jokes were ridiculous, the quips suitably offensive, the language enough to make anyone blush – all followed by a few suggestions on how to make some cash from forthcoming football fixtures. However, as entertaining as the weekly column was, Bowles was dropped from the popular site which, he suggests, was moving away from football. 'I was with them just the other day and they explained they'd just dropped out of the football thing because they've gone more for the betting side. Obviously there's more money in the racing, especially with this no-tax betting now.' Never one to flirt with negativity, however, he adds, 'But I had two good years or so of doing that.'

During that time, his comments on the website were a regular source of entertainment, offering lashings of irreverence and insight. He once wrote, 'I get asked these two questions on a regular basis: "What are you doing in my garden?" and "Have you ever considered giving up gambling?" To be perfectly honest, the answer is no, not really. I enjoy gambling. OK, I've lost a load of dough – but so what? If I died with £750,000 in the bank that too would be wasted money – a supreme act of stupidity – although my children might not be of the same opinion.' He went on to admit that he is mostly famous for his drinking and gambling, but insisted that he could not complain about the image. It's not, he joked, as if he has a hidden side and reads Tibetan poetry in the evenings while listening to violin concertos. Providing some insight into his enduring frame of mind, he added, 'I'm not really a big drinker – I only drink to make other people seem more interesting. It's not as if I like the stuff. I get bored very easily which is why I crave a constant need to be excited. The need is fulfilled by my boozing and gambling habits. Betting is always interesting because one afternoon spent in the bookie's and I don't know if I'll have enough left over for a pint down the pub. Or for food! It keeps me guessing.'

A regular income would probably scare Bowles to death, so accustomed is he to the frivolous, dangerous lifestyle he has had all his life. 'I was doing that column and I was working at QPR,' he says, 'but I lost that job at the end of last season because the club went into administration. So I lost two jobs in a week. And the after-dinner events with Charlie George have fizzled out. But new things come up all the time.'

Much of Bowles' work in recent years has been based on reliving past mistakes and past glories, a way of life former Scotland international Pat Nevin, in a collaborative book with Dr George Sik, a psychological examination of a footballer through dialogue, thinks tragic. 'There are plenty [of players] whose subsequent living is based on reminiscing about the period in which they played,' he says, and Sik replies that it's always the same names: Best, Bowles, Worthington, Hudson. 'A lot of these people,' Nevin continues, 'are continually reliving their life in the game, keeping it going by hankering back to it . . . again and again and again.'

This is a little unfair on Bowles as he uses football as a means of making money, even to this day, and if people still want to hear the stories, then why not? He is not desperately trying to turn back the clock, just clever enough to realise that interest (or gruesome curiosity) in his career has not diminished. As ever, he is taking any opportunities offered. It is not his sole means of income, and he seems to genuinely enjoy it.

Nevin's opinion on the so-called legends of the game retelling their tales is fine in theory, but doesn't quite work in practice. 'Maybe nothing can ever recapture the thrill of football and maybe nothing can replace the distinct sense of certainty that goes with it,' he wonders. This does match Bowles' steep decline after retiring from Brentford, but then again he had always found 'thrills' in other ways – in particular by gambling – and it is questionable whether he ever had any 'certainty' in his long playing career anyway. Nevin continues, striking more of a note of truth, 'The players that make me feel most sad are the ones I have very fond memories of, ones I watched play and really admired. I suppose, like most fans, I only want to see them through the idolising eyes of a starstruck child.'

One thing that Stan Bowles has never been, however, is a figure of sympathy. Yes, he lost all his money because of a compulsion to take risks and never fulfilled his potential on the football field. But such is his easy-going attitude to life and his ability and desire to laugh it off that it's impossible not to laugh with him. He has made his bed, as they say, and is comfortable lying in it.

Though Bowles' hospitality and charity work with his favourite club Rangers, where he also played a few celebrity matches, was short-lived, club officials are still trying to track him down in order to arrange more such events (one press officer mentioned he would love to know where Bowles had disappeared to and could I possibly let him know if I found out!). 'I change my telephone numbers all the time,' Bowles reveals with a big laugh. 'It's just something I always do. I'm hard to track down if I want to be.'

It's not that Bowles wants to disappear altogether, though. He is hard to track down, but not impossible. He seems to like to keep his options open, and while his life seems about as random as a horse race in the mist, he does, you have to believe, just about know what he's doing. 'I do quite a bit of business in Manchester still,' he acknowledges. This last comment amused fellow 1970s legend Frank Worthington, who roared with laughter. 'Business interests in Manchester? He's a lad, isn't he, Stanley? Ha ha! That could mean absolutely anything! The mind boggles!' The mind does indeed boggle. There's no reason to think any of those business interests are anything but above board and honest, but with a reputation like Bowles', a lot of people assume the worst.

Over the last few years Bowles has also branched out into radio and television, and has even assisted in the making of one or two football videos. He also wrote an entertaining column for *Loaded* magazine, which celebrates laddish behaviour at its worst. With these experiences under his belt and after a long period out of the limelight, Bowles has had time to ponder his varied career.

'My greatest achievement,' he decides, 'was getting myself back up to the top after Malcolm Allison said I'd never play in the First Division and I'd never play for England. But I did it. I did everything, basically, that people said I couldn't do. I'm a bit funny like that. If you tell me I can't do something I'll get it in my head that I can. After the first time I played for England, he said to me, "You f***ing done it, didn't you!" And I said, "I told you I would." People say I never won a major medal, but at the end of the day I could have won one but I didn't want one. That doesn't bother me.' Bowles has never looked at medals as proof of talent and doesn't need to convince anyone of his own ability as a player. His sometimes comically inflated opinion of his own brilliance is typical of a 1970s maverick. He really does believe that he was the most skilful player of the period (and who can argue?), but he says it with a glint in his eye.

Since retirement, he has also had plenty of time to try to put his notoriety into perspective. 'A lot of Tranmere supporters seen me at a match recently, and they were all around me. People still remember me and I haven't played for twenty years. How many of these people will be remembered in twenty years?' he asks, gesturing at the other drinkers in the pub. 'Not a lot, I can tell you. It's nice. People always say I'm an icon, but what does that mean? I need to check that in the f***ing dictionary!' Part of that notoriety stemmed from the image of Bowles as a serial gambler, which stuck from the moment he made an appearance in the newspapers announcing that he would quit gambling to take football seriously. 'If I'd have kept quiet when I was in trouble, nobody would have ever known about it, apart from close friends or people surmising that I was gambling. Even then I could have denied it. But once I put it in the paper then I was a f***ing gambler for the rest of my life.'

It is not easy to draw a line under Bowles' story. There is always another chapter waiting to be written, always trouble on the horizon. He still has star status when so many colleagues and former professionals have been demonised or have lost their appeal. He still goes to matches at Loftus Road, chats with the fans. And there aren't many football fans who wouldn't want to have a chat with him – after all, he experienced all the highs and lows as a footballer, and the end of his career was the end of the maverick era. A long-time QPR fan offered a fitting summary: 'That's the big thing about him, the relationship with the fans. The LSA [Loyal Supporters Association] had a stall at the club's open day last year and when we were packing up and almost everybody had gone, we looked over and Stan had organised a kids' football match in the corner and was refereeing it. Everyone else had gone home, but he was still there and he took the time to arrange this match. Wonderful stuff.'

'He has gambled his way through a fortune,' Hince reflected. 'He should have been comfortable after finishing in football. He could certainly have stashed away a big lump of his money but he's got no interest in it. He doesn't get miserable if he hasn't got any money, he'll just do something to get some. And if he's got it, he'll spend it. He was a kid from a working-class family without two pennies to rub together, who almost won the title with QPR and played for England. That isn't bad. There's a lot of footballers who'd settle for that.'

Perhaps the ultimate fitting conclusion to this biography, though, is this from fellow bad boy Frank Worthington: 'Bowles is one of those guys people instantly recognise. I do a lot of after-dinner speaking at functions these days, and you've only got to mention Stan's name and people smile. That's the effect Bowlesy has on people, because he played the game with a smile and used to perform magic. And that is really the essence of what football is all about, isn't it? He lived his life the way he saw it and enjoyed himself. I just take my hat off to him.'

Epilogue

A few hours into our conversation in a pub in Brentford, one of Bowles' mates – possibly one of the infamous 'shady characters' – made a grand entrance with a young blonde in tow. He cracked a few unpleasant jokes ('niggers', 'strippers', that kind of thing), discussed briefly who had been killed recently and who was in trouble with the police (I didn't like to ask for details), then dragged Bowles off to another pub. Easily led, or just bored of my incessant questioning, Bowles gulped down the rest of his pint, put on his suave long black coat – a bit of a trademark – gave me his home number with the invitation to ring him any time, and disappeared.

Before leaving, however, he showed his friend some photos from his autobiography, which I had brought with me: Bowles with Phil Lynott, Bowles dressed as Stan Laurel, etc. 'I've got the original draft of this book,' said his mate, a fearsome-looking man with a flashy earring and a nose that looked like it'd been broken a few times. 'It'll be worth a fortune when Stan's dead! Mind you, people usually only get to be legends when they are dead, but Stan's a legend when he's still alive.' Bowles half-smiled, flattered but ill at ease with the sudden sweet talk, and looked down at the old photos. 'That's lovely,' he muttered. He didn't deny his friend's words, of course, because they're true.

As his trimmed silver hair disappeared down the grey, drizzle-soaked street, I pondered our enjoyable conversation. I wondered if I'd really seen a quick look of disbelief when, with both of us standing in the pub toilets earlier on, Bowles had asked me what I wanted to drink and, considering it was eleven in the morning and I was cold and wet, I asked for a cup of tea. I felt self-conscious the instant those words slipped from my mouth, but Bowles didn't seem to mind and very quickly the barmaid, who knew him well, was bringing over our drinks. Tea with two sugars for me and a pint of lager for the legend. As the hours slipped by I soon forgot such trivial insecurities and began to enjoy Bowles' company.

As he vanished into the rain, his collar turned up to his ears, I also wondered where he was going and who he was going to see. He lives in an almost impenetrable world, a place that is at once intriguing and unnerving. I realised that there are people like Bowles in every pub in the country. It's just that very few of them can claim to be one of the best footballers Britain has ever seen.

A few minutes later, after finishing my own drink, I followed Bowles into the cold drizzle. There was no sign of him. On the train home I remembered that a few of his former team-mates, such as John McGovern and John Robertson, had asked me to pass on their telephone numbers so that they could get in touch with him again. A great many people hold Bowles in high esteem; even those he has wronged have forgiven him.

Bowles is now writing a column for *FourFourTwo* magazine. I didn't suggest it, nor did I even think of it, but he saw an opening and a way of making a few extra quid each month for very little effort. Until the end of his days he will be asked by journalists, fans and fellow drinkers about his football career, even though it's now thirty years since he began playing for Queens Park Rangers and the stories are sadly fading into distant history.

Stan Bowles was one of the best players English football has ever seen. He had the world at his feet, but, always a gambler, he gambled on his career and lost. Still, he lost with immaculate style. Hopefully this book will keep the stories alive for a while longer.

Stan Bowles Factfile

1948
24 December – born in Collyhurst, Manchester.

1967
September – makes stunning two-goal debut for Joe Mercer's Manchester City against Leicester City in the League Cup.

1969
June – marries teenage sweetheart Ann. They go on to have three children: Andrea, Carl and Tracey.

1970
August – after being sacked by City, begins a doomed spell at Bury which ends nine weeks prematurely on 5 September.
September – begins career afresh with Crewe Alexandra and manager Ernie Tagg.

1971
October – moves to Ian MacFarlane's Carlisle United for £12,000.

1972
September – joins Queens Park Rangers for a club record £112,000.

1974
April – makes England debut under Sir Alf Ramsey in friendly against Portugal in Lisbon.
May – plays against Wales in Cardiff, scoring his only England goal in a 2–0 win. In the next game, against

Northern Ireland, he is unfairly subbed and walks out on England.

1976
November – returns to the England line-up for a World Cup qualifying match against Italy, which England lose 2–0.

1977
February – plays his last game for England, another 2–0 defeat, this time at the hands of Holland in a friendly at Wembley.

1979
December – signs for reigning European Cup holders Nottingham Forest on assistant manager Peter Taylor's recommendation.

1980
May – Forest again win the European Cup, without Bowles, who fails to turn up for the match after a disagreement with manager Brian Clough.
July – joins Second Division Orient (now Leyton Orient) for a club record fee of £100,000.

1981
August – marries long-term girlfriend Jane Hayden.
October – signs for Fred Callaghan's Brentford in Division Three.

1984
February – retires from professional football at the age of 36.

Date	Club	League apps	League goals
1967–70	Manchester City	17	2
1970	Bury	5	0
1970–71	Crewe Alexandra	51	18
1971–72	Carlisle United	33	12

1972–79	Queens Park Rangers	255	70
1979–80	Nottingham Forest	19	2
1980–81	Orient	44	7
1981–84	Brentford	81	16

Bibliography

Adams, Tony and Ridley, Ian, *Addicted*, CollinsWillow, 1998

Attaway, Pete, *Nottingham Forest – A Complete Record 1865–1991*, Breedon Books, 1991

Bowler, Dave, *Winning Isn't Everything – A Biography of Alf Ramsey*, Orion Books, 1999

Bowles, Stan; Allen, Ralph and Iona, John, *The Original Stan the Man*, Paper Plane Publishing, 1996

Broughton, Chris, *Forest Ever Forest*, Tricky Red Publications, 2001

Burchill, Julie, *Burchill On Beckham*, Yellow Jersey Press, 2001

Campbell, Denis; May, Pete and Shields, Andrew, *The Lad Done Bad*, Penguin Books, 1996

Clough, Brian and Sadler, John, *Clough – The Autobiography*, Corgi Books, 1994

Crisp, Marco, *Crewe Alexandra Match by Match*, Tony Brown, 1997

Finch, Harold (ed.), *Images of Sport: Crewe Alexandra FC*, Tempus Publishing, 1999

Francis, Tony, *Clough – A Biography*, Stanley Paul & Co Ltd, 1987

Hayes, Dean, *The Craven Cottage Encyclopedia*, Mainstream Publishing, 2000
Nottingham Forest – The Unofficial A–Z, Sigma Press, 1999

Holmes, Bob (ed.), *My Greatest Game*, Mainstream Publishing, 1993

James, Gary, *Football with a Smile – The Authorised Biography of Joe Mercer OBE*, ACL and Polar Publishing, 1993

Macey, Gordon, *The Official History of Queens Park Rangers FC*, QPR FC, 1999

Marsh, Rodney, *Priceless*, Headline Publishing, 2001

Nevin, Pat and Sik, George, *In Ma Head, Son*, Headline Book Publishing, 1997

Nixon, Neil, *Singin' the Blues*, Terrace Banter, 2000

Penney, Ian, *The Maine Road Encyclopedia*, Mainstream Publishing, 1995

Manchester City: The Mercer–Allison Years, Breedon Books, 2001

Powell, William A., *Britain in Old Photographs, Queens Park Rangers*, Sutton Publishing Ltd, 2000

Pringle, Andy and Fissler, Neil, *Where Are They Now?*, Two Heads Publishing, 1996

Robinson, Michael (ed.), *Football League Tables 1888–1997*, Soccer Books Ltd, 1997

Rothmans Football Yearbook 1974–85

Shaoul, Mark and Williamson, Tony, *Forever England*, Tempus Publishing Ltd, 2000

Soar, Philip, *The Official History of Nottingham Forest*, Polar Publishing, 1998

Steen, Rob, *The Mavericks*, Mainstream Publishing, 1994

Williams, Russ, *Football Babylon*, Virgin Books, 1996

Selected newspapers and magazines
FourFourTwo
Total Football
Daily Mirror
Observer
Guardian
The Times

Index